Basic Human Rights and the Humanitarian Crises in Sub-Saharan Africa

Princeton Theological Monograph Series

K. C. Hanson, Series Editor

Recent volumes in the series:

Basic Human Rights and the Humanitarian Crises in Sub-Saharan Africa

Ethical Reflections

GABRIEL ANDREW MSOKA

Pickwick *Publications*

An imprint of *Wipf and Stock Publishers*
199 West 8th Avenue • Eugene OR 97401

BASIC HUMAN RIGHTS AND THE HUMANITARIAN CRISES IN
SUB-SAHARAN AFRICA
Ethical Reflections

Princeton Theological Monograph Series 74

ISBN 10: 1-55635-100-3
ISBN 13: 978-1-55635-100-6

Cataloging-in-Publication data:

Msoka, Gabriel Andrew
Basic human rights and the humanitarian crises in Sub-Saharan Africa:
ethical reflections / Gabriel Andrew Msoka

Princeton Theological Monograph Series 74

xvi + 184 p. ; 23 cm.

ISBN 10: 1-55635-100-3
ISBN 13: 978-1-55635-100-6

1. Human rights. 2. Basic human rights—Philosophical and religious aspects. 3. Africa,
Sub-Saharan. 4. Great Lakes Africa. 5. Rwanda. 6. Burundi. 7. Congo (Democratic Republic). 8. Uganda. 9. Somalia. 10. Sudan. 11. Kenya. 12. Tanzania. I. Title. II. Series.

BL65 C58 M80 2007

Manufactured in the U.S.A.

*To the memory of those dedicated
to the cause of protecting and promoting
the basic human rights of refugees and internally
displaced persons (IDPs) in the Great Lakes
Region of Sub-Saharan Africa.*

Contents

Acknowledgments / ix
Introduction / xi
Abbreviations / xv

▦ Part I
The Nature and Scope of the Humanitarian Crises / 1

1   The Root Causes of Refugees and Internally Displaced
     Persons / 3

▦ Part II
An Evaluative Description of the Response to the Humanitarian
Crises: Legal and Moral Criteria / 29

2   Responding to the Humanitarian Crises of Refugees and
     IDPs / 31

▦ Part III
The Ethics of Basic Human Rights / 61

3   A Philosophical Assessment of the Interpretation of
     Human Rights in International Refugee Law and Public
     Policy / 63

4   Theological Justification of Basic Human Rights / 109

▦ Part IV
Concrete Proposals and Recommendations / 151

5   Toward a Liberation Ethic of Public Policy for Refugees
     and IDPs / 153

General Conclusion / 169
Bibliography / 175

Acknowledgments

THE publication of this book has been a *cosmotheandric* effort of many hands. I express my gratitude to them all. I am especially grateful to the Superior General of the Religious and Missionary Institute of the Apostles of Jesus, AJ, Very Rev. Augustine Njuu, AJ, and the US Regional Superior, Rev. Paul O. Gaggawala, AJ, for their immeasurable support that has enabled me to realize this project. I am indebted to the faculty and administrative staff of the Jesuit School of Theology at Berkeley, California, US for their input in this major undertaking. Furthermore, without having an easy access to the Graduate Theological Union library and the University of California library, Berkeley, California this great accomplishment wouldn't have been possible. These institutions' management deserves a word of gratitude. A word of gratitude goes to the Wipf and Stock Publishing staff for their resilient spirit instilled in this venture.

My heartfelt gratitude goes to Teresa Picchi for her wholehearted commitment and dedication in editing the manuscript. Her interest in this study was the engine behind the success.

To my father, Andrew Msoka, and my mother, Esteria Andrew (RIP), for being God's effective instrument and, indeed, without them this book could have been utopia. Above all, to God who deserves all the credit as the ultimate source of life.

To all who should have been, but were not singled out by name, my apologies and a lot of thanks.

Introduction

For decades, post independent Africa has been marked by unprecedented conflicts, violence, and civil wars. Most African countries attained independence from foreign rule in the 1960's. Despite this achievement, many countries of the Great Lakes Region of Sub-Saharan Africa such as Rwanda, Democratic Republic of Congo (D.R. Congo), Uganda, Somalia, and Sudan continue to experience political instability and economic stagnation.[1] The factors that contribute to this situation are multi-faceted: tribalism and/or ethnocentricity, the Cold War and colonial legacy, poor leadership and governance, race as well as religion. The resulting strife has led to forced migrations and humanitarian catastrophe, leaving thousands of civilians as refugees and internally displaced persons (IDPs).

The 2003 UNHCR report indicated that in Africa, there were 4,593,199 persons of concern, of these 3,343,700 were refugees, 715,100 were IDPs, and 29,600 were stateless persons. The numbers are likely to rise due to persistent conflict and protracted civil wars in the Great Lakes Region, particularly in the D.R. Congo, Uganda, Somalia and Sudan. Under the auspices of United Nations High Commissioner for Refugees (UNHCR), governments and the international community have achieved some success in providing these groups with basic rights of security, subsistence, and liberty of active social participation. Despite the achievements, refugees and IDPs in the region, particularly women and children remain vulnerable to human rights' abuses.

For years, scholars engaged in various debates exploring the concept of human rights. Today, this endeavor is still relevant as a credible source of inspiration for dealing with humanitarian crises in the Great Lakes Region of Africa. This book critically examines the achievements and failure of governments and the international community to deal with human rights

---

[1] The Great Lakes Region of Sub-Saharan Africa is comprised of countries that either generate influx of refugees and/or IDPs or host refugees. The countries that generate refugees and/or IDPs are Rwanda, Burundi, D.R. Congo, Uganda, Somalia, and Sudan. The countries that host refugees are Kenya and Tanzania. The counties that generate and host refugees and/or IDPs are Rwanda, Burundi, D.R. Congo, Uganda, and Sudan.

abuses of refugees and IDPs. To achieve this objective, the book focuses on how the concept of human rights contribute to redressing the failure of governments and the international community in effectively responding to humanitarian crises in the Great Lakes Region of Africa.

In view of the prevailing crises in the region, the following questions are posed: What bearing does interpretation of human rights in international law have on public policy regarding refugees and IDPs in the Great Lake Region of Africa? What are the fundamental legal and moral limitations of such an interpretation? How can recourse to contemporary philosophical and theological study of human rights redress these limits? To effectively respond to these legal and moral questions, scientific inquiry of human rights of refugees and IDPs is a four-fold process:

In Part I, a descriptive analysis of the nature and scope of forced migrations and humanitarian crises in the Great Lakes Region of Africa is offered. The factors: tribalism and/or ethnocentricity, colonialism, political leadership, race, religion, and the Cold War are highlighted. How these factors contribute to causing the crises is demonstrated.

In Part II, a critical evaluation of governments' and the international community's responses to humanitarian crises is made. Achievements as well as the principal legal and moral limitations that contribute to the failure of governments and the international community are identified.

In Part III, philosophical and theological ethics of basic human rights is offered. From the standpoint of philosophical ethics of basic human rights, a critical ethical assessment of the interpretation of basic human rights in international law and public policy for refugees and IDPs is made. This method exposes the principal legal and moral limitations that contribute to the failure of governments and the international community to effectively protect and provide refugees and IDPs with basic human rights of security, subsistence, and liberties of active social participation and physical movement. This inquiry is made under the formal elements of human rights' theory namely, the subject, the object, the nature, the respondents of correlative duties, and the justification of human rights. Under the same formal elements, a re-interpretation of basic human rights of refugees and IDPs in international law and public policy is made from the standpoint of Henry Shue's theory of basic human rights. The ethical principles that are drawn from Shue's theory are highlighted, and applied to redress governments' and the international community's failure in the Great Lakes Region of Africa. To deal with the lacunae of Shue's argument regarding justification of rights, a theological justification of rights is offered from the standpoint of modern Roman Catholic social teaching, and thus completes the study of basic human rights of refugees and IDPs in international law and public policy. A theological interpretation of basic human rights is drawn from both general as well as Sub-Saharan Regional Catholic social teaching. The latter provides an African expression of basic human rights of refugees and IDPs. Philosophical and theological ethics of human rights provides a framework for evaluating the public policy for refugees and IDPs in the Great Lakes Region of Sub-Saharan Africa.

In Part IV, concrete proposals and recommendation are offered. Moral priorities are generated and the manner of implementing them is shown in light of philosophical and theological study of basic human rights. This approach proposes short, medium, and long-term solutions to forced migrations and humanitarian catastrophes, and thus provides a holistic and authentic liberation of refugees and IDPs in the region. It is argued that a liberation ethic of basic human rights is critical to protecting and promoting the dignity of refugees and IDPs in the Great Lakes Region of Sub-Saharan Africa.

The book is divided into four parts and five chapters:

Part I focuses on the nature and scope of humanitarian crises in the Great Lakes Region of Africa. Chapter 1 deals with the historical background of forced migrations and humanitarian crises. In this groundbreaking chapter, an in-depth analysis of the root causes of forced migrations and humanitarian crises is unearthed. Contrary to the view that the humanitarian disaster can be blamed on a single factor, the chapter shows that the social disorder in this part of Africa is the result of multifaceted conditions. Moreover, the factors: social and economic, cultural and religious, as well as racial and political are closely interrelated. This endeavor demonstrates that both internal and external factors play roles in contributing to the humanitarian crises in the Great Lakes Region of Africa.

Part II focuses on the legal and moral criteria invoked in responding to the humanitarian crises. Chapter 2 is a critical moral evaluation of governments' and the international community's responses to the humanitarian crises. Their major achievements and failures are identified. The moral failure of governments and the international community that lead to massive human rights violations of refugees and IDPs sets a platform for the discussion of basic human rights in international law and public policy.

Part III, which focuses on the ethics of basic human rights, consists of two chapters. Chapter 3 is divided into three major sections that focus on the philosophical ethics of human rights. Section A deals with the moral concerns that are raised in view of governments' and the international community's failure to effectively or adequately respond to the crises. This section establishes the rationale for considering a re-interpretation of basic human rights of refugees and IDPs in international law and public policy. Section B offers a re-interpretation of basic human rights in international law and public policy by critically analyzing Henry Shue's theory of basic human rights. Section C demonstrates the moral and legal significance of Shue's theory in redressing governments' and the international community's failure that is discussed in section A. Chapter 4 focuses on the theological justification of basic human rights from the standpoint of contemporary Roman Catholic social teaching, inculturated into an African social milieu, *cosmotheandrism*. Both the philosophical and theological study of basic human rights provides a framework for evaluating public policy for refugees and IDPs in the countries of the Great Lakes Region of Africa.

Part IV focuses on concrete proposals and recommendations. Chapter 5 deals with a liberation ethic of public policy for refugees and IDPs. In this chapter, a set of priorities is proposed and strategies to implement them are made. The chapter offers short, medium, and long-term solutions to the problems of humanitarian crises in the region. Therefore, the study of basic human rights, I argue, provides a comprehensive solution to the plight of refugees and IDPs by protecting and promoting human dignity, and thus restores justice and peace in the Great Lakes Region of Sub-Saharan Africa.

Abbreviations

ACS	*African Christian Studies*
AFER	*African Ecclesial Review*
AMSCE	American Society of Christian Ethics
ANSCE	*Annual of the Society of Christian Ethics*
AMECEA	Association of Member Episcopal Conferences in Eastern Africa
AMREF	Africa Medical Research Foundation
D. R. Congo	Democratic Republic of Congo
FAO	UN Food and Agricultural Organization
FNLC	National Front for the Liberation of Congo
IDP	Internally displaced persons
JRE	*Journal of Religious Ethics*
JRS	Jesuit Refugee Service
KANU	Kenya African National Union
LRA	Lord's Resistance Army
LWF	Lutheran World Federation
NGO	Non-governmental organization
OAU	Organization of African Unity
PI	*Promotio Iustitiae*
RPF	Rwanda Patriotic Front
SPLA	Sudanese People's Liberation Army
TS	*Theological Studies*
UN	United Nations
UNAMIR	UN Assistance Mission for Rwanda
UNDP	UN Development Program
UNHCR	UN High Commissioner for Refugees
UNICEF	UN International Children's Fund
WFP	UN World Food Program
WHO	UN World Health Organization

PART I

❖

The Nature and Scope of the Humanitarian Crises

The Root Causes of Refugees and Internally Displaced Persons

Introduction

THE crises of mass migrations are a manifestation of the social disorder that has rocked the Great Lakes Region of Sub-Saharan Africa since the 1960's. This social problem, a consequence reflected in the context of the violence, political and religious conflicts and civil wars, contributes to the humanitarian catastrophes occurring in the area. A comprehensive approach to finding a solution to these crises requires an in-depth understanding of the underlying factors that contribute to the social disorder in this region.

People are deeply divided on the root causes of conflicts and civil wars in Africa, which are a highly contested subject among historians today. Despite differences of opinion, a thorough understanding of the issues leading to conflicts and civil wars is critical to finding effective ways to bring about justice and peace in the region. Ignorance of the root causes of conflicts and civil wars tends to free those responsible for the crises of accountability and obligation to the innocent victims.[1]

In this chapter, I will examine four major combinations of factors that have contributed to the conflicts and civil wars in African countries, and have led to mass exoduses and humanitarian catastrophes in the Great Lakes Region since the 1960's. The four major combinations of factors are tribalism and colonialism, political leadership and governance, politics and religion, and the Cold War politics and regional conflicts. The social and political situations in Rwanda, the Democratic Republic of Congo

---

[1] Bulcha, "Historical, Political and Social Causes," 20.

(D.R. Congo), Somalia, Uganda, Kenya, and Sudan will be employed as examples to illustrate the factors.[2]

Conflicts and civil wars in these countries have generated refugees, internally displaced persons (IDPs) or both from the 1960's to this day. Although both groups of displaced people share the similar life condition of homelessness, their legal status varies. According to international refugee law, IDPs are not accorded the same international legal protection as refugees. To clarify the legal distinction between refugees and IDPs, it is extremely important to know the legal definition of each. A historical background of the refugee conventions and the subsequent refugee laws will be discussed.

Terminology

In the aftermath of World War II, the United Nations (UN) recognized the need to address the problems of refugees across Europe. In this context, the UN convened a conference in Geneva, Switzerland, on January 1, 1951, during which "The 1951 United Nations Convention Relating to the Status of Refugees was adopted."[3] In this convention, the term "refugee" was defined to provide a legal framework for refugees affected by World War II:

> A refugee is a person who, owing to a well-founded fear of being persecuted for reasons of race, religion, nationality, membership of a particular social group, or political opinion, is outside the country of his nationality, and is unable or, owing to such fear, is unwilling to avail himself of the protection of that country; or who, not having a nationality and being outside the country of his former habitual residence as a result of such events, is unable or, owing to such fear, is unwilling to return to it.[4]

---

[2] Some of the major root causes of conflicts, violence, and civil wars will be examined by analysis of representative countries: D.R. Congo and Somalia, and Uganda and Kenya. For example, the D.R. Congo stands as a good example of the impact of Cold War conflict from 1960's to the late 1970's in the region. Somalia stands as a good example of the impact of Cold War conflict from 1980's to 1990's in the region. Kenya and Uganda share similarities due to the fact that both were under British colonial rule. Although Rwanda and Burundi share a similar colonial history, namely, they were known as Rwanda-Urundi during the Germany occupation, Rwanda forms a category of its own in the study because it represents the countries most affected by colonial legacy and scrambles for power along tribal lines in the modern African history. The 1994 Rwanda genocide is the best illustration of the impact of colonialism and tribalism in the country.

[3] Schaeffer, *Sanctuary and Asylum,* 96.

[4] "Text of the United Nations' 1951 Convention Relating to the Status of Refugees," 97.

Historically, implementing the 1951 UN Convention was limited because it focused only on events that occurred in Europe before January 1, 1951. The operations of agencies such as the United Nations Relief and Rehabilitations Agency (UNRRA), and the International Refugee Organization and subsequently United Nations High Commissioner for Refugees (UNHCR) were limited by a three-year mandate to resettle 1.2 million European refugees left homeless by the global conflict. Over time, as the magnitude of conflicts continued to grow globally, there was a need to address the problems of refugees throughout the world that did not fall under the immediate scope of the 1951 UN Convention. To this effect, the UN General Assembly adopted the "1967 UN Protocol Relating to the Refugee Status," which expanded its mandate by including events that occurred in Europe, before 1951, and after this period, across the globe. "It is desirable that equal status should be enjoyed by all refugees covered by the definition in the Convention irrespective of the dateline January 1, 1951."[5]

While the 1951 UN definition of "refugee" is an international landmark for refugee status, it remains substantially unchanged in the face of addressing the current influx of refugees throughout the world. In response to these new realities, the African heads of state and government expanded the definition further by incorporating issues that address the problems of the contemporary Africa. In 1969 the Organization of African Unity (OAU), currently known as the African Union (AU), convened a conference in Addis Ababa, Ethiopia, in the Horn of African Region, during which a Convention that addresses the influx of refugees in Africa was adopted. Hence, "the 1969 OAU Convention Governing the Specific Aspects of Refugee Problems in Africa" is the official regional instrument for protecting refugees in Africa. The 1969 OAU Convention, Article 1, states that the term "refugee":

> Shall also apply to every person who, owing to external aggression, occupation, foreign domination or events seriously disturbing public order in either part or the whole of his country of origin or nationality, is compelled to leave his place of habitual residence in order to seek refuge in another place outside his country of origin.[6]

[5] "Text of the 1967 Protocol Relating to the Status of Refugees," 130. The 1967 UN Protocol is an additional agreement that globally extends the application of the 1951 UN Geneva Convention.

[6] "OAU Convention Governing the Specific Aspects of Refugee Problems," accessed 6/13/2003.

While the definition of the OAU reflects the essence of the UN
Convention of 1951 and the 1967 UN Protocol Relating to the Status
of Refugees, it is also specific to the African situation. The nature of the
causes of refugees in Africa is different from that in Europe. In Europe,
during the World Wars, inter-state armed conflicts were the major causes
of influx of refugees and IDPs. In the early 1960's, Africa had to cope with
the aftermath of the armed struggle of liberation movements, intra-state
conflicts, power struggles and external aggression that threatened the newly
independent African states. Often these problems led to insecurity, unrest,
violence, socio-political instability, and the internal displacement of civilians and refugees.[7] The 1969 OAU Refugee Convention is not opposed to
the 1951 UN Convention, but complements the UN Convention definition of "refugee" and the mandate to protect refugees in Africa.[8] In sum,
the 1969 OAU Refugee Convention is directed toward implementing the
African spirit of communal solidarity among states and governments by
protecting civilians who are driven from their homes because of unstable
political situations in native states.

The definition of the term "refugee" stipulated in the conventions accords refugee status only to those who have crossed an international border.
Therefore, by these definitions, IDPs do not qualify as refugees. However,
the difference between refugees and IDPs is simply geographical, namely,
the former cross an international border while the latter, for one reason or
another, remain in their countries. Although there is a geographical difference between these two groups, they suffer from the similar problem
of homelessness. The UN, however, did not initially address the need to
protect IDPs. Often IDPs are at greater risk of insecurity than refugees because IDPs remain at the mercy of their governments for protection. The
dilemma is: can the persecutor be the protector at the same time? Neither
the 1951 UN Convention and the additional 1967 UN Protocol, nor the
1969 OAU Refugee Convention addressed the need to protect IDPs who
potentially are more vulnerable to life threatening situations than refugees
because they continue to live in unstable environments. To this day, IDPs
do not qualify as refugees.

Even though IDPs do not fall under the 1951 UN Convention, they
are ultimately accorded a measure of legal protection under the international humanitarian law:

---

[7] At the time of armed struggle against colonialism, freedom fighters were perceived by
colonialists as terrorists. However, the OAU perceived them as true liberators of Africa.
Consequently, the fighters sought refuge in other states as victims of *just wars* liberation.

[8] Van Selm, et al, *Refugee Convention At Fifty*, 32–33.

Despite not being the beneficiaries of a specific convention, as is the case for refugees, internally displaced persons (IDPs) are protected by various bodies of law, principally national law, human rights law, if they are in a state experiencing an armed conflict, international humanitarian law.[9]

UNHCR has recently raised a concern for the protection of IDPs. However, this is not yet reflected in the official policy of the organization

Background Description of Conflicts and Civil Wars: A Panoramic Historical Presentation of Causal Factors in the Great Lakes Region of Sub-Saharan Africa

Tribalism and Colonialism

The cause of the conflicts and civil wars in Rwanda that have led to an influx of refugees and IDPs in the Great Lakes Region has often been attributed to tribalism. However, tribalism alone cannot account for the unstable political situation in Rwanda after independence in 1961. One must consider how the colonialists exploited socio-political and economic differences of ethnic groups for their own advantage. The scrambles for political power in the 1990's between minority Tutsis, and majority Hutus are closely linked to colonial legacy in Rwanda.

In order to determine the impact of tribalism in Rwandan political conflicts, there is need to establish the ethnological composition of the country. The history of Belgian's presence in the Great Lakes Region of Africa began during World War I, when the Belgian forces from Congo-Leopoldville[10] defeated the Germans in 1916 and took control of both Rwanda and Burundi. Under the UN League of Nations Mandate in 1923, Belgium administered both countries as a single political entity known as Rwanda-Urundi.[11] Some claim that before the Belgians came to Rwanda, the country was asymmetrically divided along tribal lines; therefore, tribalism can be considered the root cause of conflicts and civil wars in the country. Supporters of this view believe that the Hutus, Tutsis, and Twa

[9] "Legal Protection for Internally Displaced Persons," accessed 5/25/2004.

[10] The Belgian Congo is currently known as the Democratic Republic of Congo (D. R. Congo), and its capital is Kinshasa. Historically, when Congo was a Belgian colony, its capital was called Leopoldville, after King Leopold of Belgium. Distinguishing Congo-Leopoldville from Congo-Brazzaville was easy. Brazzaville was the capital's name under French rule.

[11] Kibread, *African Refugees*, 44.

are distinct tribes in Rwanda and Burundi. They argue that the Tutsis and Hutus migrated from the North East of Africa many decades ago, and settled in both Rwanda and Burundi. At that time, the dominant aristocratic minority Hamitic Tutsi cattle owners, under the leadership of their king were 14% of the population and the Bantu Hutu majority farmers were 85% of the population.[12] The minority Twa tribe, 1% of the population, was the earliest indigenous group whose main occupation was hunting and pottery making. This ethnological analysis reveals that the Tutsis, Hutus, and Twa are distinct tribes.[13] According to this theory, scrambles for political power among these tribes existed before the coming of the Belgians to Rwanda. Therefore, proponents of this theory conclude that tribalism is the root cause of the current conflicts and civil wars in Rwanda.

The speculation that these three groups were distinct tribes has been disputed. Ethnologically, tribes are known to have distinct cultures involving languages, customs, and traditions. The Hutus, Tutsis and Twa, however, speak one language and practice similar customs and traditions in Rwanda. Furthermore, they are not separated by distinct geographical boundaries.[14] It is argued that during the pre-colonial era, these groups were one people known as Banyarwanda and spoke one language, Kinyarwanda. Over time, the Tutsis, the Hutus, and the Twa became increasingly distinguishable socially and politically, not on the basis of tribe, clans, language, customs and tradition, but rather on the basis of occupations, economics, and wealth.

As noted earlier, the Tutsis traditionally were cattle owners and warriors, the Hutus were farmers, and the Twa were hunters and pottery makers. To date, little is known about the origin of the Twa people apart from the fact that they lived on hunting and fruit gathering similar to the pygmies.[15] According to this perspective, all three groups have different

---

[12]   Ibid., 42. See Sadi, "Rwanda: The Sacred and Political Violence," 16, 17. The author affirms that the Tutsis came either from Ethiopia, Egypt, or the Middle East. This is the reason that some people in Rwanda perceive Tutsis as outsiders. Tutsis are Hamitic in origin. One theory describes the term *Hamitic* as originating from *Kemit, (K)hamit,* that denotes Egypt; while another describes the term *Hamitic* as an Arabic translation of the Greek word *Ethiopia.* The term *Ethiopia* originates from *Aetiop* to signify "burnt faces." The Tutsis are also called, the "hima" (hamitic). The Hima have been associated with the Hamitic myth: that the Tutsis are superior and Hutus are inferior. Biblically, the Hamites are believed to have descended from Ham, the son of Noah (Genesis 10:6).

[13]   Kibread, *African Refugees*, 44.

[14]   Mbanda, *Committed to Conflict*, 4.

[15]   The term *pygmy* is associated with indigenous population that lives in the wild or jungles in Rwanda, Burundi, Uganda, and D.R. Congo.

historical backgrounds, origins, and occupations but all of them share the same customs and tradition. During the pre-colonial era, wealth possession was a determining factor in acquiring social status. However, through a cultural ritual, Hutus could easily become Tutsis and vice versa. Laurent Mbanda explains:

> Most people are surprised to hear that a Hutu could become a Tutsi, and vice versa. A Hutu who gained status through wealth or by becoming a chief could become a Tutsi through a ritual of Kwihutura-literally a cleansing of one's Hutuness. In like manner, if a Tutsi lost his cattle, or turned to farming for a living and married into a Hutu family, that person could become Hutu.[16]

Despite this social arrangement, very few conflicts or civil wars occurred among these three groups during the pre-colonial era. However, during the colonial period, serious conflicts began to emerge. The Germans and the Belgians politicized the socio-political and economic differentiations in Rwanda for their own strategic interests. The relations between the Tutsis and Hutus were further polarized and strained when the Belgians from Congo-Leopoldville took over after the defeat of the Germans in the World War I. Over time, tribalism became more and more accentuated in the Rwandan politics. Philip Gourevitch notes:

> By the time that the League of Nations turned Rwanda over to Belgium as a spoil of World War I, the terms Hutu and Tutsi had become clearly defined as opposing "ethnic" identities and the Belgians made this polarization the cornerstone of their colonial policy.[17]

The Belgians influenced power relations among the Tutsis and Hutus that affected the socio-political life in Rwanda. The colonial administration pursued educational, economic, and political policies that guaranteed

---

[16] Mbanda, *Committed to Conflict*, 4. For further information, see Sadi, "Rwanda," 18–19. Sadi affirms that Rwandan oral tradition does not report of any conflicts between Tutsis and Hutus. He argues that since it is possible to find people from different ethnic groups in the same family, Tutsis and Hutus have the same ethnic origins. Since a clan denotes common ancestry, it is impossible to have different clans in the same family. Colonial rulers instituted racial profiling based on physical appearance. The *drama of the body*, as Sadi describes it, was a point of reference and differentiation between the Tutsis and Hutus. Furthermore, Karegeye affirms that wealth in terms of cattle would determine social classes. "A Rwandan owning more than ten cows was specified as a Tutsi. Less than this number reduced the Rwandan to the status of Hutu."

[17] Gourevitch, *We Wish to Inform You*, 54.

the domination of the Tutsi over the Hutus in all aspects of life.[18] The few Hutu who received education came from the Catholic Church's sponsored institutions such as seminaries.[19] Since the Belgians used the indirect rule of "divide and rule," the main purpose of the colonial school system was to train intermediaries to run local administration at the lowest ranks and staff private colonial firms.[20] The Belgians' technique of using intermediaries such as Tutsi aristocratic clan leaders was a pragmatic means to colonize the people. It was viewed as more convenient and efficacious for the colonial power to depend on a tribe, clan, or a group of tribes that had the reputation of being powerful or well organized as a strategy for advancing their interests.[21]

As the minority Tutsis became increasingly powerful economically, they took control of the political life of Rwanda. The Belgian colonial authorities used indigenous political institutions under the exclusive control of the minority Tutsis, as a tool for their own administrative advantages. The majority Hutus were on the margin of society economically, socially, and politically, and they were totally excluded from the colonial administration. Due to the socio-political and economic inequalities between the two tribes, the Hutus were deliberately subjugated to degrading and humiliating treatment both at the hands of the colonialist and their Tutsi masters.[22]

The aristocratic Tutsi majority was recruited to the Belgian army and the police force, leading to resentment from the Hutu majority.[23] To add to the inequality, for a period of time in the early 1960's after the independence from Belgium, there was an unfair distribution of resources among the local communities. Consequently, the Hutus and the Twa were disenfranchised and remained at the margin of society.

Due to the political developments from colonialism and tribalism, Rwanda experienced two major mass migrations, leading to humanitarian crises. Phase one took place shortly after independence in the 1960's, and phase two in 1994. In the early 1960's, the tragic death of Mwami Mtara V in Rwanda,[24] triggered tension between the Belgian colonial adminis-

---

[18] Ibid.

[19] John, *Africa's Refugee Crisis,* 69.

[20] Rodney, *How Europe Underdeveloped Africa,* 240.

[21] John, *Africa's Refugee Crisis,* 69.

[22] Kibread, *African Refugees,* 44–45.

[23] John, *Africa's Refugee Crisis,* 70.

[24] The term *Mwami* means "king" in Rwanda and Burundi.

tration and the Tutsis. The latter believed that their king died under suspicious circumstances, most likely poisoning by a Belgium doctor. They reacted negatively to the death incident by disengaging themselves from the Belgians and formed a political party known as the National Rwandese Union (UNAR). This sequence of events sparked a serious misunderstanding that caused a rift between the Tutsis and the Belgian colonial administration.[25] Based on this state of affairs, Belgium tried to isolate the Tutsis by encouraging the Hutus to oppose the UNAR. Consequently, civil war broke out in Rwanda between the two groups, forcing thousands of Tutsis and privileged Hutus and Twa to flee the country to Tanzania.

In addition to the political turmoil, the so-called "social revolution" exacerbated conflicts in Rwanda. During the 1961 general elections, under the influence of the Belgian colonial administration, the Hutu political party, known as Party for the Liberation of the Hutu People (PALIPEHUTU), won the elections and gained 78% of the seats in the parliament.[26] At the same time, the Belgian colonial administration officially abolished feudalism and replaced it with a republic. These events marked the first social revolution of the majority rule in Rwanda. In the January 1961 general elections, Gregoire Kayibanda, a Hutu, became the first president of the Republic of Rwanda. Moreover, the social revolution favoring the oppressed Hutu majority in Rwanda was greatly influenced by the Christian missionaries from Belgium.[27]

The transition from monarchy to republic in Rwanda in the 1960's was marked by painful experiences characterized by conflicts, deaths, and the flight of civilians. During this period, political power was concentrated in the hands of the Hutus. Tensions were not only between the Tutsis, who lost the elections and their Hutus rivals, but also between the Tutsis and the Belgian colonial administration. In retaliation for the disparity of power, Tutsi commandos pillaged villages, burned houses, and killed Hutus. As the Tutsis stepped up the action against their colonial master, Belgium, "the colonial administration answered by launching abhorrent massacres of Tutsis and provoked their flight into exile."[28] Thousands of Tutsi refugees fled from Rwanda to D.R. Congo, Uganda, Burundi, and Tanzania.[29] A report by UNHCR confirmed that there was an estimated

---

[25] Gourevitch, *We Wish to Inform You*, 60.

[26] John, *Africa's Refugee Crisis*, 70.

[27] See Gourevitch, *We Wish to Inform You*, 58.

[28] John, *Africa's Refugee Crisis*, 70.

[29] Kibread, *African Refugees*, 43. At the independence in 1961, the Belgian Congo was

200,000 Rwandan refugees who fled to Burundi, 40,000 to Tanzania, and 20,000 others to Kenya.[30]

The second great mass migration took place during the 1994 genocide, a scenario that shocked the world and had the largest impact on the course of history in Rwanda since independence in 1961. In 1990, the Tutsis were persecuted through a powerful scheme designed by Hutu controlled government propaganda in both print and electronic media. For example, the journal, *Kangura,* meaning *Wake Up,* contained the so-called "Hutu Ten Commandments," urging the Hutus to dissociate themselves from the Tutsis. At the same time, the electronic media, *Radio Television Libres des Milles Collines* urged the Hutus to persecute the Tutsis.[31]

In 1994, a full-fledged conflict erupted in the wake of a plane crash that killed the Burundian president Cyprien Ntaryamira and his counterpart president of Rwanda, Juvenal Habyarimanna, both Hutus. Once again, the hostilities and tensions between the Tutsis and Hutus were brought to light. There were conflicting reports inside and outside the country about who was responsible for the plane crash. According to *A Chronology of U.S./U.N. Actions*, Hutu extremists suspecting that the Rwandan president was about to implement the Arusha Peace Accords, a treaty between the Hutus and Tutsis, were believed to be behind the plane crash. It was claimed that Rwandan political extremists did not want the peace treaty in Arusha, Tanzania, to succeed. Its success would mean that these two groups would share power in the new government, a move that displeased Hutus extremists. However, according to *Inter Press Service News Agency*, the Rwandan Patriotic Front (RPF), a Tutsi rebel group, under the leadership of Paul Kagame was to blame for the killing. The agency reported that the French daily, *Le Monde:*

> Disclosed that a French judge who investigated the crash after a call for an inquiry by the family of one of the pilots, had concluded the RPF was not only responsible but Kagame himself had ordered the shoot down . . . Le Monde's account was confirmed by a former RPF member, Abdul Ruzibiza, in an interview with the British Broadcasting Corporation (BBC) in which he claimed he had been charged with preparing the operation.[32]

changed to the Democratic Republic of the Congo.

[30] John, *Africa's Refugee Crisis*, 71.

[31] Josephat, "Crises in the Great Lakes," 26.

[32] Lobe, "Rwanda–US," accessed 2/12/2004 and 5/6/2004.

The killings of civilians began the night of April 6, 1994, when the Rwandan Armed Forces (FAR) and Hutu militia (*the interahamwe*) set up roadblocks and went from house to house, killing Tutsis and moderate Hutu politicians.[33] The killings were discriminately carried out because the Rwandan identity cards were ethnically marked.[34]

Two days later, on April 8, 1994, the Tutsi-led RPF launched a major offensive to end the killings and rescue 600 of its troops who were part of the Arusha Accord, that were surrounded in the Rwandan capital, Kigali. Thousands of refugees left their homes and fled from the advance of the Tutsi army into Tanzania, Burundi, and Zaire. Following this offensive, an estimated one million ethnic Hutu Rwandans fled the country.[35] As the RPF increased its military offensive against the defeated Hutu government, Kigali fell to the control of the Tutsi armed forces.

Hutu government officials fled the country into Zaire. The RPF set up an interim government that marked the end of the genocide in which an estimated over 800,000 Rwandans, mainly Tutsi minority, lost their lives within 100 days.[36] The Rwandan debacle is a landmark event in the history of the Great Lakes Region of the Sub-Saharan Africa.

Although the "tribal factor" contributed to the Rwandan conflict, colonialism exacerbated tribalism. The colonial legacy orchestrated the socio-political and economic disparities between the Hutus and the Tutsis that led to hostilities, revenge, conflicts, and ultimately, genocide in Rwanda. Sharp differences and hostilities between Tutsis and Hutus were non-existent in the pre-colonial era. No sooner had the Belgians occupied Rwanda, than a serious rift emerged between Tutsis and Hutus. With the departure of the Belgians in the early 1960's, the hostilities immediately became more and more conspicuous. Such politically instigated tribalism continued to erode social cohesion, and political and economic stability in Rwanda.

---

[33] "A Chronology of U.S./U.N. Actions," accessed 2/12/2004. The Arusha Accords, signed in the town of Arusha, Tanzania, signify a historic moment for peace between the Rwandan government and the rebels or opposition.

[34] Fred De Sam Lazaro, a Rwandan civilian, claims that the Hutus and Tutsis are virtually indistinguishable in physical features, language, and religion. This claim supports the view that the Tutsis and Hutus were at one time a single community of people that shared similar values, traditions, customs, and language. For more information, see "Religion and Conflicts in Rwanda," accessed 2/12/2004; see also Sadi, "Rwanda," 19.

[35] "Rwanda 2002," accessed on 10/4/2004.

[36] Ibid.

Today, as the region continues to strive for reconciliation and national unity, the adverse impact of colonialism and tribalism is far from over in Rwanda. If the negative effects of colonialism and tribalism go unchecked, they will continue to fuel civil strife and conflicts leading to humanitarian crises. Moreover, other factors such as the lack of political leadership skills and good governance contribute to conflicts, civil wars, mass migrations, and humanitarian crises in the region.

Political Leadership Skills and Governance

The strong interrelationship between political leadership, mass migrations, and humanitarian crises should be seen from a historical perspective. In the Great Lakes Region, it is impossible to dissociate African politics from the colonial past; therefore, the colonial legacy is part and parcel of contemporary African politics. People in the region have had a variety of reactions toward colonialism and African leadership, leading to a two-fold resistance: resistance against colonialism and resistance against African leadership. The situations in Uganda and Kenya, both formerly under the British rule, are good illustrations of the relationship between political leadership, mass migrations, and humanitarian crises.

In the 1950's, popular resistance against the British rule took form in a liberation movement in Kenya, known as MAUMAU.[37] This uprising caused thousands of Kenyans to become internally displaced. Several years later, a second popular uprising occurred against African leaders in independent states who were accused of political mismanagement.

Some critics point an accusing finger to colonial rulers for the unstable situation in these countries, while others accuse African leadership of being directly responsible for the state of affairs. It is claimed that during colonial rule, most of the economic policies in Africa generated underdevelopment and stagnation. For instance, some of the agricultural policies favored growing cash crops to provide raw materials for the European market industries instead of food crops to provide for the population.[38] These policies, which were a common practice in pre-colonial Kenya and other countries in the region, led to poverty, famine, and internal displace-

---

[37] MAUMAU is an acronym, which stands for the Kiswahili translation, *Mzungu Aende Ulaya, Mwafrika Apate Uhuru*. Literally, it means, "Europeans should pack and go back to their own country, so that Africans may be set free." The Kiswahili language is spoken in Kenya, Tanzania, Uganda, Rwanda, Burundi, and D.R. Congo.

[38] Nelson, *Hunger for Justice,* 11.

ment of civilians in the region.[39] This is compelling evidence that mass migrations and humanitarian crises are closely linked to colonialism and poverty. However, other critics argue that African leadership is more to blame than former colonial rulers for the current upheavals. The truth of the matter is that colonial legacy and African political leadership share the blame for the conflicts that have led to an influx of refugees and IDPs in the Great Lakes Region.

It is worth establishing that poor education for the African leaders also contributes to unstable situation in the region. After independence, there were growing expectations and desires for a better quality of life among citizens. Yet, leaders failed to fulfill them. This imbalance is attributed to insufficiently preparing African leaders with modern leadership skills. The colonial powers' failure to offer effective education to most Africans has contributed significantly to the unstable conditions of contemporary governments in Africa. Poor education led to a lack of managerial skills and ultimately contributed to political dictatorship, popular resistance, conflicts, mass migrations, and humanitarian crises in the region.[40]

Additionally, African leaders faced administrative difficulties as a result of the colonial legacy. As leaders of the independent states, they were confronted with two models of government: the traditional political system and the colonial political system. Because colonialism disrupted the African traditional political system, it was difficult for African leaders to re-establish this type of rule after independence. As a result, they resorted to the colonial system with which they were familiar. However, the lack of education as well as sociological factors posed serious obstacles to implementing effective governments. The Western economic model of organizations and structures is quite difficult to adopt in African societies, which have traditionally been agricultural, pastoral and nomadic.[41] Furthermore, colonial powers did not teach the principles of democracy, but rather, taught and practiced authoritarianism right up to the time their rule was brought to an end.[42] Ultimately, African leaders failed to create a modern political system and the result is the existence of neo-colonialism in the region. Mistaken policies have contributed to repression and popular re-

---

[39] John, *Africa's Refugee Crisis*, 61.
[40] Kibread, *African Refugees*, 37–41.
[41] Symser, *Refugees*, 65.
[42] Bulcha, "Historical, Political and Social Causes," 21.

sistance. However, more importantly, an inequitable distribution of power and wealth has led to social unrest and violence.[43]

After the attainment of political independence, there emerged two types of leadership in the region: one-party rule and military dictatorship.[44] Uganda is good example of a country that has experienced both types. Uganda gained its independence from Britain in 1962, and under the first president, Milton Obote, the country became a multi-party state. During this time, several western countries withdrew support for the government of Uganda for two reasons: First, it was alleged that during his tenure, Obote nationalized 80 British firms, sending an alarm to British entrepreneurs. Second, the West viewed Obote as a pro-socialist.[45] Following these developments, in January 1971, Idi Amin Dada led a British-supported military coup, overthrew the incumbent president and seized power. Multi-party democracy was halted and the country became a military dictatorship. Political totalitarianism under the new president, Idi Amin Dada, caused a mass exodus.[46] During his regime, there were reports of atrocities, deaths, detention and torture for political and religious reasons. Idi Amin Dada attempted to eliminate Milton Obote's elite class, fearing that they posed a political threat to his regime.

Another major factor contributing to political conflicts in Uganda during this period was religion. In the 1960's Obote, a Protestant, led a political party called the Uganda People's Congress (UPC) that drew the majority of its followers from Protestants. Likewise, Paul Ssemogerere, a Catholic, led a political party called the Democratic Party (DP) that drew the majority of its followers from Catholics. Although at this time, religious differences existed between these two parties, they did not generate serious conflicts or an influx of refugees. During Obote's presidency, there was religious tolerance and conflicts between Christians and Muslims were virtually non-existent. However, following Idi Amin Dada's coup, things changed. Amin was a Moslem and as a means of winning support in the Islamic world, he downplayed Christianity. During his tenure, the government abolished individual civil and political rights. The move was designed to eliminate specific ethnic groups, such as the Acholi and Lan'go (members of Obote's ethnic group), Christians and elite business people.[47]

---

[43] Arrupe, *Refugee Crisis in Africa,* 9.

[44] Magesa and Nthamburi, *Democracy and Reconciliation,* 15.

[45] John, *Africa's Refugee Crisis,* 62.

[46] Ibid.

[47] U.S. Senate, *World Refugee Crisis,* 106, 108.

These social changes caused fears in the country, especially among these ethnic groups, driving many of them into exile.

As the political tension mounted in Uganda, "UNHCR estimated that in the early 1979 alone, about 200 refugees per month crossed the border from Uganda into neighboring countries."[48] Under Amin's regime, an estimated 50,000 to 300,000 people were killed, and 15,000 Ugandan refugees fled to Kenya and 20,000 others to Tanzania.[49] Additionally, an estimated 40,000 to 50,000 Asian business people were expelled from Uganda during his tenure.[50]

Prior to 2005, multiparty democracy was banned in Uganda from the time Yoweri Kaguta Museveni seized power through guerrilla warfare in the 1980's. Museveni claimed that multiparty democracy would precipitate tribal conflicts and religious animosity among Ugandans. He makes reference to the tribal and religious conflicts during the regimes of Milton Obote and Idi Amin Dada. Due to both domestic and international pressure, however, Museveni reinstated multi-party democracy in 2005. The hotly contested multi-party elections were held on February 23, 2006 and, indeed, Museveni won the majority vote and retained the presidency.[51] Over the last 17 years Uganda continues to experience civil wars between the government and the rebel groups that remain opposed to Museveni. Joseph Kony's rebel movement of the Lord's Resistance Army (LRA), the main rebel group in the north, remains a major challenge to president Museveni's government.

The government reprisals against the rebel forces contribute to many deaths and massive internal displacement of innocent civilians to this day. The Global IDP Project of the Norwegian Refugee Council has urged the Ugandan government to protect IDPs who have settled in camps since the escalation of conflicts in June 2003.[52] The northern areas of Uganda, especially the districts of Gulu, Kitgum, and Pader, have been hit hardest by the conflicts. This situation is exacerbated by the hostilities between Uganda and Sudan. Each of these countries accuses the other of supporting the rebels opposed to their own governments.

According to a senior UN official, the conflicts in northern Uganda, lasting for more than 17 years, have caused an internal displacement of

[48] Ibid.
[49] Ibid.
[50] Ibid.
[51] "Uganda General Election, 2006," accessed 6/1/2006.
[52] Reliefweb, "Uganda: Mass Displacement to Unprotected Camps," accessed 12/30/2003.

civilians that in July 2002 was estimated to be 650,000 and in December 2003 soared to 1.4 million.[53] Recently, since the governments of Uganda and Sudan have reached an agreement to not support the rebels of either side, hostilities between these two countries have been dramatically reduced. Unfortunately, however, since the agreement, the LRA rebels have changed their tactics of engagement by lodging more attacks against innocent civilians inside Uganda. There are continued efforts made by the parties involved to end the hostilities.

In post-independence African states, since the 1980's, the process of transitioning from one-party rule to multiparty democracy has been painful. The political transition has contributed to the current crises of internally displaced civilians in the region. Initially, some African state leaders conceived the notion of one-party rule as a political model for achieving national unity and nation building, especially in areas where tribalism was perceived as a major problem. However, others instigated the so-called "pseudo-tribal tensions" among the populations aimed at creating the false impression that Africa was not ready to embrace multi-party democracy because it divided people along tribal lines that led to instability. The claim that political pluralism caused violence, conflicts, and civil wars and jeopardized national unity was a rationalization for protecting their own political interests (*Realpolitik*).

The political history of Kenya in 1982 is a good illustration of political leadership, leading to an internal displacement of civilians in the region. Shortly before the general elections were held in Kenya in 1982, there were reports of land based tribal clashes in the "Burnt Forest" area of Rift Valley Province. Many people suspected that the Kenya National Union (KANU) government instigated the conflicts for political gain.[54] The tribal communities of Kalenjin, Luo (Nilotic-origin), Luhya and Kikuyu (Bantu-origin) co-existed peacefully in the area for a long time. These tribes, with the exception of the Kalenjin, moved into the so-called "Burnt Forest" area several years ago in search for land.[55]

The majority of the Kikuyu, Luhya, and Luo tribes did not support the KANU-led government of the former President Daniel Toroitich Arap

---

[53] Ibid. The Norwegian Relief Council did not disclose the name of the senior UN official.

[54] *KANU* is one of the political parties in Kenya in the Great Lakes Region. The KANU-led government was in power from 1962 until 2003.

[55] Burnt Forest is a name given by the local residents in the area in which people burn wood for charcoal for business as source of energy. Kikuyu, Luhya, Luo, and Kalenjin are indigenous tribes of Kenya in the East African Region.

Moi. The government supporters clashed with the people in opposition. The KANU government lobbied for support of other political parties by using fear and intimidation. Forcing the opposing groups to move else-where-created political zones aligned to the KANU government. In a period of four years, between 1991 and 1994, an estimated 2,000 people were killed, houses were burned, and 300,000 civilians were internally displaced.[56] Human rights groups condemned those involved in these atrocities. Based on this political scenario in Kenya as well as the one in Uganda it may be concluded that conflicts and the internal displacement of civilians are a result of the lack of political leadership skills and good governance in the Great Lakes Region of Sub-Saharan Africa.

Politics, Race, and Religion

In the last three decades, violence, conflicts, and civil wars between the Arab-Moslems in the north, and the predominantly African Christians and traditional religious adherents in the south of Sudan have been the cause of internal displacement of civilians and an influx of refugees in the Great Lakes Region of Africa. African Christians and traditional religious adherents in the south continue to be victims of discrimination on the basis of race and religion by the Arab Moslems in the north. Racial discrimination is also practiced when employing for government jobs. However, one of the most severe forms of discrimination is the continued practice of slavery.

Although by international law slavery is considered a crime against humanity, the Arab-Moslems in the north continue to enslave the African blacks from the south. Young boys and girls are taken captive by Arab militias and sold to Arab merchants in the north and forced into labor in houses and on farms. While in slavery, they often endure the physical and sexual abuse of their masters.[57] This kind of discrimination created discontent among African blacks that led to the formation of the rebel movement in the 1970's known as Anya Anya I.[58]

---

[56] Okumu, "Land Clashes in Burnt Forest," 52.

[57] Prisca Tenui, "Conflicts in the Sudan," 116–17.

[58] *Anya Anya* means "warriors." It derives its name from one of the native tribes in the south that is predominantly black Africans. It is worth noting that the *Anya Anya* rebel movement was transformed into the Sudanese Peoples' Liberation Movement (SPLM), and the Sudanese Peoples' Liberation Army (SPLA). The SPLA remains the main opposition rebel group to the Arab-led government.

In addition to the racial discrimination in Sudan, the influence of religion on the day-to-day socio-political life is increasing. The imposition of Islamic Sharia law in Sudan in the 1980's has contributed greatly to the conflicts, resistance, and civil wars between Arab-Moslems in the north and African-Christians, and traditional adherents in the south. The Islamic Sharia law, introduced first in 1983 by the former President Jafar Nimeiri and reinforced by Premier Sadiq-el Mahdi in 1986, initially was binding only in the north. The Islamic Sharia law is a penal code in which flogging, stoning to death and amputation of culprits' limbs are penalties for various offenses.[59] In a twist of events in 1989, the President of Sudan, Mohamed Omar Al Bashir, declared that Islamic Sharia law would be fully implemented in the whole country.

From the moment the Arab-Moslem Khartoum government declared an enactment of Islamic Sharia law throughout the country, there has been resistance from the predominantly Christian south. In response to the resistance, the government declared Jihad against the predominantly Christian south. Confrontations between the SPLA rebel forces and the government have led to devastation, poverty, hunger, disease and a high mortality rate. Thousands of civilians are internally displaced and thousands of others are refugees in other countries in the Great Lakes Region and in the Horn of Africa.[60] The UNHCR sources indicate that as of 2002, Uganda, Kenya, and the Central African Republic have received a total number of 16,000 refugees from Sudan.[61]

From the outside, these conflicts may be perceived as being simply religiously or ethnically motivated. However, the bottom line is that the Africans in the south have been deprived of an equal opportunity to participate fully and share equally in economic resources and political decision-making.[62] Nevertheless, there is growing optimism that the peace agreement signed between the government and the SPLA on January 9, 2005 is expected bring to an end the 21 years of civil wars in Sudan. Basically, "The peace deal calls for sharing power and oil revenues and exempting Christians from Muslim Sharia law."[63]

Yet, quite recently, a new turn of events is emerging in Sudan. Persecution against the black Africans in the Western Darfur region is yet

---

[59] Tenui, "Conflicts in the Sudan," 115.

[60] Ibid., 109.

[61] "Major Refugee Arrivals 2002"; accessed 7/11/2004.

[62] Ferris, *Beyond Borders,* 137.

[63] Donnelly, "Government, Rebels," A23.

another manifestation of the racial discrimination that is pervasive in the country. Reports of recent fighting between the government army, and the opposition groups, the *Sudan Liberation Army (SLA) and the Justice of Equality Movement* in the Western Darfur region, indicate that an estimated 100,000 refugees have fled across the desert border to Chad[64] and hundreds of thousands of others are IDPs. The refugees tell horrifying stories of indiscriminate killing, torture and rapes by Arab militias, the *Janjaweed*, affiliated with the Arab-dominated government in Khartoum. Moreover, the Khartoum government is depriving refugees' relief assistance by denying humanitarian relief organizations access to Darfur region.[65] Hence, the scenarios in Sudan's political history demonstrate that mass migrations and humanitarian crises are a result of racial and religious persecution in the Great Lakes Region of Sub-Saharan Africa.

Cold War Politics and Regional Conflicts

The emergence of East-West politics in the world, following World War II, had an enormous impact on regional politics that contributed to conflicts, mass exoduses, and humanitarian crises in the Great Lakes Region, while the key countries involved, namely, the U.S. and the former U.S.S.R. remained relatively peaceful.[66] During the Cold War, the planet was divided ideologically into first and second worlds. The former represented a democratic and capitalist system, and the latter represented a communist and socialist system. The third world was often a bipolar political battleground and "the staging ground for circumscribed, surrogate wars between the two."[67] It is believed that in Africa in the 1960's, the Cold War was politically and economically motivated. The situation in the Congo-Leopoldville[68] during this time is the best illustration of the impact of the Cold War ideology on the regional politics.

---

[64] Lacey, "Uprooted Sudanese," A3. See also Lacey, "Sudan Frustrated," A6.

[65] Sengupta, "Sudan's Ethnic Strife," A20. The peace deal reached between the major rebel groups in Darfur and the Arab dominated government in Khartoum through the African Union mediation hopes to bring lasting peace and justice in the region. See Shirbon, "Sudan Signs Peace Deal," accessed 6/1/2006.

[66] Josephat, "Crisis in the Great Lakes," 12

[67] Schreiter, *New Catholicity*, 5.

[68] It is worth noting the successive changes of names for the country of the Democratic Republic of Congo (D.R. Congo) in the Great Lakes Region of Sub-Saharan Africa. Before independence, the Belgian Congo was known as Congo-Leopoldville. After independence, it was named, Democratic Republic of the Congo. Then, in 1965, the former president Mobutu Sese Seko re-named it, Zaire. When Joseph Desire Kabila seized power in 2000,

Bipolar politics in the Congo during the 1960's contributed to a war between the nationalist movement, headed by Patrice Lumumba, and the western allies. Because of rich mineral resources such as copper and uranium, especially in the Katanga Province, Congo was very attractive economically to outside countries. From colonial times, trade in precious minerals (gems) has been at the heart of conflicts and civil wars in Africa, particularly in the Congo. In the 1960's, the Belgian colonial administration instigated an uprising in Katanga Province, aimed at dividing the country for an economic gain. The colonial regime with the support of some African puppets crushed Patrice Lumumba's nationalist movement, which was intended to liberate the Congo completely from external political influence. It is apparent that external geo-strategic economic interests became intertwined with regional politics and conflicts in the Congo. Michael John notes:

> The exploitation of the mines was a strategic necessity for the economy of the capitalist countries and faced with the strength and the determination of Congolese nationalism, the directors of the mining companies obliged the industrial region of Katanga to proclaim its secession.[69]

It is worth noting that the Katanga conflict was a legacy of Belgium colonialism. On June 30, 1960, the Republic of Congo gained independence from Belgium. Joseph Kasavubu became the first president, and Patrice Lumumba, his prime minister. During this time, a serious power struggle between the president and the premier occurred due to differences in political opinions and strategies for the country.[70] Lumumba requested UN intervention in the Congo conflict, but this was futile because the West viewed his nationalist movement as a pro-communist.[71] The UN was controlled by powerful western nations, so it was partial to their geo-strategic interests in the region. Lumumba was seen as a serious obstacle to western interests because his liberation movement was a push for the good of not only the Congo, but also for the rest of the region, which was still under the colonial rule (Northern and Southern Rhodesia, Mozambique,

he restored its post-independence name, Democratic Republic of the Congo (D.R. Congo). For further information on the history of D.R. Congo, see "Key Events," accessed 9/13/2004.

[69] John, *Africa's Refugee Crisis*, 44–45.

[70] "Key Events," accessed 9/13/2004.

[71] For a detailed information of UN military intervention in the Congo, see Bloomer, "Violence in the Congo."

Angola, and South Africa).[72] Western countries regarded the nationalists as communist agents, therefore, they felt a need to install a puppet candidate to run the country and protect their interests. Conflicts of interests between the West and Patrice Lumumba's nationalist movement led to frictions, hostilities, clashes, fears, and the internal displacement of civilians. Refugees fled to Angola as well as other neighboring countries.[73]

On January 17, 1961, Patrice Lumumba was assassinated and a second round of civil war erupted in the Katanga Province of Zaire between the National Front for Liberation of Congo (FNLC) and the government forces led by the Army Chief, Mobutu Sese Seko. Some believed that the FNLC, belonging to the former exiled Katanga insurgents and perhaps also to the Lumumba and Moise Tshombe loyalists, invaded Katanga Province (Shaba) from Angola.[74] As a result, the country became deeply divided politically. An association between the communists and Zairian politicians was made based on allegations that the Soviets were assisting Lumumba. In order to maintain law and order necessary for political survival, Mobutu and his western allies crushed the Katanga uprising. Nevertheless, this incident of repression and reprisal caused thousands of refugees to flee into Angola and Zambia once more.[75]

It is generally assumed that the Soviets were chiefly responsible for the two incidents of civil wars in the Congo.[76] However, the U.S. is partly to blame. The conflicts that caused an influx of refugees were a result of the hostilities between the two super-powers. One must consider that the super-power military presence in the region, highly motivated by strategic economic interests, added more turmoil in the area. U.S. military spending was increased under the disguise of deterring the imminent threat of nuclear war. In fact, increased military spending was an impetus to stimulate economic growth in the U.S. The strategy of using arms proliferation to improve the economy in the country was successful in the past when "World War II brought the United States out of depression."[77] From this

---

[72] Fanon, *Toward the African Revolution*, 193–96.

[73] John, *Africa's Refugee Crisis*, 45. No reports are available on the number of IDPs and refugees.

[74] "Key Events," accessed 9/13/2004.

[75] John, *Africa's Refugee Crisis*, 45.

[76] Ibid. The civil wars that Michael John is referring to took place in the early 1960's (between Patrice Lumumba's nationalist movement and Moise Tshombe's Belgium backed separatist forces in Katanga Province) and in the mid 1970's (between Mobutu government and former Katanga separatists, and remnants of Lumumba nationalist movement).

[77] Nelson, *Hunger for Justice*, 76.

historical perspective, I can conclude that all parties in the Cold War conflicts, the U.S. and the former U.S.S.R., bear responsibility for the state of
affairs in the Congo.

Players in the West-East confrontational politics continued to influence regional politics throughout the 1980's. Each side supported policies
that protected its own interests in Zaire. For example, the West continued
to provide military and economic support to Mobutu's dictatorial regime,
despite his repressive policies. Lack of firm democratic structures has largely contributed to socio-political and economic instability, conflicts and
civil wars in the country. The UNHCR report indicates that as of 2002,
there were 39,000 Zairian refugees in Burundi, Tanzania, and Zambia as
a result of the situation.[78] Unfortunately, Zaire was not the only African
country to experience the impact of the West-East conflict.

The Cold War conflict reached its climax in the 1990's in Somalia,
generating another influx of refugees and humanitarian crises in the Great
Lakes Region. In 1977 war broke out over the Ethiopian Ogaden area between Somalia, a firm ally of the former U.S.S.R., and Ethiopia. Somalia
claimed that Ogaden, an area rich in mineral resources, was part of its territory. Rather than siding with Somalia, the former U.S.S.R. gave support
to Ethiopia and, with the help of Cuban soldiers, drove out the Somali
invaders. The war forced more than a million people to flee their homes
and seek refuge in the neighboring countries.[79] On October 21, 1982,
in the wake of the Soviet action against Somalia, on October 21, 1982,
U.S. President Ronald Reagan signed an agreement with Somali President
Mohamed Siedd Barre, giving U.S. military and economic assistance to
Somalia for fighting their aggressor, the U.S.S.R.[80] Consequently, the
Horn of Africa was diametrically divided along West-East ideologies. In
1991, the central Somali government collapsed. Two major factors caused
internal conflict and civil war leading to the collapse of Mohamed Siade
Barre's government on January 5, 1991; one was the termination of all
western economic and military aid, and the second, was the decline in
world prices of Somalia's main export, livestock:

---

[78] *Refugees by Numbers* 2003, accessed 9/11/2004.

[79] John, *Africa's Refugee Crisis*, 46. Also see Bulcha's views on the Cold War as one of the
root causes of refugee influx in the Horn of African Region in which Somalia is located.
"In their efforts to solicit support they ally themselves with local power-holders and supply
them with large amounts of sophisticated war weapons with which the local power-holders
seek to maintain their control over their subjects." Bulcha, "Historical, Political and Social
Causes," 20.

[80] John, *Africa's Refugee Crisis*, 46.

Once the global military rivalry between the United States and the Soviet Union receded, there was no geo-strategic reason for either nation to supply aid to countries in the horn of Africa.[81]

During Mohamed Siedd Barre's administration, the U.S. government publicly expressed dismay over increasing reports of human rights deprivations due to undemocratic policies. Notwithstanding these violations, for years the U.S. government continued to support the Somali government as part of its Cold War strategy in East Africa.[82] As the threat of the Soviet Union to the U.S. receded, and Soviet support for its allies diminished, human rights deprivations came to dwarf the strategic significance of Somalia. Due to the absence of compelling strategic need, the U.S. cut off all military aid to Somalia in mid-1988 and diverted US $21 million in economic aid to other African nations. The U.S. closed the door to Somalia in October 1989.[83]

Lack of financial support had a devastating effect on Mohamed Siedd Barre's administration. The entire Somali infrastructure became paralyzed leading to full-scale civil war between warring factional clans and warlords, and the government. This in turn led to the total collapse of the Somali central government. In the aftermath of the collapse, the country was fractured between clans and warlords. Internal conflicts and civil wars among different warlords caused loss of life, poverty, and the destruction of infrastructures. It is estimated that more than 600,000 refugees crossed the border into Ethiopia, Yemen, and Djibouti in the Horn of Africa and Kenya in the Great Lakes Region as a consequence.[84] Moreover, hundreds of Somali refugees have sought asylum overseas principally in the United Kingdom and in the U.S.

The Cold War politics, compounded by political mismanagement and the lack of democratic reforms by the Somali government, have contributed to the internal conflicts, civil wars, mass exoduses, and humanitarian crises in Great Lakes Region, characterizing the current situation. The U.S. and the former U.S.S.R. protected their geo-strategic interests in Somalia, and the government of Siedd Barre protected his own interests. Despite its abhorrent human rights record, the Somali government

---

[81] Blakley, "Somalia, Case Preview," accessed 7/11/2004.

[82] Ibid. The phrase, "The Horn of Africa" connotes an area of Eastern Africa that derives that name from its geographical shape on the map. Somalia is located in this area. However, Blakely refers to Somalia, as part of Eastern Africa since the phrase, "The Horn of Africa" is not commonly used.

[83] Blakley, "Somalia, Case Preview."

[84] Ibid.

enjoyed full political and military support from its allies. The Somali government used the support to suppress political opponents who demanded a fair share in the country's resources and full participation in the democratic process of the country.

Maintaining a balance of power between foreign geo-strategic and domestic interests vis-à-vis internal democratic reforms and the promotion of human rights may not have been easy. However, a balance of power and interests was essential to avert civil war and prevent the collapse of Somalia, mass migrations, and humanitarian crises in the region. Thomas Knight in his seminar course on *US Intervention in Failed States at the National Defense University National War College* affirms the notion that Somalia is one of the failed states and a victim of the Cold War conflict in the Horn of Africa.[85] Since the current Transitional Government (TNG) is extremely weak and controls only half of the city of Mogadishu, the ongoing conflicts between warring Somali factions continue to pose a security threat to people's lives in Somalia.[86]

Conclusion

In this chapter, I have argued that conflicts, violence, and civil wars triggering mass migrations and humanitarian crises in the Great Lakes Region are multi-faceted, and cannot be blamed solely on tribalism. Neither can we exclusively regard colonialism as the cause of the unstable social conditions. The 1994 Rwandan genocide is the best illustration of how both tribalism and colonialism caused devastating violence, deaths, mass migrations, and humanitarian crises in the Great Lakes Region.

Lack of political leadership skills and good governance contributed to the unstable situation in the region. The conflicts in Uganda in the 1970's, and in Kenya in the 1980's were a consequence of a combination of these factors that ultimately led to internal displacement of civilians and the flight of refugees into exile.

The link between Cold War politics, conflicts and civil wars leading to mass migrations and humanitarian crises has been established. This link was illustrated by the socio-political situations in Zaire and Somalia. The collapse of the Somali central government in 1991, remains a good illustration of the impact Cold War politics had on regional conflicts in the region.

---

[85] Knight, *Fundamentals of Strategic Logic*, 2.

[86] Menkhaus, "Somalia at Crossroad," accessed 2/21/2004.

There is a close link between politics, race, and religion, and civil wars, mass migrations, and humanitarian crises in the region. This link has been illustrated by the state of affairs in Sudan where religion and race are the basis for persecution and discrimination in government jobs. For almost three decades, race and religion are at the root of insurgence, resistance, and humanitarian crises among the black Africans in the south. The current crisis in western Darfur region is another demonstration of racial discrimination in the Great Lakes Region of Africa.

As seen in the cases of Rwanda, D.R. Congo, Uganda, and Kenya, the colonial legacy is a *leitmotif* in the current conflicts and civil wars in the region. As an expression of neo-colonialism and globalization, the economics of war as well as the lack of control over arms and precious minerals trade contribute to the problem and the current escalation of conflicts and civil wars in the region. Lack of positive action continues to create huge humanitarian crises in the region. Because the refugee problem is multi-dimensional, it requires a multi-dimensional approach to solve it. Finding a lasting solution to the humanitarian crises in the region requires a long-term commitment, aimed at bringing about a holistic liberation in the region. In the next chapter, I will examine the legal and moral criteria in responding to humanitarian crises in the Great Lakes Region of Sub-Saharan Africa.

PART II

An Evaluative Description of the
Response to the Humanitarian Crises:
Legal and Moral Criteria

2

Responding to the Humanitarian Crises of Refugees and IDPs

Introduction

In the previous chapter, I argued that conflicts and civil wars causing the migration crises and humanitarian catastrophe in the Great Lakes Region of the Sub-Saharan Africa stem from historical, socio-political and economic factors. As victims of war and persecution, refugees and IDPs are orphans of the state system and thus are highly vulnerable to the deprivation of basic rights such as security, subsistence and liberty of social participation. The most vulnerable persons are children, women, the disabled, and the elderly. In this chapter, I provide an evaluative description of the response to the humanitarian crises by examining the legal and moral criteria for implementing international law and policy.

Two conditions are critical. The first condition, human rights' deprivations that occur during armed conflict is discussed using the events in Rwanda and Somalia as illustrations. The situations in Tanzania and Uganda are used to illustrate the second condition: human rights' deprivations that occur in settlement camps. The way in which the problems under both conditions are addressed by UNHCR is highlighted, and the achievements, constraints, and setbacks of administering to refugees and IDPs are identified. Both local and international constraints are discussed.

The Nature and Scope of UNHCR and the Global Picture of Refugees and IDPs

The office of the United Nations High Commissioner for Refugees (UNHCR) was created in December 1950 by Resolution 428 (V) of the United Nations General Assembly, and began its operations on January 1,

1951.[1] UNHCR is a humanitarian, strictly non-political agency, devoted to providing protection not only to refugees, but also to asylum seekers, stateless persons and IDPs. Internal conflicts are of great concern within the international community because they displace an enormous number of people, and thus deserve special mention in emerging new contexts. UNHCR notes:

> As the cold war ended, the nature of conflict began to change, from superpower confrontation to smaller, internal struggles. These wars have helped produce far larger numbers of internally displaced persons. Civilians become internationally recognized as refugees when they cross a national frontier to seek sanctuary in another country.[2]

International Refugee Law requires the host country to meet the needs of vulnerable and threatened individuals to ensure that their basic rights are protected in accordance with international standards. According to the UNHCR mandate, refugee protection is considered in a broad context that includes not only meeting the physical needs of vulnerable groups, but also implementing measures to strengthen protection capacity, and finding durable solutions to their resettlement.[3]

It is worth examining the scope of the UNHCR mandate using both the global and local statistics of refugees and internally displaced persons (IDPs). Africa, and the Great Lakes Region in particular, contributes to a large portion of the world's refugees and IDPs. A global survey of refugees and IDPs by UNHCR indicated that as of January 1, 2003, approximately 20,556,781 were "persons of concern" worldwide.[4] Among these, there were an estimated 5,777,200 IDPs. In Africa, there were 4,593,199 persons of concern, of which 3,343,700 were refugees, 715,100 were IDPs, and 29,600 were stateless persons. An estimated 159,600 persons were asylum seekers, and 354,300 had been repatriated.[5] However, as of July 12, 2004, the number of persons of concern worldwide had declined by 3,463,381 to 17,093,400 compared to 20,556,781 in 2003. The decrease is attributed to repatriation of refugees to their homeland. Asia ranks first

---

[1] "Protecting Refugees, 2002," accessed 12/19/2003.

[2] Ibid.

[3] *UNHCR 2002 Global Report*, accessed 12/19/2004.

[4] The phrase, "persons of concern" is generally used to cover refugees, stateless persons, asylum seekers, and IDPs.

[5] "Basic Facts," *Refugees by Numbers, 2004*, accessed 7/11/2004.

with the greatest number of "persons of concern" globally followed by Africa then Europe (Tables 1 and 2).

Table 1—Global Report of Persons of Concern: 2002–2003

Region	Total of Concern 1st January 2002	Total of Concern 1st January 2003
Asia	8,820,700	9,378,900
Africa	4,152,300	4,593,200
Europe	4,855,400	4,403,900
North America	1,086,800	1,061,200
Latin America & Caribbean	765,400	1,050,300
Oceania	81,300	69,200
TOTAL	19,761,900	20,556,700

Sources: 2004 UNHCR Refugee Population

Table 2—Global Report of Persons of Concern: 2004

Region	Total of Concern 12 July 2004
Asia	6,187,800
Africa	4,285,100
Europe	4,268,000
Latin America and Caribbean	1,316,400
North America	962,000
Oceania	74,100
TOTAL	17,093,400

Sources: 2004 UNHCR Refugee Population

The 1951 UN Convention and the 1967 Protocol relating to the Status of Refugees remain, to date, the legal milestones that are the international standards for protecting refugees. As such, UNHCR plays a pivotal coordinating role:

This often involves securing the rights to life (which includes basic assistance with food, shelter and health care), safety and liberty, through political approaches to governments, mobilization of other actors in the national and international arena, or through physical intervention, such as transfer of refugees to safer locations, or resettlement to another country.[6]

Refugees fall under the 1951 UN Convention and the 1967 Protocol relating to the Status of Refugees, which makes humanitarian response an issue of international justice. To effectively carry out its mandate of providing refugees and IDPs with basic needs, and respond adequately to humanitarian crises, UNHCR requires sufficient resources at its disposal.

As a non-political and humanitarian agency, "UNHCR is almost entirely funded by direct, voluntary contributions from governments, non-governmental organizations and private individuals."[7] The international community and individual governments have made concerted efforts over the years, under the auspices of the UNHCR and its sister agencies, to raise both awareness of the issues and the funds to protect "persons of concern." The funds subsidize a significant portion of the administrative costs of the organization. UNHCR's budget peaked in 1994 when its requirements worldwide exceeded US $1.4 billion, primarily due to refugee emergencies in both the former Yugoslavia and the Great Lakes Region of Africa. It declined over the next years, and in 2002 the budget stood at US $843.2 million.[8]

Sources estimate that as of July 14, 2004, UNHCR global financial requirement is US $1,177,488,731. Financial requirements for Africa in 2004 are US $475,194,214 to cover humanitarian needs in Central Africa and the Great Lakes Region, East Africa and Horn of Africa, and Southern Africa[9] (Table 3).

[6] *UNHCR 2002 Global Report*, accessed 12/19/2004.

[7] Ibid.

[8] "Donors/Partners, Sunday, March 21, 2004," accessed 8/4/2004.

[9] *Financial Requirements for 2004.*

Table 3—UNHCR Financial Requirement for Africa: 2004

Regional Programs	Annual Programs (USD)	Supplementary Programs (USD)	TOTAL (USD)
West Africa	92,266,318	39,241,983	131,508,301
Central Africa and Great Lakes Region	85,718,718	81,246,716	166,965,434
East and Horn of Africa	100,480,653	23,767,928	124,248,581
Southern Africa	52,471,898	–	52,471,898
Sub-total	330,937,587	144,256,627	475,194,214

Source: 2004 UNHCR Report

As of December 31, 2003, a total of 94 countries and private organizations contributed US $957,093,313 to 2003 UNHCR programs. However, as of June 25, 2004, a total of 66 countries and private organizations contributed US $769,535,757 to 2004 UNHCR programs.[10] The number of contributors decreased by 28 compared to 2003 causing a predicted shortfall of US $187,557,556 for the year 2004. Given the 2004 UNHCR budget of US $1,177,488,731, the global financial shortfall for 2004 UNHCR programs stands at US $407,952,974. This financial situation negatively affects the humanitarian needs of refugees and IDPs in the Great Lakes Region of Sub-Saharan Africa.

The UNHCR response to the humanitarian needs of refugees and IDPs in areas of armed conflicts in Rwanda, Burundi and Somalia is examined in the following sections. Achievements, setbacks and constraints that have been encountered will be discussed.

The Approaches to Humanitarian Crises of Displaced Civilian Populations in Armed Conflict Areas: Legal and Moral Criteria

UNHCR is dedicated to protecting displaced persons in areas where there are armed conflicts and in earmarked settlement areas. At times, the UNHCR and non-governmental organizations operate in extremely

[10] "Donors/Partners, Situation as of June 25, 2004," accessed 8/4/2004.

dangerous environments. UNHCR success with humanitarian operations largely depends on the cooperation of governments to provide security for workers. In the 1990's, the UN established a mission to protect the lives of the most vulnerable people that were displaced by conflicts, violence, and civil wars in Rwanda. However, the volatility of the conflicts in Rwanda, the limited access to affected civilian populations and deteriorating security situations often make the UNHCR operations difficult in the country.

The UN Assistance Mission for Rwanda (UNAMIR), enacted by Security Council resolution 87 on October 5, 1993, was designed to help implement the Arusha Peace Agreement that had been signed on August 4, 1993 by both parties in the Rwandan conflict.[11] The UNAMIR and Rwandan parties failed to implement the Arusha Peace Accord. This failure led to an escalation of the conflict between the Rwandan government and warring factions. The deaths of Rwandan and Burundian presidents in a plane crash ultimately triggered the 1994 Rwandan genocide. The Rwandan Patriotic Front (RPF) claimed that it tried to stop the genocide, however, Human Rights Watch and the International Commission on Human Rights Abuses in Rwanda charged that, according to their investigations, the military wing of the RPF, (RPA) was responsible for human rights violations.

Furthermore, the report alleged that between 1990 and 1993, RPF soldiers abducted and killed civilians, and pillaged property in northeastern Rwanda.[12] While it is believed that some of the casualties and deaths were a result of collateral damage in the conflicts between the RPF and the former Hutu government army, other casualties were a result of the indiscriminate killing of non-combatant civilians. Human Rights Watch claims that the massacre of groups of unarmed civilians in eastern, central and southern Rwanda, which continued even "after the combat was finished were clear violations of international humanitarian law."[13]

The RPF opposed enlarging international forces, specifically UNAMIR II, a move aimed at facilitating their victory. They alleged that genocide had already been completed and there was nothing left to protect. Meanwhile, when the UNHCR brought the need for international intervention to the attention of the international community, the UN Security Council suppressed it.[14]

---

[11] "Rwanda-UNAMIR Mandate," accessed 2/22/2004.

[12] *Leave None to Tell*, accessed 2/22/2004.

[13] Ibid.

[14] Ibid.

Attempts were made to improve security in Rwanda, but with little success.[15] Multiple complications impeded plans, including financial constraints. Most importantly, the UN report that was commissioned by the OAU revealed that other crucial factors were involved in the failure of outside interventions: double standards for implementing international law, the split of opinion within UN Security Council, and *Realpolitik*.[16] These factors may have contributed to the UN refusal to acknowledge the existence of genocide in Rwanda, and the unwillingness of powerful and influential nations to use political and moral authority to challenge the legitimacy of the genocidal government. Furthermore, the governments of Great Britain, France, and Belgium lobbied for the withdrawal of their peacekeeping forces in Rwanda-an action that illustrates the use of double standards and *Realpolitik*.

According to the judgment of Romeo Dallaire, the Commander General of UNAMIR, if 5,000 UN peacekeeping forces had been sent to Rwanda between April 7 and April 21, 1994, genocide could have been averted. [17] The urgent need to expand UNAMIR to about 5,000 and its immediate dispatch to the country was delayed adding to the problem. Contributing to the delay was the fact that "the Pentagon required an additional seven weeks to negotiate a contract for delivering armed personnel carriers to the field."[18] The report added, "when the genocide ended in mid-July 1994 with the final RPF victory, not a single additional UN soldier had landed in Kigali."[19]

Furthermore, according to the Carlsson Inquiry, which was appointed by UN Secretary- General Kofi Annan in 1999 to look into the role of UN in the genocide, revealed that on April 9, 1994, a cable message from the UN Chief to UNAMIR General Commander stated:

> You should make every effort not to compromise your impartiality or to act beyond your mandate . . . but you should exercise your discretion to do [so] should this be essential for the evacuation of foreign nationals. This should not, repeat not, extend to participating in possible combat except in self-defense.[20]

---

[15] "Rwanda-UNAMIR Mandate," accessed 2/22/2004. See also Smith, "Need for Humanitarian Intervention," accessed 2/15/2004.

[16] "Rwanda: OAU," accessed 9/11/2004.

[17] Ibid.

[18] Ibid.

[19] Ibid.

[20] Ibid.

It was clear that during the conflict, the Rwandan civilians felt safe when they gathered under the United Nations' protection. Unexpectedly, Hutu militia extremists, *interahamwe*, massacred thousands of Tutsis and moderate Hutus when the UN withdrew from the areas such as the Kigali Technical School.[21] The UNAMIR ended its mission in Rwanda and was replaced by Ethiopian UN troops in 1995. Unfortunately, due to the magnitude of violence in the country, and the reduction in number of troops, those that remained had little impact on protecting the civilians, particularly IDPs in camps. Consequently, IDPs suffered from the lack of security and subsistence.[22] Additionally, the UNHCR operations in Rwanda faced serious obstacles because humanitarian relief organizations were denied protection by the RPF. A number of Belgium and French non-governmental organizations (NGO's) were denied access to Rwanda based on allegations that they were supporters of the slain President Juvenal Habyarimana, and had ties to the former Hutu government exiled in D. R. Congo.[23]

The Carlsson's Inquiry report also indicated that RPF human rights violations needed urgent attention. The report noted that the RPF soldiers reportedly killed dozens of people, most likely Burundian refugees, who had sought shelter in Rwanda at the Nzangwa mosque of Bugesera because of armed conflict in their own country.[24] A spokesman for the UN in Geneva, Switzerland, reported that a field officer at the Tanzania border had witnessed RPF soldiers shooting at refugees as they tried to flee from Rwanda across the Kagera River into Tanzania.[25] The RPF interim government dismissed these allegations as mere fabrication. And the information by the Tanzanian field officer was unclear whether those who were fleeing into Tanzania were the alleged perpetrators of the genocide or innocent civilians running for their lives. In general, we may say that the international community turned a deaf ear to these violations. Human Rights Watch explains:

> When the team and head of the UNHRC attempted responsibly to bring the information to the attention of the international community, the U.N. decided to suppress it, not just in the interest of

---

[21] Ibid.

[22] Smith, "Need for Humanitarian Intervention," accessed 2004.

[23] *Leave None To Tell*, accessed 2/22/2004. In April 2004, during the occasion to mark the tenth anniversary of the 1994 Rwandan genocide, the Rwandan president, Paul Kagame, blamed the international community for failing to prevent the genocide, though he also noted that all failed to prevent the atrocities, including Africa and the people of Rwanda.

[24] Ibid.

[25] Ibid.

the recently established Rwandan government but also to avoid further discredit to its self.[26]

Moreover, although the involvement by the Organization of African Unity (OAU) in resolving the Rwandan conflict was primarily at the level of negotiating peace between the warring factions in Arusha, Tanzania, it failed in its responsibility to provide some peacekeeping forces in Rwanda when the Peace Accords were not effective. This would not have undermined the mission of the UN. On the contrary, it would have contributed to the success of its mission. The lack of collective action by OAU contradicts the very spirit of African solidarity in protecting the lives of those threatened by civil strife and wars in the region as stipulated in the OAU Charter:

> . . . The Charter of the Organization of African Unity . . . [African Union] stipulates that 'freedom, equality, justice, and dignity' are essential objectives for the achievement of the legitimate aspirations of the African peoples.[27]

However, the international panel commissioned by OAU placed the blame on the United Nations Security Council, the United States, France, and Belgium for the failure to prevent the Rwandan genocide. In 1998, US president Bill Clinton, and UN Secretary General Kofi Annan, apologized to the victims of the genocide.[28]

The OAU report reveals that the need for security, particularly for IDPs in camps in Rwanda, was perceived as less important than the safety of expatriates and foreign nationals. In this case, the mission of UN was no longer seen as an impartial instrument for protecting the lives of all, in accordance with the UN Universal Declaration of Human Rights, but rather, it was reduced to an instrument for defending the interests of a few powerful nations and individuals. There is no doubt that the few deaths of Belgium UN peacekeeping forces in Rwanda are regrettable, but this is the risk that comes in the line of duty. However, the lives of 800,000 Tutsis and moderate Hutus, and the safety of IDPs should have been considered to be as important as those of foreign nationals and expatriates. The use of double standards demonstrates how seriously flawed the legal and moral criteria of UN Security Council were when responding to the humanitarian crisis in Rwanda.

---

[26] Ibid.

[27] "African Charter on Human and Peoples' Rights," 137.

[28] "Chronology of U.S./U.N Actions," accessed 2/12/2004.

Another case of humanitarian crisis unfolds in Somalia where the security situation remains extremely dangerous for UNHCR operations and for non-governmental organizations working on relief efforts in this country. Historically, dramatic events taking place in Somalia in the early 1990's brought the country to its knees and paralyzed social life. Socio-political and economic factors brought millions of civilians to the brink of starvation, many were displaced and others became refugees across the Horn of Africa,[29] and the Great Lakes Region. The repressive policies of Mohamed Siedd Barre's administration between 1988 and 1991 brought suffering to the population and contributed to the rebellion and resistance against him in Somalia. Despite human rights deprivations, his government received military support from the United States for many years as part of the US Cold War strategy in East Africa.[30] Foreign aid was used to sustain a strong army that controlled political opponents and clan rivals, thus keeping him in power. During this period, Somalia had the best-equipped military in the entire region.

Although the greatest share of foreign aid was invested in the military, Mohamed Siedd Barre did reserve a portion of the foreign assistance coming into his country to maintain a subsistence level of nutrition for most of the populace.[31] Consequently, when foreign aid and foreign investment were withdrawn suddenly and unexpectedly in 1989, the Somali government eventually collapsed in 1991, leaving the country in chaos. When the Somali government fell, there were no institutions to take over the critical functions of providing public order, enforcing laws and contracts throughout the country, or administering food aid.[32] A full-scale war over the capital city, Mogadishu, broke out. In November 1991, there were more than 25,000 civilian casualties, 600,000 cross-border refugees and several thousand IDPs as a result of the strife.[33] Adding to the turmoil, the UN peacekeeping forces departed in 1994, hampering humanitarian assistance in Somalia. The security situation continued to deteriorate, leading to serious constraints for the UN World Food Program and other non-governmental organizations responsible for protecting innocent lives and dispatching humanitarian assistance to thousands of refugees and IDPs. Consequently, refugees and IDPs suffered from lack of physical safety, loss

---

[29] The Horn of Africa consists of the countries of Somalia, Ethiopia, and Djibouti.

[30] Blakley, "Somalia Case Preview," accessed 7/11/2004.

[31] Ibid.

[32] Ibid.

[33] Ibid.

of life, pillaging, rape, and other sexual violence.[34] Today, displacement of civilians in this country is a major problem and will remain so until a political solution is found.

Although IDPs do not fall under the 1951 UN Convention and its additional Protocol of 1967, "they are protected by various bodies of law, principally national law, human rights law and, if they are in a State undergoing armed conflict, international humanitarian law."[35] During peaceful periods, national and human rights laws protect civilian populations, thus respect for these laws prevents displacement. However, violation of the laws often leads to civilian displacement. In the circumstances of the Somali armed conflict, displaced civilian populations who got caught in the hostilities were under the protection of humanitarian law. One humanitarian law prohibits the "starvation of civilian populations . . . and requires parties to the conflict to allow humanitarian relief assistance to reach affected civilians."[36]

UNHCR raised concern about the forceful displacement and security of civilian populations in areas of armed conflict. The organization also drew attention to those involved in the conflict and requested that they adhere to the guiding principles prepared by the Representative of the Secretary General on internally displaced persons and contained in document E/CN.4/1998/53/Add.2. In part, principle 3 of the document states:

> National authorities have the primary duty and responsibility to provide protection and humanitarian assistance to internally displaced persons within their jurisdiction . . . [37]

Principle 5 states:

> All authorities and international actors shall respect and ensure for their obligations under the international law, including human rights and humanitarian law, in all circumstances, so as to prevent and avoid conditions that might lead to displacement of persons.[38]

Nevertheless, there is a major problem obstructing implementation of these principles. Successful UN relief operations go hand in hand

[34] United Nations Economic and Social Council, *Situation of Human Rights in Somalia.*
[35] "How Does Humanitarian Law," accessed 5/24/2004.
[36] Ibid.
[37] Ibid.
[38] Ibid.

with effective security, which should be provided by the host government. Demanding that the dysfunctional Somali government implement the UNHCR guiding principles is futile since functioning government institutions do not exist. Despite efforts by UNHCR to raise concerns for protecting the displaced civilian population, the social and political instability in this country makes it exceedingly dangerous for humanitarian relief organizations to administer their programs. Most importantly, the withdrawal of UN peacekeeping forces exacerbated the insecurity situation in Somalia, thus making IDPs vulnerable.[39] The case of Somalia establishes the fact that lack of security is detrimental to the safety and well being of refugees and IDPs in the Great Lakes Region of the Sub-Saharan Africa.

Humanitarian Responses to the Plight of Refugees and Internally Displaced Persons in Settlement Camp Areas: Legal and Moral Criteria

The preceding section focused on the humanitarian response by UNHCR in the armed conflict in Rwanda and Somalia. It was argued that security takes a top priority for the success of the UNHCR mission and safety of civilian populations in flight for asylum. In this section, the humanitarian response to the situation of IDPs and refugees in Uganda and Tanzania is examined.

A UNHCR survey on refugees provides us with the magnitude of the task of protecting refugees in camps. According to the 2003 UNHCR report, as of 2002, Tanzania and D.R. Congo hosted a total of 574,000 Burundian refugees, Tanzania and Uganda hosted a total of 6,000 Rwandans refugees, and Burundi, Tanzania, and Zambia hosted 39,000 refugees from D.R. Congo. Meanwhile, 505,200 Sudanese refugees sought sanctuary in Uganda, Ethiopia, D.R. Congo, Kenya and the Central African Republic. There were a total of 429,000 Somali refugees in Kenya, Yemen, Ethiopia, Djibouti, United Kingdom, and USA (See Table 4).[40]

---

[39] For historical factors surrounding the pullout of UN keeping forces in Somalia, see chapter 1.

[40] *Refugees by Numbers 2003*, accessed 9/11/2004.

Table 4—Major Refugees Arrivals During 2002 (10 Largest Groups)

Origin	Main Countries of Asylum	Total
Afghanistan	Pakistan/Iran	2,481,000
Burundi	Tanzania/D.R. Congo	574,000
Sudan	Uganda/Ethiopia/D.R. Congo/ Namibia/Congo/Kenya/ Central Republic	505,200
Angola	Zambia/D.R. Congo/Namibia/ Congo/	433,200
Somalia	Kenya/Yemen/Ethiopia/U.K/ US/Djibouti	429,000
D.R. Congo	Tanzania/Congo/Zambia/ Burundi/Rwanda	415,000
Iraq	Iran/Germany/Netherlands/Sweden	401,000
Bosnia-Herzegovina	Serbia-Montenegro/US/Sweden/ Denmark/Netherlands	372,000
Vietnam	China/US	348,000
Eritrea	Sudan/Ethiopia	316,000

Sources: UNHCR 2003 Report

The Representative of the UN Secretary-General on Internally Displaced Persons estimates there are between 20–25 million displaced persons worldwide, with major concentrations in Sudan, Angola, Colombia, D.R. Congo, Afghanistan, Sri Lanka, Bosnia-Herzegovina and countries of the former Soviet Union. The debate continues about how the international community can provide more sustained and comprehensive assistance to IDPs.[41] Although there are estimated to be 20–25 million displaced persons worldwide, UNHCR has been able to assist only about one quarter of them (5,777,200). As conflicts worldwide continue to escalate, there is growing fear that the numbers of IDPs will keep rising making the situation even more dire. The circumstances of IDPs in Uganda illustrate the magnitude of the problem.

---

[41] "Basic Facts, Sunday, 1 February 2004," accessed 7/11/2004.

Response to Basic Needs of IDPs in Ugandan Camps

GENERAL SITUATION

The 17 years of civil war in Uganda have left hundreds of thousands of innocent civilians internally displaced and homeless. Camps set up in the Lira district house more than a million people uprooted by rebel attacks in the north. Recently, the escalation of conflicts in the northern districts of the country, Gulu, Kitgum, Pader, and Lira coupled with lack of security have led to the deaths of many IDPs, generating renewed concern for their protection. According to the Uganda daily, the *New Vision*, and posted to the web this same date on February 27, 2004, nearly 200 innocent civilians staying at Barlonyo camp near Lira were attacked and killed by the LRA rebels.[42] Many Ugandan citizens blamed the government, which should have prevented the attacks, for the lack of adequate security in the camps. The *New Vision* news that posted the information to *allAfrica.com* states:

> The fact of the matter is that the government of Uganda must bear part of the blame for what happened at Barlonyo and all other camps that have been attacked and pillaged over the years. There is absolutely no question that the LRA attacks could and should have been prevented.[43]

Following these recent attacks, Reuters reported that on February 28, 2004, the Ugandan army launched massive counter attacks against rebel positions killing 30 LRA rebels.[44] The insurgency continues, causing people to live in constant fear for their lives in those areas of the country.

During the period from July 2002 to December 2003, there have been an estimated 650,000 to 1.4 million IDPs residing in the northern districts of Uganda.[45] Furthermore, the number of IDPs rose from 1.4 million in 2003 to 1.6 million by April 2004 causing the biggest humanitarian catastrophe since the civil war broke out 17 years ago. The Global IDP Project of the Norwegian Refugee Council providing humanitarian assistance in Northern Uganda is unable to cope with relief assistance due to the overwhelming numbers of IDPs. Based on the UN Guiding Principles

[42] "Let Barlonyo Camp Attack Be the Last," accessed 2/29/2004.
[43] Ibid.
[44] "Uganda Rebels Feeling the Heat," accessed 2/29/2004.
[45] Reliefweb, "Uganda: Mass Displacement to Uprooted Camps," accessed 6/14/2004. The Global IDP Project of the Norwegian Refugee Council monitors and analyses internal displacement in over fifty countries worldwide.

on IDPs, the Ugandan national authorities have the primary duty to provide protection and humanitarian assistance to IDPs. The compelling evidence of the conditions in Uganda demonstrates that international action is urgently needed when governments are unable to protect their own civilians from life threatening situations. How the international community responds to humanitarian crisis is highlighted in the next section.

SUBSISTENCE AND SECURITY RIGHTS

The UN Office for the Coordination of Humanitarian Affairs (UN OCHA) reveals that IDPs in camps in the northern districts of Uganda are currently receiving humanitarian relief from the following organizations: United Nations International Children's Fund (UNICEF), Africa Medical Research Foundation (AMREF), World Food Program (WFP), and Food and Agricultural Organization (FAO). In 2004, UNICEF succeeded in delivering supplies for shelter and non-food items worth US $214,150 as well as education materials to displaced 7,200 school children in nine schools worth US $19,600.[46] AMREF provides water, sanitation and health related assistance; drilling boreholes and mobile toilets, providing medicine and vaccines, and administering care for the HIV/AIDS patients in camps.

Rebel incursions have destroyed infrastructure: roads, bridges, and buildings, causing such a disruption in farming activities, that IDPs must rely heavily on humanitarian relief for food. WFP provides food assistance to over 1.6 million IDPs in four districts: Gulu, Kitgum, Pader, and Lira.[47] It is estimated that "WFP faces a serious shortfall of 106,338 tons of food commodities worth US $56 million to assist over 1.6 million IDPs through December 2004"[48] to contain the crisis. In 2004, the Uganda government approved a total of Shs 1.2 billion (more than US $600,000) to cater to the nutritional needs of IDPs in the affected areas of the country.[49] As a move to reduce dependence on the distribution of humanitarian assistance, FAO in conjunction with OXFAM, CARITAS, and other organizations, introduced self-help crop production projects such as supplying seeds and other farm materials to 88,000 households in the districts of Gulu, Pader, Kitgum, Lira, Apac, and Teso. The project aims to provide

---

[46] *Humanitarian Update Uganda* 6, no. 4, accessed 6/14/2004.

[47] Ibid.

[48] Ibid.

[49] Ibid. The term Shs. stands for "shillings," the local currency denomination of East Africa, comprising Uganda, Kenya and Tanzania.

nutritional resources to children and other needy groups in the camps.[50] Table 4 below illustrates the affected population of IDPs in the Northern Uganda at the end of April 2004.

Table 5—Report of IDPs in Uganda: 2004

District	April/March/April 2004
Gulu	438,639
Katakwi	144,945
Soroti	88,000
Kaberamaido	97,561
Kitgum	267,078
Pader	279,589
Lira rural camps	212,139
Lira Municipality	81,857
Total IDPs	1,609,807

Sources: Government of Uganda, UN, NGOs, and Donors, Ios, and News Agencies

Although subsistence is a critical part of humanitarian aid for people in camps, physical safety is equally important both for IDPs and humanitarian relief workers. The most pressing issue in Northern Uganda is the lack of adequate security. The lives of displaced men, women and children are destroyed through torture, sexual molestation and HIV/AIDS related illnesses when, due to inadequate protection, LRA abduct women for sexual exploitation or forced marriage and kidnap children to use as child soldiers and sexual objects. To address the needs and concern of abducted men, women and children, UNICEF has established rehabilitation programs for those who return to the country.

The UN Security Council has warned LRA rebels to stop committing atrocities and has urged the Ugandan government to initiate effective means to protect innocent civilians. In early 2004, President Yoweri Museveni expressed a willingness to negotiate for peace with the LRA rebels and end the conflict and prevailing insecurity in northern Uganda. The UN Secretary General, Koffi Annan, praised the President's move, encouraging both parties to end hostilities through peaceful means. Some LRA

[50] Ibid. OXFAM is a British non-governmental organization for overseas development. CARITAS is a Catholic Church non-profit relief organization.

rebel commanders agreed to participate in the peace process following the president's offer of negotiations.[51] This is a step in the right direction; however, such treaties in the past have not lasted long. In March 2003 the LRA rebels and the Ugandan government agreed upon a cessation of military hostilities, and the LRA broke the truce in the same month.

Responding to the humanitarian situation requires a lot of resources. In the fiscal year 2003, the US Agency for International Development (USAID), through the Bureau for Democracy, Conflict, and Humanitarian Assistance (DCHA), offered humanitarian assistance worth US $3,715,622 to Uganda. The humanitarian assistance is not only limited to IDPs, but is also to aid refugees in the country from Sudan and D.R. Congo. This is about 15% of the total US Government Humanitarian Assistance in the 2003 fiscal year, which was US $59,405,551.[52] For now, the UN Secretary General is urging the international community to continue with their efforts in strengthening security capacity and measures, and in providing humanitarian relief to the affected populations in northern Uganda.

Elsewhere in places such as the Western Darfur region in Sudan, IDPs are also experiencing inadequate security, subsistence, and liberties of social participation and physical movement. In this region, there are reports of killings, tortures, and rapes by Arab-militias, the *Janjaweed*, affiliated with the Arab-dominated government in Khartoum. At the outset of the crises, the government denied humanitarian agencies access to the most severely affected IDPs. The government's policy led to starvation, malnutrition, diseases, and deaths. Following the pressure by the international community, the government relaxed its restrictions on humanitarian agencies and human rights groups. Consequently, recently IDPs are receiving some humanitarian relief such as food and medical supplies in Darfur.

Despite the presence of a small African Union peacekeeping force in Darfur, IDPs still suffer from the lack of adequate security and endure constant attacks by the *Janjaweed* and the government's aerial bombardments. In addition, humanitarian aid is still inadequate to ameliorate the subsistence needs of IDPs in the area. It is hoped that the peace deal signed by the Khartoum government and the main rebel groups in 2006 will restore security in Darfur.[53] Based on this scenario, it can be argued that security is prerequisite for subsistence in the Great Lakes Region of Sub-Saharan Africa.

---

[51] Ibid.

[52] "Uganda Complex Situation Report #3," accessed 6/13/2003.

[53] See chapter 1 under "Race, Politics, and Religion."

The Human Rights Situation in Refugee Camps in Tanzania

GENERAL SITUATION

Historically, Tanzania has been the home of thousands of refugees since the 1960's;[54] the result of continued internal conflicts, violence, and civil wars in Rwanda, Burundi, the D.R. Congo, and Uganda. Liberation movements in two southern African states, Mozambique and Southern Rhodesia (Zimbabwe) in the1970's[55] produced additional refugee influxes to Tanzania. Consequently, resources for assisting these displaced people have been stretched thin.

A 2002 UNHCR report indicated that Tanzania has hosted a total of 686,770 refugees and 160 asylum seekers, and 416,879 refugees as well as all asylum seekers have been assisted. Table 6 below shows that of 540,900 Burundian refugees, 370,900 have been assisted, as have 140,300 refugees from D.R. Congo, 3,400 refugees from Somalia, and 2,270 refugees from Rwanda. Additionally, all asylum seekers have been assisted.

Table 6—The United Republic of Tanzania
Report of Persons of Concern: 2002

Main origin/Type of Population	Total in Country	Of Whom UNHCR Assisted	Percent Female	Percent under 18
Burundi (Refugees	540,900	370,900	51	56
DRC (Refugees)	140,300	140,300	51	57
Somalia (Refugees)	3,490	3,490	53	62
Rwanda (Refugees)	2,720	2,720	48	53
Asylum-seekers	160	160	19	–

Sources: UNHCR Global Report 2002

Most refugee camps in Tanzania are located in the Kagera and Kigoma Regions in the northwest, along the common border with Burundi, Rwanda, and the D.R. Congo. Most Burundian refugees live in nine refugee camps, one of which hosts both Burundians and Rwandans. In Kagera Region, there are two Burundian refugee camps located in Ngara District. These camps are Lukole A and Lukole B. In Kigoma Region, there are sev-

---

[54] Gasarasi "Tripartite Approach," 99.
[55] UNHCR, *Global Report 2002*, accessed 12/19/2004.

en Burundian refugee camps in Kigoma, Kasulu, and Kibondo Districts. These camps are Karago, Mtendeli, Kanembwa, Mkugwa (Burundians and Rwandans), Nduta, Mtabila, and Muyovosi. There are two Congolese refugee camps in Kigoma Region. These camps are Nyarugusu, and Lugufu. The Somali Bantu refugees are located in the Tanga Region, eastern Tanzania.

Partner agencies to UNHCR in Tanzania include government agencies (Ministry of Home Affairs, Principal Commissioner of Prisons, Kigoma Principal Administrative Secretary, Tanga Regional Administrative Secretary) and NGOs (Africare, Assist Road Foundation, Atlas Logistique, Caritas Kigoma and Rulenge, Chama Cha Uzazi na Malezi Bora Tanzania [Tanzania National Family Planning Association], Tanganyika Christian Refugee Services, and World Vision Tanzania). Other groups working with UNHCR are FAO, UNDP, UNICEF, WFP and WHO.[56]

The UNHCR and the Tanzanian government face serious challenges of physical security. Women and young girls in the camps suffer from domestic violence, physical harm, and sexual abuse. Additionally, there is widespread fear that some of the former officials and armed militia (*interahamwe*) of the Hutu government, alleged to have been involved in the 1994 genocide in Rwanda, are politically active in refugee camps in Tanzania. The unstable situation creates fear and poses a security threat to refugees and humanitarian relief organizations, and civilian populations in the Kigoma and in the Kagera Regions.[57] Life in the Tanzanian refugee camps will be described in the next two sections.

SECURITY RIGHTS

In "Impoverished Tanzania Still Bears Heavy Refugee Problem" reveals that while most of its eight neighboring countries have experienced civil war, Tanzania has been a haven of relative peace and political stability.[58] However, there is a question as to whether or not the situation in the refugee camps reflects this positive image of Tanzania. A Human Rights Watch report indicates that women and young girls suffer from domestic violence, and physical and sexual abuse in refugee camps despite the presence of the UNHCR and government representatives in the camps. A 1999 survey by Refugee International, a US based non-governmental advocacy group, estimated that "one in every four Burundian refugee women

---

[56] Ibid.

[57] *African Exodus*, 187.

[58] Carperson, "Impoverished Tanzania," accessed 3/16/2003.

in northern Tanzania had been the victim of rape or serious sexual harassment."[59] The International Rescue Committee (IRC), a US based humanitarian organization that provides health services to refugees in Tanzania camps, "in 1998 documented 122 cases of rape and 613 cases of gender-based violence in four refugee camps-Kanebwa, Mkungwa, Mtendeli, and Nduta."[60]

Human Rights Watch blames UNHCR and the Tanzanian government for the assaults against women and girls and their inaction in preventing them. Clearly, it is their utmost duty to protect human life and dignity. Yet, protecting human dignity is often compromised for refugees, who are considered "orphans of the state system."[61] According to Human Rights Watch, each camp has a UNHCR protection officer to ensure the safety of refugees and a UNHCR community service officer to design and run community services. As the host country, the Tanzanian government provides police, magistrates, and camp commanders.[62]

So where is the system failing and what can be done to improve the security and conditions in the camps? The problem is complex; a combination of social and cultural issues, namely African family structure, women's role in society, social relations between refugees and local communities, and circumstances in the camps. Spouses and close relatives are often the perpetrators in violence against women, and cases of physical or sexual abuse often go unreported for fear of reprisals by family members. In Burundian patriarchal society, as in many African societies, gender equality does not exist. Because they are not considered equal to men, women are frequently subjected to inhumane treatment by their spouses or other male relatives without fear of reprisal. Moreover, men are considered to be in charge of their families, and as breadwinners, they have control of all aspects of family life including sex. Therefore, contrary to human rights groups' definition, Burundian men do not believe that having non-consensual sex with one's wife constitutes rape.

While in exile in the Tanzanian refugee camps, traditional family hierarchy can break down. When UNHCR becomes the epicenter for food distribution, men lose their social status as the family breadwinner. At the same time, Burundian women in the camps are encouraged to participate

[59] Mabuwa, *Seeking Protection*, 2.

[60] Ibid.

[61] O'Neill and Spohn, "Rights of Passage," 94. Also see reference made to the work of Carens, "States and Refugees," 23.

[62] Mabuwa, *Seeking Protection*, 16.

in community leadership roles that may be in conflict with their homeland traditions. As the men's traditional social status declines, women's status improves; women begin to take control of their lives, and no longer view themselves as subservient to their husbands. Consequently, family conflicts between husbands and wives develop.

This situation is not unique to the Burundian refugee camps in Tanzania, however. In refugee camps in Sudan, Ethiopian women have similar stressful family experiences. Mekuria Bulcha reports that the Ethiopian refugee women's new roles as leaders of households in Sudan often lead to social maladjustments. As a gender-structured society, Ethiopian women are mainly administrators of home and family and nurturers of both their children and their spouses, while the role of breadwinner is the responsibility of the men.[63] Conflicts between spouses occur as the Ethiopian women assume leadership roles in refugee camps in Sudan. Experience with groups of refugees leads human rights organizations to conclude that a gender-structured society often exacerbates domestic violence and sexual abuse of women in refugee camps.

It is believed that unfriendly relations between refugees and local residents in surrounding areas near the camps often result in physical attacks and sexual violence against women.[64] Furthermore, the presence of large numbers of refugees (demographics) often exerts pressure on the environment (ecology) and on the limited resources (economics). Sharing resources among refugees and the local community may lead to a scarcity of resources, and intense competition for them. The effects of the three factors: demographics, ecology, and economics contribute to xenophobia, hostilities and conflicts.[65]

According to the UN Refugee Convention, it is the responsibility of the host government to provide access to the state justice system. However, in a gender-structured society, access to the system is not usually equal for men and women. Moreover, a Human Rights Watch report indicates that the attitudes of law enforcement agents frequently serve the interests of the abuser, not the abused in these societies. The report also shows that this is a problem worldwide not just in Africa.[66]

Tanzania ratified the 1951 UN Refugee Convention in 1993 and is party to the 1969 OAU (AU) Convention Governing the Specific Aspects

---

[63] Bulcha, "Sociological and Economic Factors," 88.

[64] Ibid., 40.

[65] Ibid., 87.

[66] Ibid., 21

of Refugees in Africa. Additionally, the country ratified the 1969 OAU Refugee Convention on January 10, 1975. Human Rights Watch states that as a party to the 1951 UN Convention Tanzania has an obligation to ensure that refugees, including women who are victims of domestic violence or sexual abuses, are protected under the national laws and have access to the courts.[67]

Lack of fair treatment by law enforcement agents and fair access to the judicial system has undermined the security rights and dignity of women refugees in Tanzania. However, Human Rights Watch recognizes the fact that the Tanzanian government has faced constraints in carrying out its obligations; among them are limited resources to train adequate and sustainable law enforcement personnel and legal experts, such as the police force and magistrates. In 1999 there were reports of some improvement in access because of funding improved by the UNHCR.[68] The organization refers to "Guidelines on the Protection of Refugee Women" issued in 1991 and "Sexual Violence Guidelines" issued in 1995 as documents that have been in place to protect women's rights. However, to this day these documents remain simply inspirational because countries fail to implement them.

Human Rights Watch also raised concern about the Tanzanian government's harassment of locally integrated Burundian refugees in the country since the 1970's. Following escalation of conflict in Burundi in late 1997, the Burundi government alleged that Burundian rebels were engaged in arms trafficking and cross border incursions. In response to the situation, Tanzanian government security arbitrarily rounded up thousands of foreigners, including the so-called "old caseload refugees" in towns and villages close to the Burundian and Rwandan borders and confined them in refugee camps. Although they were later released and returned home, these refugees lost property through looting and vandalism, were separated from their families, and saw their schools and other community institutions closed.[69] Human Rights Watch claims that the "old caseload refugees" had

---

[67] "Burundian Women," accessed 3/16/2003.

[68] Ibid., 56.

[69] "Tanzania in the Name of Security," accessed 3/14/03. Human Rights Watch interviewed approximately 200 Burundians subjected to the round-ups. These are refugees who have been in the country for almost forty years and had integrated into Tanzanian society. Under UNHCR, the Tanzanian government was able to re-locate them by providing them with necessary provisions. With the "Ujamaa System," they had obtained land from the government to grow their own food as part of self-reliance program, attended school, and had access to health care. See Gasarasi, "Tripartite Approach," 99–114.

been self-sufficient, productive and paid taxes; indeed contributed positively to development in Tanzania.[70] The government justified its actions as concern for national security, claiming that the Burundian insurgents posed serious dangers to local populations living along its common border with Burundi. However, among those rounded by government security forces were the elderly, women, and children. It was inconceivable that these people would be involved in criminal activities.

After the 1994 Rwandan genocide, the Tanzanian government addressed a similar security situation pertaining to Rwandan refugees in the country. Because criminals are not accorded refugee status, scrutiny of any subversive elements in the camps and especially alleged perpetrators of the genocide in Rwanda, falls under the jurisdiction of the Tanzanian government. Under the provision of OAU refugee law, Article 3 (2), signatory states ought to:

> Prohibit refugees residing in their respective territories from attacking any State Member of the OAU, by any activity likely to cause tension between Member States, and in particular by use of arms, through the press, or radio.[71]

Most importantly, international humanitarian law demands that host governments protect refugees from attacks.[72] Tanzania's Refugee Control Act prohibits refugees from entering the country with arms.[73] To enforce the act, the government, in conjunction with UNHCR, requires that refugees be disarmed at the port of entry into the country to ensure security of both the state and refugee camps. However, this strategy is hampered by the overwhelming influx of refugees, limited personnel and logistical support, and the porous borders.

While the Tanzanian government has the right to protect its citizens against possible threats from within or without, the security measures could easily undermine physical safety and subsistence rights of refugees, as shown by the round-ups of the Burundians in 1997. Once these refugees returned home, the government should have compensated them for damaged or lost property or at least made a public apology; neither happened. Although as strangers, refugees are more likely to be suspected of criminal behavior than citizens, rather than subjecting the entire refugee

[70] "Interview, Refugee Nduta Camp," accessed 3/14/2003.

[71] "OAU Convention Governing the Specific Aspects of Refugee Problems in Africa," entered into force June 20, 1974. Accessed 6/13/2003.

[72] "Legal Protection of Internally Displaced Persons," accessed 5/25/2004.

[73] *African Exodus*, 188.

community to arbitrary arrests and harassments, the Tanzanian government should have sorted out suspected criminals, arrested them and charged them in the court of law. The government, accused of inappropriately harassing and arresting refugees, claimed that there was insufficient time to conduct a search for alleged criminals. Increasing security patrols, they argued, required more funding in the face of limited resources already shrunken due to the huge presence of refugees in the country. The Tanzanian government's top priority is to protect its own citizens. But according to international law, the host government also must protect refugees residing in the country.

In addition to security issues in Tanzania, there is growing concern about the health risks of refugees and humanitarian relief personnel in this country. A 2001 study by the United Nations Development Program (UNDP) indicated, "Hundreds of women and young girls from rural Tanzania are streaming to refugee camps, located in the western Kigoma Province, to engage in commercial sex."[74] The big salaries paid to staff of UNHCR and non-governmental organizations (NGOs) have attracted sex workers. Pregnancies and sexually transmitted diseases, including HIV and AIDS, that result from the commercial sex trade have a devastating effect on the victims and society. Teenage pregnancies, school drop-outs, AIDS related diseases have had a negative socio-economic impact on families and the nation.[75] The National Society of Tanzania Red Cross, with financial assistance of US $507,600 by the United Nations Family Planning (UNFP) launched a health project, to improve the availability of reproductive health services and strengthen efforts against sexual violence in the refugee camps. Workshops to promote adolescent reproductive health and responsible sexual behavior are being conducted.[76] Programs like these can only be successfully implemented in a secure environment. Therefore, every effort to enhance security forces and stabilize the judicial system in Tanzania will be one step forward to ensuring justice and peace for the most vulnerable persons in the Great Lakes Region of Africa.

Subsistence Rights

Food shortages in Africa due to drought, economic instability, and insufficient aid affect 38 million people on the continent, including more than one million refugees, according to 2003 World Food Program (WFP)

---

[74] Nuhu, "Refugee Camps Attract Sex Workers and AIDS," accessed 3/16/2003.

[75] Ibid.

[76] "UNFPA Sponsors Services," accessed 3/14/2003.

reports. Reuters reported in February 2003, "the WFP urgently needs 112,000 tons of food, worth an estimated US $84 million, over the next six months to avert severe hunger among refugees."[77] To make matters worse at this time in Tanzania the maize allotment for more than 515,000 refugees from Burundi and D.R. Congo was cut for the second time since November 2002.[78] In March 2003, a joint statement made in Washington D.C. by the Jesuit Refugee Service-USA, International Rescue Committee, Refugees International and US Committee urged the international community to respond to an urgent UN appeal for US $84 million.[79] The statement revealed that shortages of food had already made desperate refugees vulnerable to finding alternative ways to provide for their families and was leading to, among other things, the sexual exploitation of young women in return for food.

Riots for food in camps have fueled conflicts and clashes among refugees. There are few, if any, income-generating projects within the camps, and no freedom for people to move to other locations where food may be available. This situation causes increasing hardships on refugees, particularly children and the elderly who are at high risk for malnutrition. The concern for food is genuine both for refugees and local residents. Provision of this basic need is crucial to ensuring that peace between refugees and local residents and security is maintained.

The Tanzanian government raised the possibility of repatriating refugees to avert the escalation of violence in the camps if the shortage of food is not immediately addressed.[80] In 2002, UNHRC and the government of Tanzania agreed on steps to accelerate the voluntary repatriation of 23,534 Rwandan refugees to ease the financial strain on the country and avert possible violence caused by food shortages. The lack of adequate international financial support as well as the continuing internal conflicts in the region, poses serious challenges for the UNHCR and the Tanzanian government in accomplishing this task.

In the face of reduced international assistance and donor fatigue, in 2000, UNHCR and the Tanzanian government stepped up measures to assist refugees with providing for their own basic needs; food, shelter, water, health care and education. The Self-Reliance Initiative Community aims to make refugees self-reliant in crop production and provides assis-

---

[77] "UN Urges Urgent Aid," accessed 3/14/2003.

[78] Ibid.

[79] "African Refugees Face," accessed 5/9/2003.

[80] Ibid.

tance in education, forestry (environment preservation), health and nutrition, and the maintenance and repair of water distribution points.[81] The success of the refugee camp project, made possible with the collaboration of United Nations Food Program (FAO), is the first of its kind in Africa. It is estimated that 50,000 refugees have benefited from the project by learning how to grow their own food, thus improving the nutrition and health of the families.

Achievements, Constraints, and Setbacks

Achievements

From the previous discussion it is clear that, over the last three decades, the UNHCR, governments (both regional and foreign), and non-governmental organizations have made a tremendous effort to provide for the basic needs of hundreds of thousands of refugees and IDPs in the Great Lakes Region of the Sub-Saharan Africa. The success of their efforts has been possible with the collaboration of governments and partner agencies: UN World Food Program (WFP), the UN Children's Fund (UNICEF), the UN World Health Organization (WHO), the UN Development Program (UNDP), the UN Food and Agricultural Organization (FAO), the Office for the Coordination of Humanitarian Affairs (OCHA), and the UN High Commissioner for Human Rights (UNHCHR). The non-governmental organizations providing humanitarian assistance include: the International Committee for Red Cross (ICRC), International Organization of Red Cross and Red Crescent Societies (IFRC) and the International Organization for Migration (IOM).

With contributions from these organizations, most refugees and some IDPs have access to a measure of physical security, food, shelter, health care, and education. Moreover, 50,000 refugees have benefited from the 2000 refugee-camp project known as Self-Reliance Initiative Community. In addition, through the efforts of these agencies, thousands of refugees have been repatriated, re-settled, or re-integrated into communities in their countries of origin.

UNHCR and FAO in cooperation with the Tanzanian government have been able to alleviate food shortages by providing land for crop production; thus curbing hunger and malnutrition in refugee camps. Based on the success of the program in the Tanzanian refugee camps, UNHCR initiated similar programs in other countries in the region. The initiatives

---

[81] *UNHCR, Global Report 2002*, accessed 12/19/2004.

by the UNHCR, with the support of governments and the international community, have improved the lives of refugees and helped them to retain their self-respect and dignity. However, UNHCR still faces difficult challenges in the days ahead.

Constraints and Setbacks of International Character

Enormous contributions by governments, non-governmental organizations and private organizations have made the operations of UNHCR in the Great Lakes Region a commendable success story. Despite the successes, however, UNHCR faces a number of setbacks due to international and local constraints. The major problems facing the organization are scarcity of resources, budget cuts, and donor fatigue. For instance, the global 2004 UNHCR budget stands at US $1,177,488,731 yet only US $769,535,757 is available, causing an estimated shortfall of US $407,952,974.[82] Regionally, out of 540,900 Burundian refugees in Tanzania, only 370,900 have been assisted so far, leaving 170,000 refugees still in need. Tanzania alone, in 2002, required US $28,897,701 yet only US $27,716,307 was available.[83] The budget gaps are indicative of the shortfall of funding that is detrimental to the day-to-day UNHCR operations, and the lives of refugees and IDPs in the Great Lakes Region. Jesuit Refugee Service (JRS) notes:

> We are also beginning to look into the impact of such cuts from a human rights perspective, and we are trying to raise awareness of human rights impact of these budget cuts in the UN Human Rights mechanisms.[84]

Table 7 below illustrates the budget shortfall of the 2002 UNHCR in Tanzanian refugee camps:

Table 7—Income and Expenditure (USD)
Annual Program Budget in Tanzania: 2002

Revised Budget	Income from Contribution	Other Funds Available	Total Funds Available	Total Expenditure
28,897,701	22,979,081	4,815,934	27,795,015	27,716,307

Sources: UNHCR Global Report 2002

---

[82] See "Donors/Partners, June 25, 2004," accessed 8/4/2004.

[83] See *UNHCR Global Report 2002*, accessed 12/19/2004, as reflected in Table 6.

[84] *Update on the Work of the JRS*, accessed 12/19/2003.

Recently, the international community shifted its focus from Africa to the refugee crises in Eastern Europe, the Middle East, and Afghanistan as conflicts in those areas grow. The new wave of refugee crises has had a negative impact on humanitarian relief operations in Africa, and the Great Lakes Region in particular. Consequently, there is a shortage of food and other vital supplies for refugees. The Tanzanian government is concerned about riots in the refugee camps that occur when humanitarian aid is inadequate. The government threatens that forceful repatriation of refugees will be the only option if the situation is not addressed immediately. Adding to the problem, military support of dictatorial regimes or rebel groups ultimately exacerbates conflicts and humanitarian crises in the region requiring humanitarian assistance. This situation contributes to the severe budget constraints of the UNHCR mission operations in the Great Lakes Region of Sub-Saharan Africa. In addition to budgetary obstacles, a limited understanding of human rights in international law and the lack of political will for implementation are major constraints in providing refugees and IDPs with adequate security and subsistence rights. This problem will be discussed in great detail in the next chapter.

Constraints and Setbacks of Local Character

UNHCR operations in the Great Lakes Region of Africa are being hampered by a variety of constraints; the inability and/or refusal of the host country's government to provide adequate security to UNHCR workers in Rwanda, Somalia, and Sudan; inability and /or refusal by the Ugandan government to implement the new guidelines for the protection of IDPs; the absence of a central government and institutions in Somalia, and malpractice by some of the UN staff affecting the credibility of the organization (raised by the UNHCR Standing Committee in 2003).[85]

Human Rights Watch criticized the Tanzanian government and UNHCR for inadequately protecting refugees particularly, women and young girls. The lack of equal access to the legal system by the latter exacerbates vulnerability to domestic violence, physical and sexual abuse. A variety of factors hamper efforts to protect refugees or IDPs; among them, insufficient numbers and inadequate training of staff in the refugee camps. So, the government has demanded that the necessary resources to train sufficient and efficient security forces and law court personnel be made available to provide optimum security for refugees. Scarcity of resources, security concerns, and environmental degradation contribute to

[85] Ibid.

an unfriendly atmosphere between the local communities and refugees in Tanzania, the phenomenon of xenophobia. Despite the inadequacies discussed above, the latest report indicates that the security situation in and around refugee camps is improving. This is "attributed to the increased police patrol and a newly introduced system whereby police and refugee volunteers are guarding all unofficial entrances to the camps."[86] The collaboration between government personnel and refugees to fill the security void is leading to a more peaceful situation in the camps.

By contrast, the situation in Sudan is deteriorating and deserves special mention here. It is charged that the Sudanese government's obstruction of humanitarian relief organizations from aiding IDPs in Darfur is a matter of *Realpolitik*[87] and motivated by two reasons. First, the Sudanese government has sought to block bad publicity and ensure that no information about atrocities being committed against their own civilians is available to the outside world; thus avoiding condemnation from human rights groups and the international community. Second, the government is determined to refute claims that it is involved in racial segregation in Western Darfur region in Sudan. In sum, the government, which is supposed to protect its own citizens from standard threats, is actually causing systemic deprivations of basic rights of security and subsistence through its domestic policy. This situation in Sudan illustrates the use of double standards by which the government protects some citizens and commits atrocities against others on the basis of race.

Conclusion

Although UNHCR is making great strides in providing for the vital needs of refugees, asylum seekers, and IDPs, these people in the Great Lakes Region of the Sub-Saharan Africa remain vulnerable. Contributions by governments, non-governmental organizations, and private organizations have led to some successful achievements. For example, the introduction of self-reliance projects for food crop production, which supplements donors' effort, has been a great part of the success in providing basic needs to those in refugee and IDPs camps.

Despite the accomplishments of the organization, UNHCR faces serious challenges that undermine its mission. First, there is a limited understanding of human rights in international law and policy, and a lack of

---

[86] "WFP Emergence Report No. 20," accessed 6/24/2004.

[87] The move by the Sudanese government was meant to prevent any publicity that could jeopardize its strategic agenda in Western Darfur.

political will to implement international standards and guidelines. This leads to inadequate security, exposing refugees and IDPs, particularly women and young girls, vulnerable to domestic violence, and physical and sexual abuse. In some situation, law enforcement agents and the judiciary system in host countries do not accord female refugees fair treatment, particularly when it comes to issues related to sexual abuse. Second, limited resources; budget cuts, famine, donor fatigue, and reduced funding put relief efforts in jeopardy. Third, the persistent escalation of conflicts in the region, and around the world poses financial constraints on limited resources. Military support for repressive African governments and rebel groups or insurgents continues to cause humanitarian crises in the region. Fourth, the failure of UNHCR to develop staff guidelines for dealing with domestic violence causes a miscarriage of justice by putting women in the hands of mediating local councils who lack expertise and the jurisdiction to preside over criminal cases in refugee camps. Fifth, the failure of some UNHCR personnel to adhere to the professional code of ethics undermines the credibility of this organization. Six, lack of protection and/or access by the UNHCR personnel to afflicted areas hampers humanitarian relief operations especially in Rwanda, Somalia, and Sudan.

UNHCR remains optimistic that its mission will be successful if measures are taken to address these constraints. Achieving their objective requires cooperation in solidarity, not only from the international community, but also from the African Union and individual governments. Considering not only the people who have been deprived of their security and subsistence but also to the factors, forces, and conditions that cause, contribute, precipitate, or exacerbate such deprivations is fundamental to the success of the UNHCR mission in this region of Africa. In the next chapter, a philosophical ethics of human rights for assessing the interpretation of human rights in international law and policy, and how it affects public policy for refugees and IDPs in the Great Lakes Region of Africa will be offered. This approach is aimed at redressing government's and the international community's failure when responding to the humanitarian crises of refugees and IDPs in the region.

PART III

The Ethics of Basic Human Rights

3

A Philosophical Assessment of the Interpretation of Human Rights in International Refugee Law and Public Policy

Introduction

THE prevailing humanitarian crises of refugees and IDPs in the Great Lakes Region of Africa, described in chapter 1, and the failures of states and the international community to respond effectively, shown in chapter 2, call for a critical assessment of the human rights of refugees and IDPs. A revised interpretation of rights, drawing upon the critique of Henry Shue, which is proposed in this chapter, provides a better understanding of the moral responsibilities of all parties, and serves as a critical framework for evaluating public policy.

Chapter 3 consists of three sections. In section A, I argue that an adequate account of human rights is urgently needed to redress the failures of states and the international community. Moral questions regarding the failures vis-à-vis international refugee law and policy are discussed under the following formal elements: the subject of rights (the bearer of rights), the object of rights, the nature or moral force accorded rights claims, the respondents or recipients of rights' claims (the bearers of the correlative duties), and the justifying basis or ground of rights' claims. In section B, an adequate understanding of human rights to effectively protect and provide refugees and IDPs with basic rights is presented. A philosophical analysis of human rights is developed in light of Henry Shue's critique of basic human rights for addressing the fundamental moral questions: the subject of rights, the object of rights, the nature of rights, the respondent of rights' claims and the justifying grounds of rights' claims. In section C, it is shown how Shue's theory of rights contributes to dealing with the crises by offering an adequate response for protecting and providing refugees and IDPs in the Great Lakes Region of Sub-Saharan Africa with basic rights.[1]

SECTION A
The Rationale for Developing a Revised Interpretation of Rights of Refugees and IDPs in International Refugee law and Public Policy

The Subject of Rights or Bearer of Rights

The legal and moral criteria employed by states and the international community for responding to the plight of refugees and IDPs raise serious moral questions regarding the subject of rights in international refugee law and public policy. The limits of these criteria contribute significantly to the failures in dealing with the prevailing humanitarian crises in the Great Lakes Region of Africa.

A brief glimpse of the failures helps establish a basis for discussing the moral questions involved. The extensive humanitarian crises in the Great Lakes Region of Africa deserve our utmost attention, and the manner in which they have been handled calls for a critical moral evaluation. Protecting human life in these circumstances is, indeed, a serious moral responsibility. There have been some substantive achievements in providing refugees and IDPs with a level of security, subsistence, and social participation through financial and logistic support from governments, NGOs, and international organizations. Despite these achievements, the mission of UNHCR is failing both locally and internationally when it comes to effectively addressing the crises in the Great Lakes Region of Africa. What is the ultimate reason for the failures? Is it financial constraints, lack of political will or an inadequate understanding of the appropriate role of human rights in international refugee law and public policy? A critical examination of the current responses to the crises may ultimately provide answers to the moral concerns that are raised.

Examples of the shortcomings in international law and policy regarding refugees and IDPs are abundant. The lack of UN humanitarian inter-

---

[1] The formal elements of rights theory are drawn from Gewirth, *Human Rights*, 1–30; Gewirth, *Reason and Morality*, 63–102; and Gewirth, *Community of Rights*, 8–13.

vention in the 1994 Rwandan genocide is a symptom of a deeper problem than inadequate resources or the lack of political will. The unwillingness to increase the size of UNAMIR, coupled with evacuation of foreign nationals and staff while ignoring protection for Tutsis and moderate Hutus exposes the double standards in international law and policy. In Sudan, the government's refusal to allow humanitarian relief to reach thousands of IDPs in the Western Darfur region illustrates racial and religious discrimination implicit in domestic law and policy. In another situation, the unwillingness of the Ugandan government to seek international protection poses a security threat to thousands of IDPs in this country. Gender discrimination, demonstrated in Tanzanian refugee camps where victims of violence, physical and sexual abuse have very little access to the justice system, jeopardizes the rights of security. In Somalia, the withdrawal of UN peacekeeping forces rendered IDPs vulnerable to insecurity.[2]

The response to the plight of refugees and IDPs in which discrimination is based on religion, race, ethnicity, and gender that is implicit in governments' and the international community's policy not only affects the lives of these groups of people, but also indicates an inadequate understanding of the subject of rights in international law and public policy. The failure by governments and the international community portrayed in the examples above raises a fundamental moral question; what legal and moral criteria are invoked when determining the subject of rights in international law and policy? To shed some light onto this fundamental question, the subject of rights in both international law and domestic policy must be explored.

According to the 1948 UN Universal Declaration of Human Rights, every person is a moral subject entitled to equal dignity and respect (Article 1).[3] Every person has the right to seek asylum when his/her life is threatened by conflicts and violence (Article 14.1).[4] The Declaration leads to the consideration that refugees are moral subjects of equal legal entitlements. However, the scenarios described above that demonstrate the failure to protect the rights to security in Tanzania, Uganda, Rwanda, and Sudan, raise a serious moral question regarding the subject of rights in both international law and domestic policy. This moral concern becomes even

---

[2] For the responses accorded refugees and IDPs in Rwanda, Somalia, Tanzania, Uganda, and Sudan, see the in-depth analysis of the humanitarian crises in chapter 2.

[3] "United Nations' 1948 Universal Declaration of Human Rights," 84.

[4] Ibid. Although the Declaration is not a legally binding Treaty internationally, member state parties explicitly express its legal force in the ratification of the International Covenants on social, economic, and cultural rights as well as civil and political rights.

more relevant if one considers whether or not IDPs are subjects of rights in international law and domestic policy.

Demographics provide an illustration of why the subject of rights is of serious moral concern. In 2003 there were an estimated 715,100 IDPs in Africa. The persistent escalation of armed conflicts and violence continues to depict a somber picture in the Great Lakes Region. In Uganda, the number of IDPs rose from 1.4 million in 2003 to 1.6 million in April 2004. In Sudan, there are estimated 1.6 million displaced persons since the conflict broke out in the Western Darfur region in 2003.[5]

A critical look at the magnitude of such crises reveals that IDPs outnumber refugees, and IDPs are more vulnerable to human rights deprivations than refugees. Due to the restrictive definition of refugee status in the 1951 UN Refugee Convention and its 1967 Protocol, which excludes the legal rights of IDPs, the group lacks legal recognition in international refugee law, and are thus at a disadvantage. The recent development of UNHCR Guidelines to protect IDPs is a good step in the right direction. Unfortunately, this measure does not suggest that the IDPs Guidelines are legally binding internationally. Yet, IDPs suffer from life threatening conditions that are similar to refugees.

Furthermore, the analysis of the nature and scope of humanitarian crises discussed in chapter 1 demonstrates the magnitude of the problem; the causes of the crises are not rooted simply in politics, but in economics as well. The restrictive definition of refugee in the 1951 UN Refugee Convention does not recognize victims of social and economic deprivation, natural disaster, political instability or internal armed conflict as the subject of rights. Adopting a more inclusive definition of refugee, such as the one that is accepted by the 1969 OAU Convention Governing the Specific Aspects of Refugee Problems in Africa (Articles 1.1 and 1. 2), would recognize a broader range of the subject of rights. This definition includes victims of general political instability and internal armed conflict, as well as natural disaster and social and economic deprivation in Africa.[6]

Partly, the reason for inadequate responses to the plight of refugees and IDPs is the narrow interpretation of who is legally and morally en-

---

[5] For an in-depth analysis of the nature and scope of the humanitarian crises in Rwanda, Somalia, Uganda, and Sudan, see chapter 1. With respect to 1.6 million displaced civilian populations, it is unclear how many people are refugees and IDPs in Sudan. For more information on the current growing problem of IDPs in Africa, see "Internally Displaced," accessed 3/14/03.

[6] See chapter 1 on the description of the root causes of refugees and IDPs in the Great Lakes Region of Africa.

titled to security, subsistence, and liberty of active social participation in international refugee law and public policy. Therefore, the manner in which refugees and IDPs, the moral subjects, are recognized and protected by states and the international community contributes to the failures in responding to the crises. These failures raise serious moral questions in the field of philosophical ethics of rights.

The Object of Rights

The object of rights is intimately connected to the subject of rights. Although governments and the international community provide basic needs to refugees and IDPs in the Great Lakes Region of Africa the efforts are barely adequate. The failure to fully protect these people, particularly women and children, raises a serious moral concern about their entitlements to security, subsistence, and liberty of social participation. People become refugees and IDPs because of the governments' inability or unwillingness to protect them. Considering refugees and IDPs to be 'orphans of the state system'[7] generates moral claim-rights to security, subsistence, and liberty of social participation.

The analysis of the responses to humanitarian crises presented in chapter 2, suggests that security, subsistence, and liberty of social participation are closely linked. Enjoying subsistence rights heavily depends on an adequate level of security, and satisfying security and subsistence rights demands active involvement of all the parties concerned: governments, NGOs, and the international community.

Participatory involvement in providing security and subsistence to civilian populations is key for governments, NGOs, and the international community to be successful in fulfilling their moral responsibility. This did not happen in the 1994 Rwandan genocide. Poor security caused thousands of innocent civilians to lose their lives, thousands of civilians were internally displaced, and thousands of others crossed the border as refugees. Again, the current situation in the Western Darfur region and in southern Sudan demonstrates how inadequate security contributes to the humanitarian catastrophe. Fundamentally, failure to recognize the need for security rights of refugees and IDPs in domestic law and policy contributes to the crises in this country, which are being perpetuated by the Sudanese government. This situation leads to a deterioration of the quality of life in camps.

---

[7] O'Neill and Spohn, "Rights of Passage," 94.

The humanitarian crisis in northern Uganda is another example of the consequences of the government's failure to protect human rights, particularly security and subsistence rights of women and children in IDPs camps. The unwillingness of the Ugandan government to involve the international community in providing security to IDPs raises the same moral concern once again. When governments fail to guarantee adequate security to refugees or IDPs, the well-being of these groups becomes threatened by violence. Furthermore, humanitarian aid organizations are unable to provide relief assistance to refugees or IDPs in armed conflict areas because of insecurity. Consequently, these people, particularly children, suffer from severe malnutrition, preventable diseases, and even death.[8]

The joint efforts of the parties concerned; UNHCR, governments, NGOs and international aid organizations have resulted in the successful security programs instituted in the Tanzanian refugee camps where refugees actively participate in leadership roles and organize security measures within the camps. This initiative has also provided some opportunity for refugees, particularly women, to actively participate in self-reliance projects, which include growing food, improving sanitation, and educational programs. In general, the presence of security in and around the camps allows refugees to enjoy freedom of movement and find work in order to support their families.[9]

Because security is intimately linked to subsistence, the presence of insecurity in Uganda is a major stumbling block to the quality of life in camps. The failure to adequately respond to the crisis is attributed to the Ugandan government's unwillingness to take moral responsibility for providing adequate security for innocent civilians in armed conflict areas or in camps. Government's failure to recognize the need for security and subsistence rights poses the serious moral problem that impedes satisfying rights-claims in international law and public policy.

The success story of the Tanzanian participatory programs does not suggest that the cooperation of the parties concerned has succeeded to root out all the possible injustices surrounding the lives of refugees in camps. Women who are not adequately given fair access to the Tanzanian justice system when they become victims of violence, physical or sexual abuse are

[8] For further information regarding security problems in Rwanda and Somalia, see chapter 2, "The Approaches to Humanitarian Crises of Displaced Civilian Populations in Armed Conflict Areas," 35–42. For security problems in Uganda, see chapter 2, "Response to Basic Needs of IPDs in Ugandan Camps," 44–47.

[9] For further information regarding the link between security and subsistence, see chapter 2, "The Human Rights Situation in Refugee Camps in Tanzania," 48–56.

another cause for serious moral concern about the failure of governments and social institutions to recognize equal rights to legal protection.[10]

The restrictive definition of refugee status in the 1951 UN Geneva Convention contributes to these moral concerns, by failing to recognize the security, subsistence, and liberty rights of persons or groups suffering from general political insecurity and internal armed conflict, as well as natural disaster and economic deprivation in Africa.

Basic rights of security, subsistence, and social participation are part of broader social, economic, and cultural rights, as well as civil and political rights. The inadequate understanding of these rights in international refugee law and public policy raises fundamental moral concerns when it comes to effectively protecting refugees and IDPs in the Great Lakes Region of Africa. In addition to poorly interpreting and inadequately defining the subject and object of rights in international refugee law and public policy, recognition of these rights is at stake because the 1948 UN Universal Declaration of Human Rights is not a legally binding treaty, and thus does not impose strict legal force upon member states. On the other hand, the 1966 UN Covenants on Social, Economic, and Cultural Rights, as well as Civil and Political Rights are legally binding documents for those members who have ratified them.[11] However, unless the International Covenant is ratified by member states, enjoying these rights may not be legally guaranteed. Consequently, lack of recognition of these rights in international law and public policy renders refugees and IDPs vulnerable to human rights' deprivations. This situation raises serious moral concerns regarding the object of rights demonstrated by the scenarios of the crises in the Great Lakes Region of Africa.

Nevertheless, there is a sign of hope for refugees in Africa. Social, economic, and cultural rights, as well as civil and political rights are implicit in the 1969 OAU Refugee Convention. The inclusive definition of refugee status in the Convention demonstrates recognition of these rights. The OAU Convention also recognizes general social-political instability and armed conflict, as well as natural disaster and economic deprivation

---

[10] For further information regarding this matter, see chapter 2, "The Human Rights Situation in Refugee Camps in Tanzania," 48–56.

[11] For example, the failure of the US Government to recognize social, economic and cultural rights demonstrates that the lack of legal recognition of these rights has a serious impact on domestic and foreign policy. The US does not recognize these rights; nevertheless, it is the major contributor of funds to the mission of UNHCR worldwide. In context, the total US Government humanitarian assistance to refugees and IDPs in Uganda stood at US $ 59,405,551 in the fiscal year. See information in chapter 2, "Subsistence and Security Rights in Northern Uganda."

as the root cause of refugee crises in Africa.[12] Moreover, the 1981 OAU Charter on Human and Peoples' Rights, which is a legally binding treaty, explicitly recognizes social, economic, and cultural rights as well as civil and political rights.[13] Hence, when compared to UN regime of rights, the OAU Charter is an international (regional) legal instrument that better safeguards refugee rights of security, subsistence, and liberty of social participation.

Although there is legal recognition of these rights in the OAU Charter and OAU Refugee Convention, the problem remains that there is no legal recognition of IDPs in the OAU Refugee Convention. This situation contributes to the inadequate moral force accorded security, subsistence, and liberty of social participation of IDPs, and raises fundamental moral concerns in international law and public policy.

The Nature or Force of Rights

Because refugees and IDPs are victims of the state system, they have the strongest moral rights-claims for security, subsistence, and liberty of social participation. In view of the prevailing responses by governments and the international community for satisfying these rights, the question regarding priority of these rights vis-à-vis other competing legal and moral rights' claims raises serious legal and moral concerns. The analysis of the nature and scope of the crisis in Rwanda shows that conflict of rights' moral claims in political and economic power between Tutsi minority and Hutu majority is a historical problem. At the local level, the Rwandan government's response to these conflicts is morally questionable. The conflicts that led to the 1994 genocide and the manner in which they were handled, morally cannot remain unchallenged. The rights of the most vulnerable deserve the greatest attention of governments and the international community. This did not occur in Rwanda, however. The Tutsi minority and moderate Hutus suffered at the hands of their government. In a situation such as this the dilemma is: how can the perpetrator of human rights abuses at the same time become the protector of these rights?

---

[12] For an in depth comparative analysis of the 1951 UN Refugee Convention and the 1967 Protocol and the 1969 OAU Refugee Convention, see chapter 1. Also see an in-depth analysis of the root causes of humanitarian crises in the same chapter.

[13] "African Charter on Human and Peoples' Rights, Articles 6 and 22 (1) in John, *Africa's Refugee Crisis*, 138, 141. The Charter was adopted June 27, 1981, and entered into force October 21, 1986 (ratification). As of July 30, 1992, the total numbers of states parties are 50. For further information, see "African [Banjul] Charter," accessed 12/9/2004.

On the international level (both regional and universal), the absence of prompt humanitarian intervention to resolve the conflicts of rights' claims between the unlimited power of the extremists and their victims, raises a legitimate moral concern in international law and public policy. For example, the massacres of Tutsis and moderate Hutus under the watch of UNAMIR, cast serious doubts on the legal force accorded security rights of the most vulnerable persons in international law. Moreover, the order given to the UNAMIR General Commander by the UN Secretariat to evacuate foreign nationals, while neglecting to protect the lives of those threatened by violence, deserves moral scrutiny. The question regarding the legal and moral priority accorded rights of refugees and IDPs is a legitimate question in the philosophical ethics of rights.

In Tanzania, as a response to curtailing violence as well as physical and sexual abuses against women, women are encouraged to participate in leadership roles in refugee camps. This is key for them to enjoy the substance of security and subsistence rights. However, as was shown, the state's justice system makes women vulnerable to unequal entitlement of security rights.[14] The lack of equal legal and moral entitlement to these rights on the basis of gender is a legitimate moral concern of the philosophical ethics of rights.

The rights to security, subsistence, and liberty of social participation of IDPs are at high risk after 17 years of civil war in Uganda. The Ugandan government's inability to adequately protect its civilian populations would seem to legitimize humanitarian intervention in the country. That the UN or the African Union (AU) are unwilling to do so raises a legitimate moral question with regard to resolving competing rights' claims between the relative sovereignty of the Ugandan state, and security and subsistence rights of the defenseless IDPs. This negligent response to the security concerns of IDPs demonstrates the lack of sufficient legal recognition of priority of such rights in international refugee law and public policy. A major contributing part to the moral problem is that IDPs are not the subject of rights in international refugee law. With this in mind, the issue of priority of rights accorded security, subsistence, and liberty of social participation, raises a further moral concern in the philosophical ethics of human rights.

The humanitarian crisis in the Western Darfur region is unprecedented in recent memory. The failure of the Sudanese government to provide security to its own citizens is a major moral concern from the

---

[14] See the analysis of the situation of women in the Tanzanian refugee camps, as well as the constraints faced by the Tanzanian Government regarding the provision of security in refugee camps as noted in chapter 2, "Security Rights."

human rights' perspective. The *Janjaweed militia,* believed to be part of government's plan to quell the rebellion in the region, presents more evidence of conflicts of rights' claims in the country. The Sudanese government sees the Darfurians' legitimate moral claims for equal entitlement to the country's resources as insignificant and trivial. This neglect by government brings up a moral concern regarding the priority of rights' claims accorded IDPs in domestic law and policy. When governments fail to enforce the national law and policy to protect IDPs, the latter are accorded legal protection under the international humanitarian law of the Geneva Convention. Furthermore, in some cases, the law also protects refugees if the host country is experiencing armed conflict and violence.[15]

The Sudanese government's refusal to allow international humanitarian assistance to thousands of IDPs and refugees, poses serious doubts regarding absolute right of state sovereignty over those of the vulnerable groups. In competing rights' claims it appears that, from the government's view point international humanitarian intervention interferes with the domestic affairs, and thus state sovereignty becomes a top moral priority. The government's policy towards the crisis is indicative of whose moral rights' claims prevail, raising a legitimate moral concern of the priority rights of IDPs, particularly women and children.

The Respondent/Recipient or Bearer of Rights' Claims

Previously, it was argued that conflict of rights of refugees and IDPs vis-à-vis relative state sovereignty is a moral issue, and that the demand for an appropriate response to moral claims is a legitimate subject in the philosophical ethics of rights. At this point, the moral responsibility to give priority to the moral rights claims of refugees and IDPs assigned to governments and the international community is worth examining. To what extent can deprivations of the rights of security, subsistence, and liberty of social participation warrant a legal and moral response? What moral obligations do rights' claims impose upon individuals, groups, governments or the international community? Recognition and implementation of moral rights largely depend on the interpretation of the respondent or recipient of rights in international law and public policy. When the lives of refugees and IDPs are threatened by violence, conflict and war, governments and the international community have a moral responsibility to protect the

---

[15] The international humanitarian law is supposed to protect IDPs in countries, which are undergoing conflict due to governments' failure to do so, as the scenarios of Rwanda, Sudan, Somalia, and Uganda have shown in chapter in 2.

rights of security, subsistence, and liberty of social participation, particularly for women and children. Satisfying these rights may override other competing moral rights claims. In some cases, a choice has to be made between protecting the relative state sovereignty and the rights of refugees and/or IDPs.

Because, in general, IDPs are not accorded refugee status, their basic rights to security, subsistence, and liberty of active social participation are not fully recognized. However, when IDPs are in a state where armed conflict in occurring, they are protected by the international humanitarian law.[16] Of course, fulfillment of rights' claims requires availability of necessary capacity to fulfill them. Given the assumption that protecting and aiding refugees and IDPs is a top priority, making the necessary contributions becomes a significant part of assigning moral responsibility to governments, NGOs, private individuals and groups, and the international community.

The duty to provide basic rights to refugees and IDPs is hampered by financial crises. The 2003 UNHCR report shows that in this year a total of 94 countries and organizations contributed US $957,093,313 to the global fund for humanitarian relief operations. Unfortunately, the number of contributors declined by 28 in 2004 with a fall in contribution of US $187,557,556. Such a decline has an impact on the lives of refugees and IDPs who live in the poorest nations on the planet, and which are, in fact, the hardest hit by the crises. The protracted armed conflict in these areas exacerbates the financial constraints.

Based on financial constraints and persistent escalation of conflicts, the inadequate attention given to humanitarian crises in Africa, for example in the 1994 Rwandan conflict, casts doubts on the response of governments and the international community when compared to the response given elsewhere in the world; for instance, the 1994 conflict in Yugoslavia. The double standards prevailing when handling the crises set the platform for philosophical criticism of human rights. A serious moral question is raised regarding the interpretation of rights and correlative duties of governments and the international community in international law and public policy. Furthermore, unbalanced interpretation of rights points once again to the issues raised in the earlier sections of this chapter concerning the subject of rights, the object of rights, as well as the nature of rights in international law. Insufficient legal recognition of rights and correlative duties contributes largely to failure to resolve conflicts of moral rights claims.

---

[16] See the analysis of rights of IDPs in international humanitarian law in chapter 2.

The situation demonstrates the deficit of collective moral responsibility in international law and public policy, which in turn becomes detrimental to the lives of the most vulnerable persons, and raises significant moral concerns in the philosophical ethics of rights. Moral responsibilities assigned to governments, social institutions, and the international community, are crucial for satisfying the basic rights of refugees and IDPs.

The Justifying Basis or Ground of Human Rights

The significant concerns regarding collective moral responsibility assigned to governments, social institutions, and the international community have been identified. The justifying basis of the rights' claims of refugees and IDPs is another very important and controversial question that needs addressing. In general, moral philosophers agree that humans have basic human rights. What is highly disputed, however, are the moral criteria that ground these rights in international law and public policy. The ambivalence in international law and practice regarding the subject, object, force, and respondent of human rights' claims is reflected in prevailing controversies about the justification of human rights.

The Universal Declaration of Human Rights appeals to the equal dignity of moral persons as the ground of ascribing human rights. The initial clause of the Preamble of United Nations' Universal Declaration of Human Rights in 1948 solemnly recognizes "the inherent dignity" and "equal and inalienable rights of all members of the human family."[17] Yet international human rights law does not specify the philosophical or religious foundations of such attributions. Indeed, what the Universal Declaration calls our common "faith in fundamental human rights, in the dignity and worth of the human person," as the drafters recognized, is rooted in differing sacred and secular traditions.[18]

Some communitarian philosophers, however, have questioned whether the discourse of human rights constitutes a "common standard of achievement for all peoples and all nations."[19]

From such a perspective, the justification of rights is not common humanity, but rather it is membership in a particular community. Members

[17] "United Nations General Assembly Resolution 217A," 153–56. "Convention against Torture," 151–53, recognizes explicitly that "the equal and inalienable rights of all members of the human family . . . derive from the inherent dignity of the human person." Cf. Glendon, *A World Made New*, 172–91.

[18] Preamble, "Universal Declaration of Human Rights," 153.

[19] Ibid.

are entitled to rights because they have a shared understanding of these rights as social goods. Michael Walzer explains:

> Men and women do indeed have rights beyond life and liberty, but these do not follow from our common humanity; they follow from shared conception of social goods; they are local and particular in character.[20]

Since membership is the basis for the distribution of rights and duties in society, according to this theory, understanding and exercising these rights differs from time to place, and among people.

Thus, Alasdair MacIntyre dismisses "faith in human rights" as "one with belief in witches and in unicorns."[21] For Richard Rorty, rights are not self-evident or sacred truths, but "local and ethnocentric" customs, "the tradition of a particular community, the consensus of a particular culture."[22] Rights' talk, like edifying discourse generally, would be "relative to the group to which we think it is necessary to justify ourselves--to the body of shared belief which determines the reference of the word 'we'."[23]

In chapter 4, we will consider how "faith in human rights" generally, and in the rights of refugees and IDPs in particular, is supported by an inculturated understanding of Roman Catholic social teaching. Both culture and religion thus contribute to a "body of shared belief" in human rights.

Conclusion

An argument in favor of the need for a re-interpretation of human rights in international law and public policy has been laid out. Effective moral response to the prevailing humanitarian crises in the Great Lakes Region of Africa fell short, necessitating a critical assessment of the moral criteria and strategies that were invoked. A limited understanding of the subject, object, nature, respondent, and justification of human rights in international refugee law and public policy contribute to the moral failure of governments and the international community in adequately responding to the plight of refugees. Moreover, the lack of legal recognition of IDPs in international refugee law and public policy makes this group more vulnerable to human rights deprivations than refugees. Under the current

---

[20] Walzer, *Spheres of Justice*, xv.
[21] MacIntyre, *After Virtue*, 69.
[22] Rorty, "Priority of Democracy to Philosophy," 259.
[23] Ibid.

understanding of human rights, refugees and IDPs suffer when they are denied equal entitlements as moral subject of rights. An effective strategy to protect refugees and IDPs requires the establishment of a re-interpretation of human rights in international refugee law and public policy.

The question of the object of rights is intimately connected to the subject of rights, specifically, equal entitlement to social and economic rights, as well as civil and political rights. However, insufficient legal recognition of these social and economic rights in international law as stated in the 1951 UN Geneva Convention leaves refugees and IDPs vulnerable to human rights' deprivations. When one considers that these groups are victims of the state system, the failure of governments and the international community to recognize their rights becomes a major concern for the philosophical ethics of rights.

Because refugees and IDPs are victims of the state system, the rights of security, subsistence, and liberty of social participation need to be given top priority by states and the international community. The failure by governments and the international community in their duty to accord a moral priority to these rights (between relative sovereignty of states and rights of refugees and IDPs to security) makes refugees and IDPs vulnerable to human rights deprivation. From the standpoint of the philosophical ethics of human rights, failing to recognize the priority of these rights, moreover, raises serious moral concerns, regarding the bearers of correlative duties. The situation calls for a re-interpretation of the priority of basic human rights and correlative duty to aid refugee and IDPs in international law and public policy for the Great Lakes Region of Africa.

The justifying basis of human rights in international law is highly disputed today among philosophers. Although the Universal Declaration of Human Rights appeals to the equal dignity of moral persons as the basis for ascribing human rights, it does not provide a further justifying ground for such a claim. Some communitarians, however, deny the role of human rights' norms in international law. Both of these views raise a moral concern regarding the criteria for the justification of human rights in international law. To adequately address these moral concerns, a re-interpretation of human rights is urgently needed.

Section B
A Re-Interpretation of Human Rights in International Refugee Law and Public Policy

---

> If a person has a particular right, the demand that the enjoyment of the substance of the right be socially guaranteed is justified by good reasons, and the guarantees ought, therefore to be provided.[24]

Introduction

Legal rights are those that are present in the positive law, while moral human rights are claims that ought to be present in the positive law.[25] An analysis of the humanitarian crises concludes that the narrow understanding of the moral rights of refugees and IDPs that prevails in international law and public policy contributes to governments' and the international community's failure in responding to human rights' abuses of refugees and IDPs in the Great Lakes Region of Africa. It was established in section A that the rationale for an adequate theory of human rights is necessary to redress the moral failure in the region. In this section, an adequate conception of human rights of refugees and IDPs in international law and policy is offered from the perspective of philosophical ethics of rights.

    Human rights in international law and public policy are re-interpreted in light of Henry Shue's theory of basic human rights. The critique is two-fold: internal and external. The internal critique examines the coherency and consistency of arguments regarding human rights' issues. The external critique examines the views of human rights from the perspective of other philosophical critics. The critiques are evaluated under the formal features of rights' moral claims: the subject of rights, the object of rights, the nature of rights, the respondent of rights' claims and the justifying ground or basis of rights. Strengths and weaknesses present in Shue's theory of basic human rights are identified. Finally, the significance and the bearing upon rights of refugees and IDPs in international refugee law and public policy are shown.

---

[24] Shue, *Basic Rights*, 13.

[25] Ilesanmi, "Human Rights Discourse," 289. Regarding the relationship between legal rights and human rights, see the argument of Dworkin, *Taking Rights Seriously*, 185–204.

The Subject of Basic Rights

The notion of human rights is highly contested in modern scholarship, creating controversy regarding the definition of human rights. In the debate it is argued that a universally accepted standard of human rights cannot be achieved due to differing views of whether the subjects of rights are individuals, groups, or communities. Even among individuals or within groups, it is unclear whether moral or legal rights are distributed equally. This dilemma is illustrated in feudalistic society, where lords had superior rights to their subjects.[26] Perhaps the issue of equal or unequal distribution of rights depends on the particular conception of rights involved. Regardless of the controversy, human rights are considered critical for social, political, and economic life, and are thus the subject of philosophical inquiry. With this in mind, the concept of the subject of rights and bearing upon refugees and IDPs in international refugee law and policy will be examined using Shue's philosophical theory of human rights as well other relevant ethical theorists.

It was argued that the narrow understanding of the subject of rights in international refugee law and public policy contributes to the moral failure of governments, social institutions, and the international community in responding to human rights' abuses of refugees and IDPs in the Great Lakes Region of Africa. In such laws and policies, there is a narrow understanding of the moral identity or status of refugees and IDPs and equality of their moral and legal entitlements. This understanding is either explicit or implicit in the public policy for refugees and IDPs in which race, ethnicity, sex, religion, social class, or political affiliations are the determining factors and not the principles of human rights.[27]

In *Basic Rights*, Henry Shue defines human rights as "the rational basis . . . for a justified demand."[28] Shue's analysis of human rights is quite significant regarding the question of the bearers of human rights in international law and policy. A person is the subject of rights precisely because of being a person. The concept of the human person is central in his analysis; rights are ascribed to the human person, which implies that, regardless

[26] Gewirth, *Human Rights*, 3.

[27] The scenarios of the humanitarian crises in Sudan and Rwanda are a good illustration of such an understanding. In the Western Darfur region of Sudan, IDPs are being discriminated against on the basis of race. In southern Sudan, the blacks are being discriminated against on the basis of race and religion. In Rwanda, the lack of an adequate humanitarian response by the international community was influenced by race. This situation will be discussed in detail later in this section.

[28] Shue, *Basic Rights*, 14.

of personal or social attributes of the person, a human person is the subject of rights.[29] The concept of the human person's moral status requires that a demand is a demand and should not be construed as a favor or privilege, but rather, as "one's due." As such, when a demand is satisfied, there is no need for appreciation or gratitude.[30] Because human persons are "dignified objects of respect," their moral entitlements do not admit a substitute, whatsoever.[31]

Since every person possesses moral rights, making a distinction between a right and the enjoyment of a right is warranted. A right in itself does not guarantee fulfillment just because it is considered to be a declaration or proclamation.[32] Another crucial distinction must be made between a right and substance of a right. Shue writes. "A right is not a right to enjoy a right-it is a right to enjoy something else."[33]

In order to enjoy the substance of a right, the bearer of rights demands that social arrangements be made especially for those who cannot secure a right on their own.[34] Because he regards social arrangements as the prerequisite for enjoying the substance of a right, Shue is critical of liberalism. He claims that individual rights that are divorced from society are morally deficient because negative liberties to forbearance take priority over other rights. It must be noted, however, that society does not make human rights, but rather, it protects them by providing effective social arrangements. Contributing to Shue's argument, John Langan notes, "Human rights are neither granted nor abolished in such actions, though they may be acknowledged or violated . . ."[35] Enjoying human rights requires effective social arrangements, thus human rights are essentially social rights.

The humanitarian crises in the Great Lakes Region of Africa and resulting human rights' violations are attributed to governments and international community's failure to recognize and acknowledge refugees and IDPs as the subject of human rights. In international refugee law, refugees are the subject of legal entitlements. Such entitlements, in turn, derive in international law from the status of moral persons as human subjects, ac-

---

[29] Ibid. See also the definition of human right, which hinges on the concept of the human person by Langan, "Defining Human Rights," 70.

[30] Shue, *Basic Rights*, 15

[31] Ibid.

[32] Ibid.

[33] Ibid.

[34] Ibid., 16.

[35] Langan, "Defining Human Rights," 72.

corded equal respect and consideration. Yet the crises in Rwanda and the Sudan display a fundamental lack of such recognition. In these countries, refugees who are a result of social and economic deprivations as well as internal armed conflicts and political instability are not considered equal subject of basic human rights of security, subsistence, and civil-political rights. Moreover, IDPs are not accorded equal legal protection in both 1951 UN and 1969 OAU Refugee Conventions. The critique on Shue's theory of human rights provides an adequate moral standard for ascribing human rights.[36] Indeed, as human persons, governments, social institutions, and the international community must regard refugees and IDPs as the moral subjects with equal entitlements to enjoy the substances of human rights. Recognition of refugees and IDPs as the subject of human rights ought to be the objective moral standard in international refugee law and policy.

The Object of Basic Human Rights

It was previously noted that a right is not a right to enjoy a right, but rather, it is a right to enjoy something else. The object of human rights can be described as the good or goods that the human person, (the subject of rights) enjoys, asserts, or enforces for its own sake.[37] Philosophical ethics of human rights identifies "the morality of the depths" by distinguishing the basic rights that someone is entitled to enjoy, assert, or enforce, from less necessary or expedient moral or legal rights.[38] Such rights can be described as non-basic rights because they are not the necessary goods or values for the person's moral action.[39] Basic rights are like fence-points, so to speak, and they provide a minimum protection for the powerless.[40] The philosophical ethics of human rights examines which rights have more weight to be called basic rights and what manner they can be fulfilled. Fulfilling

[36] See how Shue's theory of basic human rights is successful in providing the appropriate moral and legal responses to human rights' abuses of refugees and IDPs in the Great Lakes Region of Africa, in section C.

[37] For example, the Utility Principle of the classical Utilitarian theory that the great happiness for the greatest number considers rights not in terms of the individual good as such, rather, it is considered in terms of the general social benefit. For an in-depth analysis of utilitarianism, see Mill, *Utilitarianism*, 185–202. For a critical analysis of utilitarianism and its direct impact on economic rights, see Sen, *Development as Freedom*, 60–62.

[38] Shue, *Basic Rights*, 18. By "the morality of the depths" is meant ethical principles or norms, which provide a benchmark or baseline for human conduct.

[39] See the analysis made on "the object of rights" by Gewirth, *Human Rights*, 4–9.

[40] Shue, *Basic Rights*, 18.

basic rights is reserved for the bearers of correlative duties, a topic, which will be taken up later.

Based on the general notion that a right is a rational basis for a justified demand, Shue starts by identifying basic rights and non-basic rights. He regards basic rights as "essential to the enjoyment of all other rights," and argues that they cannot be sacrificed to obtain, protect, or provide for non-basic rights.[41] Basic rights represent fundamental intrinsic values that are critical to human life: security, subsistence, and liberties of active social participation and physical movement.

Security Rights

Among the rights considered to promote intrinsic moral values critical to human life are the basic rights to security because "being physically secure is a necessary condition for the exercise of any right, and guaranteeing physical security must be part of guaranteeing anything else as a right."[42] The human person is entitled to equal dignity and respect, hence violence and physical and sexual abuse, torture, harassment, and rape are degrading and humiliating actions. The right to physical security is basic because it protects one from fundamental threats to the intrinsic moral value of physical integrity. When the moral value of basic rights to security is considered, all necessary conditions must be present and stumbling blocks must be removed.[43] Basic rights to security are not simply rights to forbearance; rather, they are basic entitlements that should be socially guaranteed. Basic rights of physical security are not merely positive or legal rights; they transcend cultures and their validity is independent of positive law. However, enjoying the substance of basic rights to security demands effective social guarantees, including legal guarantees.

Shue's understanding of the object of rights bears a great significance on the rights of refugees and IDPs. Failure to recognize basic security rights, as the object of rights, in international law and policy contributes to human rights' violation of refugees and IDPs in the Great Lakes Region of Africa. Basic security is one of the principal objects of human rights, and as such, it is necessary to effectively protect those who cannot protect themselves, particularly women and children in armed conflict areas or in camps. Hence, basic security rights ought to be the objective moral standard in international law and policy.

[41] Ibid., 19.
[42] Ibid., 22.
[43] Ibid.

Subsistence Rights

It was shown earlier, basic human rights are the moral minima; they are the most fundamental rights that can be claimed and the least that can be demanded from individuals or society.[44] Subsistence rights entail the minimal conditions of economic security, i.e. claims to adequate nutrition, basic health care, and access to basic education, and as such, should be distinguished from broader social and economic rights.[45] Shue's analysis of basic subsistence rights addresses the issue of minimal economic protection for the good of the powerless and marginalized, the absence of which could cause severe impairment of a person's physical, mental, and psychological integrity.[46] Based on its crucial role, subsistence is considered a basic right, without which other rights cannot be enjoyed. One view is that security rights take a moral priority over subsistence rights. However, deprivation of subsistence rights can be life-threatening and even lead to death from malnutrition as it is apparent in the Great Lakes Region of Africa. Deprivation of this right can be especially detrimental to those who cannot provide for themselves for some reason.[47] However, security and subsistence rights are intimately connected, not as means to an end, but rather, as an essential part of enjoying other rights: physical integrity, bodily health, and mental and psychological wellness.

The recognition of basic subsistence rights, however, differs from one society to another. For example, western liberalism does not give a serious consideration to subsistence as a basic right because such rights are thought to impose an unbearable burden on individuals and social institutions. Non-western societies, on the other hand, often recognize basic subsistence rights and regard them highly.[48]

Subsistence rights are so basic that deprivation of these rights must be protected against any serious threats that interfere with enjoying them. To get a better grasp of various kinds of human rights' deprivations, a distinction must be drawn between remediable, predictable, inexcusable, preventable, and non-preventable, and excusable threats.[49] Because basic rights are the moral minima, the least individuals, groups, or institutions are expected to do is to ensure that social guarantees are in place as de-

---

[44] Ibid., 18.
[45] Ibid.
[46] Ibid., 24.
[47] Ibid., 26.
[48] Ibid., 27–28.
[49] Ibid., 29–33.

fenses, not against every imaginable threat but, "against predictable reme-diable threats."[50] The issue of various kinds of deprivations and their due remedies will be taken up later in the section.

When subsistence rights are threatened, life as whole is fundamen-tally threatened. Therefore, in conflicts of rights, it is morally unjustifiable to prefer non-basic subsistence rights to basic subsistence rights because such ranking undermines the lives of those who cannot provide for them-selves. The failure to recognize basic subsistence rights as the object of rights in international law and policy contributes to human rights' viola-tion of refugees and IDPs. Women and children in the Great Lakes Region of Africa are particularly vulnerable. Basic subsistence rights are the prin-cipal objects of human rights, thus they ought to be the objective moral standard in international law and policy. While basic subsistence rights are critical to the lives of refugees and IDPs (the subject of rights), basic liber-ties, are prerequisite for an effective enjoyment of subsistence and security basic rights. Hence, subsistence and security rights as well as basic liberties of social participation and physical freedom are interrelated.

Liberty

Enjoying the substance of basic rights of security and subsistence demands appropriate social arrangements. Lack of social participation in these ar-rangements is likely to threaten the enjoyment of these other basic rights. It is often claimed that subsistence rights have moral priority over any other rights; liberties may be considered non-basic rights, and thus regard-ed as secondary or less important rights. Others argue that liberties take a moral priority over subsistence rights. However, the criterion of a right to be considered basic right applies equally to subsistence and liberty; liberty is basic because it is a requirement for enjoying any other rights. It is worth examining some liberties that qualify as the substances of basic rights. The significance of an interdependence of basic rights of security, subsistence, and liberties will be shown.

Considering the significance of the interdependence of basic rights is critical for refugees and IDPs, since serious predictable or unpredictable threats upon one kind of rights are likely to affect the other. Shue shows the significance when he writes, "The enjoyment of rights of security and subsistence depends upon the enjoyment of some liberties."[51] To Shue's understanding of human rights, two minimal liberties are considered the

[50] Ibid., 33.
[51] Ibid., 70.

substances of basic rights: effective social participation and freedom of physical movement. Shue describes liberty of effective participation as:

> Genuine influence upon the fundamental choices among the social institutions and the social policies that control security and subsistence and, where the person is directly affected, genuine influence upon the operation of institutions and the implementation of policy.[52]

To enjoy the substance of a right is to freely exercise it. There is a huge discrepancy between merely enjoying the substances of security and subsistence, and enjoying them as rights. When one is not able to enjoy security and subsistence as rights, there is a danger that these rights may be enjoyed at the liberty of someone else.[53] If rights are construed as privileges, benefits, favors, and tokens, one can be deprived of them at anytime without a prior notification and moral justification.

Inasmuch as security and subsistence are basic rights, one must have the freedom to effectively exercise these rights, making free choices, setting meaningful goals for the good of the individual and society. Enjoying the substance of rights requires social guarantees, and therefore liberty of social participation, through which the demands are channeled, is critical for providing the deprived persons with basic rights of security and subsistence. Collaborative actions of governments and NGOs, intergovernmental organizations, as well as international social institutions are thus critical for ensuring that there is equal opportunity for those deprived to participate in organizing effective social arrangements. In extreme cases, governments, individuals, and social organizations may need to exclude those who are incapacitated from taking part in organizing social arrangements. In such situations, an active social participation may not be required in order to enjoy security and subsistence rights.[54] In general, however, it is critically important that those who suffer from human rights' deprivations be empowered by actively participating in actions and policies that are aimed at strengthening or securing security and subsistence rights. This concept is aimed at avoiding paternalism by the providers of basic rights and passivity by the victims. Ultimately, the victims cease to be perceived as the receiving end at the mercy of their providers; but rather, they gain the capacity to take control of their lives, history, and destiny.

---

[52] Ibid., 71.

[53] Ibid., 78.

[54] Ibid., 76.

Freedom of physical movement, another basic liberty, can be described as an absence of arbitrary constraints upon the human person.[55] As part of basic liberties, physical movement is regarded to be an essential component to enjoying other rights. Because exercising a right usually requires social arrangements, effective social participation demands physical presence. When individuals are subjected to arbitrary confinement, where freedom of physical movement is hindered, exercising security and subsistence rights is impeded. Hence, the social responsibility to assert, enjoy, or enforce basic rights is ineffective. Exercising liberties of social participation and physical movement is a requirement for enjoying other rights, which makes these rights indispensable. Considering the interdependence of rights, Shue argues, "the absence of these rights is sufficient to allow the thwarting of the enjoyment of any other rights, and that is why each of these rights is a basic right."[56] When rights are regarded as a rational basis for a justified demand, effective social participation and freedom of physical movement become necessary for enjoying security and subsistence rights.

Basic liberties to security and subsistence are pivotal in the philosophical ethics of human rights. If basic rights are "the morality of the depths," basic freedoms are the *conditio sine qua non* of the realization of human morality. Basic liberties may be enjoyed in a restricted manner given the conditions in which victims of human rights' abuses live. Yet, as human persons, they have rights to a spectrum of basic liberties that are necessary for a human flourishing; freedom from fundamental threats of torture, assault, rape, physical and sexual abuse to freedom for enjoying, asserting, or enforcing physical integrity; and freedom from fundamental threats of malnutrition, sickness, and death, to freedom for enjoying bodily health, mental and psychological integrity. Liberties of exercising basic rights of security and subsistence imply that social arrangements be guaranteed and that the necessary conditions to move freely to find work and earn a good living be provided. If security and subsistence rights are threatened or denied, basic liberties become tools that enable victims to press charges to secure them.

Because knowledge of basic liberties facilitates awareness of security and subsistence rights, education, as part of subsistence rights, is necessary for exercising basic liberties. The importance of basic liberties to security and subsistence rights is critical to the lives of those deprived of basic

---

[55] Ibid., 78.
[56] Ibid., 76.

rights particularly refugees and IDPs.[57] For this reason, basic liberties of social participation and physical movement must be included among the principal object of rights.

Basic rights of security, subsistence, and liberties are critical for refugees and IDPs in international law and policy. Unlike the 1969 OAU Refugee Convention, which extends rights discourse to include social and economic rights as well as civil and political rights, the 1951 UN Refugee Convention does not adequately recognize these rights. To adequately exercise the basic rights of security, subsistence, and civil liberties, legal recognition of these rights ought to become the objective moral standard in international refugee law and public policy.

The Nature of Basic Human Rights

Human persons, the subject of rights, ought to enjoy equal moral entitlements precisely because they are persons, independent of social status or personal attributes. Security, subsistence, and basic liberties of social participation and physical movement are basic objects of rights because they are prerequisite for the enjoyment of other rights. It was argued that rights of security, subsistence, and liberty of social participation and freedom of physical movement are intimately interrelated.

Although these rights are interrelated, a number of questions must be addressed regarding the priority of human rights: Is there a possibility of conflict of rights' claims within human rights' system and policy? Are there genuine reasons that cause human rights to override other rights' claims in order to protect the basic rights of the most vulnerable persons? If so, what are the morally justifiable criteria for resolving conflicts of rights in such circumstances? Does a theory of basic human rights grant a priority of claims and urgency of satisfying moral demands consonant with equal moral status of refugees or IDPs, as the subject of rights?

In the preceding sections, it was argued that a theory of human rights ought to distinguish basic rights from non-basic rights. However, a philosophical controversy exists regarding the notion of positive and negative rights. Some critics accord moral priority of negative rights over positive rights partly because it is assumed that security rights, for example, are less demanding to enforce or fulfill than subsistence rights. Others argue that

---

[57] See the importance of the interrelation of basic rights of security, subsistence, social participation, and physical movement in reference to the success story of women in the Tanzanian refugee camps illustrated in chapter 2.

subsistence rights take a moral priority over security rights or civil liberties because they are central to human life.

In response to these views, Shue argues that placing priority on security, a "negative" right, over subsistence, a "positive" right, is a morally misguided distinction. What is worth considering is whether security rights are purely negative and subsistence rights are purely positive. To grasp the difference between positive and negative rights, it is appropriate to note whether or not there is a real distinction between them. Positive rights are thought to require actions of people, groups or institutions to satisfy moral claims, whereas negative rights require them to refrain from actions that would cause human rights' deprivation. Yet effective protection against violations of security rights does not simply mean refraining from interfering with the enjoyment of human rights. Rather, effective social guarantees are prerequisite for satisfying security rights.[58] Consequently, a distinction between positive and negative rights collapses, and thus must be rejected when this analysis is considered.[59]

The rejection of a pseudo-distinction between positive and negative rights has a moral significance when basic rights need to be protected from essential and systematic deprivations in society. The character of such rights' deprivations needs to be clarified. Essential and systematic deprivations consist of fundamental elements inherent in a system that are detrimental to enjoying the substance of rights of security, subsistence, and liberties. Eliminating the essential deprivations demands replacing those elements that are inherent in the system.[60] Accidental deprivations, however, are less detrimental to enjoying the substance of rights. Eliminating such deprivations consists of eliminating the elements that are non-essential to the system, without changing the fundamental elements therein.[61]

Achieving the objective requires not only refraining from actions that cause essential deprivations, but also demands positive actions to redress the deprivations. Individuals, groups, governments, and social institutions ought to actively get involved in eliminating essential deprivations. Civil liberties are critical for ensuring that refugees and IDPs are able to take an active part in exercising security and subsistence rights in camps. This is done when these groups in general, and women in particular, in conjunc-

---

[58] Shue, *Basic Rights*, 39.

[59] Ibid., 51.

[60] Ibid., 47.

[61] Ibid.

tion with governments, NGOs, and UNHCR, are actively involved in leadership roles to plan and implement security measures. Likewise, this process enables them to take initiative in self-reliance projects: farming, primary health care, and sanitation.[62] Because satisfying negative rights require positive actions, distinction between positive and negative rights is morally irrelevant, thus security and subsistence have equal priority.

The Bearers of Correlative Duties

It was established that security, subsistence, and liberty of social participation and physical movement are basic rights; satisfaction of these rights is prerequisite for the enjoyment of other rights. Every human person, precisely as a person, is entitled to enjoy equal basic human rights. It was also established that the argument opposed to distinguishing positive and negative rights is morally significant because negative rights do not only require forbearance but demands positive actions as well. By this argument, the distinction between duties rather than between rights becomes morally relevant from the perspective of the philosophical ethics of human rights.

According to Shue, every basic right generates three correlative duties: the duty to avoid depriving (negative), the duty to protect against deprivation (positive), and the duty to aid or provide (positive). Hence, enjoying the substance of basic rights of security, subsistence, and liberties of active social participation and physical movement require both positive and negative duties. It is worth noting, however, that the same individuals, groups or social institutions need not necessarily implement these duties.[63] Because the duty to provide refugees and IDPs is a result of the failures of governments and social institutions to avoid depriving and protect from deprivation, this duty takes moral and legal priority over the relative sovereignty of states in international law and public policy, and thus ought to be the objective moral criterion for international humanitarian assistance in the Great Lakes Region of Africa.

The primary aim of enforcing correlative duties is to ensure that every person enjoys the substance of basic rights and that actual or potential essential deprivations are eliminated or minimized. If the source of deprivation or harm is the individual, group, or institution, it is the duty of a national government, as the primary institution, to protect from depriva-

---

[62] See the success story of these initiatives in the Tanzanian refugee camps illustrated in chapter 2.

[63] Shue, *Basic Rights*, 52.

tion by enforcing the duty to avoid depriving.[64] If a government neglects its duty to avoid depriving, or even becomes the source of deprivation, then social institutions through "multilateral intervention" must assume the moral responsibility of enforcing the duty to protect against deprivation by enforcing the duty to avoid depriving.[65] Enforcing these duties may present various problems. On the one hand, due to failure of governments to avoid depriving, it may be difficult to convince social institutions or the international community to assume moral responsibility to protect people against deprivations by enforcing the duty to avoid depriving.[66] On the other hand, providing the means for protecting people whose only source of livelihood is threatened by essential and systematic deprivations may be complicated. This presents a moral dilemma for the bearers of such duties particularly when governments neglect or are unwilling to enforce the duties to avoid depriving and duties to protect against essential and systematic deprivations.

Shue responds to this dilemma by saying that "some provision must be made for enforcing this duty on behalf of the rest of humanity upon those who would not otherwise fulfill it."[67] In such cases, the international community bears the moral responsibility to protect the victims of persecution against essential and systematic deprivations by enforcing the duty to avoid depriving. As a last resort, the multinational peacekeeping force, for example, becomes a relevant bearer of duties in resolving conflicts of rights between the relative state sovereignty and refugees and IDPs; the subject of basic rights.

The issue of primary and secondary duties needs further clarification vis-à-vis protection from essential and systematic deprivations. Shue's view regarding correlative duties may suffice when applied to subsistence rights, for example, where public policy may discourage subsistence crop farming in favor of cash crop (agribusiness). Prices of food may likely go up due to a short food supply. In such a case, despite the fact that some

[64] Ibid., 56.

[65] Ibid.

[66] Ibid.

[67] Ibid. See Langan, "Defining Human Rights," 77. Langan's argument in favor of social institutions as the bearers of correlative duties to prevent human rights' deprivations reinforces Shue's analysis of human rights. It is in Langan's understanding that the moral responsibility invoked is not a matter of some acts of charity, so to speak. Rather, it is a matter of moral obligation to defend people for whom the only source of livelihood is at stake. Langan's view is counter-argument against Nozick's philosophy of philanthropic charity. Also see Nozick, *Anarchy, State, and Utopia,* 265–68.

of the consequences may be unintentional, deprivations of basic subsistence rights caused by the policy may be detrimental to individuals whose lives depend totally on small-scale subsistence farming.[68] To address the deprivations, Shue distinguishes two features of duties: the primary duty, which is designing institutions that can avoid the creation of "strong incentives to violate duty," and the secondary duty, which is enforcing the duty to avoid depriving.[69] The primary duty ascribed to social institutions becomes morally significant when considering the scope and magnitude of deprivations and harm (essential and systematic) these institutions can cause to individuals or society when they are not restrained. Elimination of essential and systematic deprivations largely depends on governments designing effective social institutions.

Duty to aid the deprived (positive) is a result of the failure to avoid depriving (negative) and protect against deprivation (positive).[70] The failure of the duty to avoid depriving imposes severe consequences on those whose alternative source of livelihood is at stake. Shue believes that "to eliminate the only realistic means a person has for obtaining food or other physical necessities is to cause that person, for example, the physical harm of malnutrition or of death by starvation."[71] In this situation, it is inappropriate to conclude that no one is responsible for protecting and providing assistance to the deprived. Rather, deprivations resulting from the failure of duty to avoid or protect should be viewed as the collective moral responsibility of social institutions to provide for those deprived. Therefore, institutions designed to carry out moral responsibility are critical to the task of aiding the victims of failures to avoid depriving and protecting from deprivations.

To eliminate essential and systematic deprivations of human rights requires effective cooperation of governments, NGOs, private individuals, and international organizations. It is for this reason that the distinction of duties (positive and negative duties) becomes more morally relevant than

---

[68] See in chapter 1 under the sub-section, "Tribalism and Colonialism" regarding the description on forced migration of Rwandans due to famine. This was caused by the Belgian agricultural policy that favored the cultivation of cash crops for export to the European industries, which disregarded subsistence farming for domestic consumption. The famine caused by the Belgians' agricultural policy in Rwanda illustrates how social institutions can cause essential and systematic deprivations of subsistence rights. In such a case, designing social institutions that can curb deprivations is prerequisite for enjoying the substance of basic rights of subsistence and other rights.

[69] Shue, *Basic Rights*, 60.

[70] Ibid., 57.

[71] Ibid.

the distinction between rights (positive and negative rights). The cooperation among duty bearers is key to preventing occurrence of human rights' abuses.[72] If duties to avoid depriving were always effectively fulfilled, duties to protect against deprivation and to provide assistance to the deprived would become unnecessary.[73] Yet, when massive failures of duty to avoid and protect occur, duty to provide fitting assistance becomes morally compelling. The more failures of duties to avoid and protect, the more burdensome the duties to provide become.[74] However, when the failure of duty to avoid depriving is minimized, the burden of moral responsibility to provide diminishes.[75] Since this scenario rarely occurs particularly in areas of armed conflict, socio-economic insecurity, and political instability, duties to aid the deprived are a moral priority in international law and policy. Shue's understanding of assigning moral responsibility becomes relevant here; the bearers of duties to shoulder the burdens related to subsistence rights "do not fall primarily upon isolated individuals…but primarily upon human communities…"[76] The assertion that a right is a rational basis for a justified moral claim gets a nod here; social arrangements including legal guarantees are prerequisite for satisfying basic rights of security, subsistence, and liberties of social participation and physical movement particularly, for victims of failure of governments to avoid depriving and protect against deprivations.

Because the duty to provide for the deprived is a result of the failures of governments and social institutions to avoid depriving and protect from deprivation, this duty to provide ought to be the moral responsibility of the international community. Therefore, the international community ought to be a bearer of duty to provide refugees and IDPs with basic rights in international law and public policy.

---

[72] Due to the current divisions in the UN Security Council, measures to curb human rights' abuses of refugees and IDPs across the globe are difficult to implement. Recent discussion and disagreement in the Security Council on whether or not to impose global economic sanctions on the Sudanese Government illustrates the ineffectiveness of the international regime of rights, particularly when there are conflicts of rights' claims between invested interests and IDPs' basic rights of security, subsistence, participation, and physical freedom in the region.

[73] Shue, *Basic Rights*, 61.

[74] Ibid., 63.

[75] Ibid.

[76] Ibid., 64.

The Justifying Ground of Basic Human Rights

Four moral affirmations have been made regarding basic human rights (1) The human person is the subject of rights (2) Basic security, subsistence, and liberties of social participation and physical movement are the principal objects of human rights (3) By nature, these rights are basic and hence enjoy a moral priority (4) Basic rights generate three duties: the duty to avoid depriving, the duty to protect from deprivation, and the duty to aid the deprived. It is the moral and legal priority for the international community to become a bearer of correlative duties to aid the deprived when governments and social institutions fail to do so.

The fundamental principles mentioned above require supporting proof, which is critical to the philosophical ethics of rights. The issue of justification of human rights is not explicit in Shue's theory of human rights. He simply talks of "compelling reasons, especially deep principles" for satisfying rights' moral claims.[77] His theory is justified with the assumption that basic human rights exist because they are necessary demands for the enjoyment of other rights, and every human person is entitled to them.[78] The questions of basic human rights (the nature and the object of rights) and correlative duties (the respondent of rights) are grounded in the human person (the subject of rights). In order to prevent deprivations, individuals, governments, and other social institutions bear moral responsibility (the bearers of correlative duties) to protect the basic rights. Shue's moral argument for the justification of rights is based on his treatment of basic rights and correlative duties.

Duties correlative to subsistence rights are often in dispute. The claim that adequate nutrition would likely trigger a population explosion in developing countries is used to support the view that security rights take priority over subsistence rights.[79] Subsistence rights are interpreted as relative, therefore able to be overridden, ensuring that security and other rights are not overlooked. This is a narrow-minded argument, which is subject to moral criticism. In perspective, the overpopulation argument in and by itself is morally insufficient to justify the denial of people's subsistence rights. On the other hand, the argument in favor of subsistence rights should not be used to ignore the question of population growth.[80]

---

[77] Ibid., 13.

[78] Ibid., 14.

[79] Ibid., 92.

[80] Ibid., 100–101.

Handling both issues proportionately offers the best solution to protecting subsistence rights. Shue writes:

> The best hopes of controlling population through discouraging births, instead of encouraging deaths by refraining from protecting subsistence, depends on simultaneous, if not prior, improvements in living standards. The protection of subsistence rights, therefore, may be part of the solution, not part of the problem, as presumed by the population objection.[81]

Given the magnitude of the problem of poverty in developing nations, acts of charity alone can hardly improve people's standards of living.[82] The moral responsibility of avoiding depriving, protecting against deprivation, and providing for the deprived falls indirectly upon the affluent nations or individuals. This includes designing social institutions both nationally and internationally that prevent deprivations of subsistence rights. This moral responsibility implies that "the affluent are expected not to enjoy less, but only to acquire more at somewhat slower rate than they would if they maximized their own interests, as narrowly construed."[83] The point is whether or not subsistence basic rights of nationals take a moral and legal priority over those of non-nationals. Some views are that factors of shared nationality, history, culture, traditions, social economic and political visions or interests are a legitimate justification to avoid depriving, protecting from deprivation and provide for the deprived.[84]

However, it is also possible that individuals in one nation forge social and moral bonds with members of other nations not necessarily based on the values above, but rather, on a mutually-shared understanding of social, moral, and religions principles, and may consider this a moral justification for undertaking moral responsibilities toward certain groups. This suggests that shared nationality may not be the only moral justification for duties to avoid, protect, and aid the deprived.[85] What is the moral justification for avoiding depriving, protecting from deprivation, and aiding the deprived, particularly people who are in no way related to each other historically, socially, culturally, politically, economically, and religiously? There seem to be factors that stand a chance of being regarded as a moral justification apart from those mentioned previously. Shue argues that fulfilling

---

[81] Ibid., 102.
[82] Ibid., 104.
[83] Ibid., 108.
[84] Ibid., 133.
[85] Ibid., 136.

subsistence duties toward the needy beyond one's own territory is a "sacred honor."[86] This conclusion is rooted in Shue's claim that human persons are the subjects of rights, and as such, they ought to be treated as "dignified objects of respect both in their own eyes and in the view of others."[87]

Fulfilling correlative duties based on philanthropic charity, as Robert Nozick claims, may result in further deprivations due to unequal distribution or overlap of duties, and may end with no moral responsibility being assigned.[88] It was argued rather that the moral responsibility of the duties to provide and to aid the deprived falls upon the affluent. Shue notes, "It is they upon whom duties to aid in the fulfillment of basic rights fall first, other things being equal."[89] If so, what is the justifying basis for "transferring"[90] non-basic rights to satisfy the basic rights, particularly of refugees and IDPs? Shue refers to a "degradation prohibition principle" that is the justifying basis for subsistence basic duties of governments and the international community; inequalities that are degrading are morally unjustifiable and unacceptable because the "affluent" are protected and the subsistence rights of the deprived are unprotected.[91] The principle of "degrading prohibition" does not advocate for the existence of simple ethical egalitarianism; that all inequalities are morally unacceptable. Rather, what the principle advocates is complex ethical egalitarianism; "inequalities that are incompatible with self-respect-that are humiliating-are impermissible. Inequality is not prohibited by the principle but limited."[92]

Although, it was argued that basic rights are universal and that social arrangements are required to enjoy the substance of these rights; it does not necessarily follow that the correlative duties must be assigned to every person in society. What is apparent, however, is that, duties to avoid depriving are universal.[93] So, who are the bearers of duties to protect from deprivation and provide assistance to the deprived? Because positive duties are often better served through effective social institutions as we have

---

[86] Ibid., 113.

[87] Ibid., 15.

[88] Nozick, *Anarchy, State, and Utopia*, 265.

[89] Shue, *Basic Rights*, 119.

[90] The term, "transfer" is often used by Shue in *Basic Rights*, chapter 5. The use of this term is maintained throughout section B of this work. Throughout chapter 5, Shue does not provide the meaning of the word "transfer." However, from the context, the term is presumed to mean, "giving away non-basic rights to satisfy basic rights of someone else's."

[91] Shue, *Basic Rights*, 119.

[92] Ibid., 120.

[93] Ibid.

seen, the answer is at least indirectly the affluent nations or individuals, who spend large amount of resources to satisfy "mere preferences."[94] Basic rights and correlative duties are misplaced when the satisfaction of mere preferences takes priority over the basic rights of the deprived, and leads to "the extreme inequalities in security or subsistence [which are] subversive of the dignity of the deprived…"[95] Physical security of the person is intimately connected to the person's integrity, which justifies the duties to security.[96] In cases where refugees and IDPs, particularly women and children, are threatened by violence, physical abuse, sexual abuse, and rape, the victims are so profoundly traumatized that "the person may not survive even if he or she is not killed."[97]

This situation leads to "degrading inequality: not the more obvious case of treating equals unequally, but the case of treating extreme unequals equally."[98] Fairness and equality is not the same thing. What does fairness mean regarding equal protection of basic rights? The Rawlsian theory of justice as fairness is not a theory of the moral minima such as the one Shue proposes; according to the theory of justice as fairness distributing rights and duties is contingent upon the procedural justice. Inequalities can be morally justified through the "difference principle": social benefits of the well-off are maximized for the benefits of the least advantaged.[99] Shue argues that Rawls simply proposes a "rope of justice" because those who are at the bottom will go up, provided those at the top pull it up. However, in this scenario, there is the possibility for those who are at the lower end of the rope to drown when it is not high enough. Hence, the "difference principle" does not guarantee eliminating extreme inequalities. Contrary to this principle, those who are about to drown ought to be lifted up, at least high enough to keep their heads above water. The concept of basic rights and correlative duties provides that role. Shue criticizes Rawls' "difference principle" and declares, "Social institutions…used to preserve rather than to eliminate extreme and degradingly unfair inequalities is beyond rational justifications."[100]

---

[94] Ibid.

[95] Ibid.

[96] Ibid., 121–22.

[97] Ibid., 122.

[98] Ibid., 127.

[99] For an in-depth analysis of "difference principle" and its application, see Rawls, *Theory of Justice*, 73–74.

[100] Shue, *Basic Rights*, 130.

Bear in mind that failure of duties by governments and the international community to avoid, protect, and aid the deprived contributes to extreme inequalities due to poor social arrangements. At present, it is regrettable that effective and sustainable international social institutions designed to carry out the moral responsibility to prevent deprivations are all too often absent in the world of globalization. Currently, the most crucial task of international relations is recognizing and implementing the duties to provide for basic rights as the results of the failure of duties to avoid depriving and protect from deprivation. According to the "degradation prohibition principle," Shue argues that duties to aid the deprived are transnational:

> A government that does violate, or assist in violating, the rights of people outside its own territory is failing in its duties both to the victims of the deprivations and, as an agent with service duties to its own population.[101]

To uphold transnational duties may require a new international moral order. A distinction was drawn earlier between legal rights and moral human rights; the former deals with rights as defined by positive law or custom, whereas the latter deals with moral claims, which ought to be present in legal rights.[102] The re-interpretation of human rights through the prism of Shue's theory of rights provides international law and policy with objective moral criteria for dealing with the problems of human rights' abuses in the Great Lakes Region of Africa. The human person, the subject of equal basic rights, becomes the prime moral principle for international law regarding forced migration. Implementing the moral principle is a step forward toward realizing basic rights as "morality of the depths" in international refugee law and policy in the Great Lakes Region of Sub-Saharan Africa.

Shue shows how his "degradation prohibition principle" supports our "faith in basic human rights." Yet Shue does not himself offer a further grounding or foundation for our "shared beliefs" in "the inherent dignity" and "equal and inalienable rights of all members of the human family."[103]

---

[101] Ibid., 152.

[102] The relationship between moral norms and positive law is described above in the "Introduction" of section B.

[103] "United Nations General Assembly Resolution 217A," 153–56.

Conclusion

Objective moral criteria have been drawn to redress human rights' abuses of refugees and IDPs in the Great Lakes Region of Africa, based on the revised interpretation of human rights in international law and policy from the perspective of Shue's theory of rights. (1) Every person is the moral subject of rights and, as such, is entitled to enjoy equal entitlements, which ought to be a guiding moral criterion in protecting the rights of refugees and IDPs in international refugee law and policy. (2) A right is a right not to enjoy a right; rather, it is a right to enjoy something else. Security, subsistence, as well as liberties of social participation and physical movement are considered basic rights because they are necessary to enjoy other rights. On the grounds that basic rights are interrelated, liberty of social participation in exercising basic rights of security and subsistence rights ought to be a moral priority in international refugee law and policy. In order to enjoy the substance of basic rights, active social participation of all parties concerned in designing effective social institutions and implementing social arrangements is expeditiously needed. (3) In view of the notion that enjoying the substance of rights requires social arrangements, a distinction between positive and negative rights is no longer considered to be of primary relevance. The emphasis can no longer be placed only on negative rights and negative duties, but rather, must be placed on positive and negative duties. Based on the failure of duties by governments and social institutions to avoid depriving and protect from essential and systematic deprivation, the duty to guarantee basic rights of security, subsistence, and liberties ought to be the collective moral responsibility of the international community. Recognizing duties correlative to basic rights resolves the conflicts of rights' claims by overriding rights of relative state sovereignty in favor of basic rights of the deprived. (4) Consequently, basic rights generate three correlative duties: the duty to avoid depriving (negative), the duty to protect from deprivation (positive), and the duty to provide assistance to the deprived (positive). Because of governments' and social institutions' failure of duties to avoid depriving and protect from deprivation causes humanitarian crises, the duty to aid the deprived ought to be given a moral priority. (5) Shue's justification of human rights is closely related to duties correlative to basic rights, and is aimed at eliminating extreme inequalities that contribute to human degradation, especially among those who have been deprived of their sole source of livelihood due to social-economic and political persecutions. Although Shue believes that the "degradation prohibition principle" promotes equality and dignity of the human person, Shue does not offer a further grounding for such a claim.

SECTION C
The Moral and Legal Significance of Henry Shue's
Theory of Basic Human Rights in International Refugee
Law and Policy for the Great Lakes Region of Africa

Introduction

In the preceding section, a revised interpretation of human rights was made and five objective ethical principles were drawn, based on Shue's theory of human rights. This section examines how the ethical principles are successful in addressing five major moral and legal concerns mentioned in section A, regarding the subject of rights, the object of rights, the nature of rights, the bearers of correlative duties, and the justification of human rights in international law and policy. This approach redresses the failures of governments, social institutions, and the international community, and thus prevents the abuses of human rights of refugees and IDPs in the Great Lakes Region of Africa. The "ethical" principles become the framework for evaluating moral and legal policy of refugees and IDPs in the region.[104]

The Subject of Basic Human Rights

Principle 1: Every person is the moral subject of rights.

Shue's view that a right is a rational basis for a justified demand is a significant contribution towards dealing with violations of human rights of refugees and IDPs in the Great Lakes Region of Sub-Saharan Africa. Shue strongly affirms that every human person is the subject of rights, and thus ought to enjoy equal entitlements in positive law. Governments, social institutions, and the international community's failure to recognize refugees and IDPs as the bearers of equal legal rights in international refugee law and policy contributes to human rights' abuses in these groups in the Great Lakes Region of Africa.[105] In part, the reason

---

[104] In this chapter, although the terms, "ethics" and "morality" are closely interrelated, they are, however, not used interchangeably. Ethics deals with the scientific evaluative study of human conduct judged under certain moral norms, which determine human actions in terms of "right" and "wrong" or "good" or "bad." Morality is the material object of the study of ethics.

[105] For an in-depth analysis of the evaluative description of responses to the humanitarian crises of refugees and IDPs, see chapter 2. Also, see the rationale for re-interpreting human rights of refugees and IDPs in international refugee law and policy in section A of chapter 3.

for failure is that international refugee law and policy (universal) as stipulated in the 1951 UN Geneva Refugee Convention is too restrictive. The Convention does not recognize equal legal rights of refugees and IDPs who are victims of social, economic, political, and internal armed conflicts in the region.[106]

To redress the failure of governments and the international community to intervene in such situations such as the 1994 Rwandan genocide and the Sudan's conflict, refugees and IDPs ought to be recognized as the subjects of rights, and thus bearers of equal legal rights in international refugee law and policy (universal). The 1969 OAU Convention Governing the Specific Aspects of Refugee Problem in Africa demonstrates this recognition; the Convention (Article 1 [2]) is broader and considers a variety of forced migrations. The Convention accepts those individuals who are refugees as a result of the "events seriously disturbing public order…" particularly the victims of social, economic, political instability, and internal armed conflicts.[107] The demographic data shows that IDPs are outnumbering refugees in Africa. However, the factor common to both the 1951 UN Geneva Convention and the 1969 OAU Refugee Convention is that IDPs are not legally recognized as the subject of rights. Despite the lack of legal recognition of IDPs, UNHCR has created some awareness of the need to protect and provide them with basic rights under the international humanitarian law of the Geneva Convention. As seen in chapter 2, the IDPs Guidelines developed recently are a step forward; nevertheless, they may be ineffective because they are not an internationally legally binding document.[108]

The concept that every human person is the subject of basic human rights allows refugees and IDPs to become the bearers of these rights regardless of race, color, sex, religion, ethnicity, nationality, social status, and political affiliations.[109] Therefore, to avoid double standards in international law and domestic policy, legal recognition of refugees and IDPs as the sub-

---

[106] For an in-depth analysis of the humanitarian crises of refugees and IDPs in the Great Lakes Region of Sub-Saharan Africa, see chapter 1.

[107] See the definition of the status of refugee stated in the 1969 OAU Convention in chapter 1.

[108] See the IDPs Guidelines in chapter 2, "Humanitarian Response to Displaced Populations in Armed Conflict Areas."

[109] The ethical principle of equal moral and legal rights is a universal standard which will help redress sexual discrimination, and thus contributes to an effective protection of women and children who are often affected by violence, physical, sexual abuse, and rape in armed conflicts and in settlement areas in the region.

ject of rights by governments and the international community is the objective international moral standard in redressing the problems of human rights' abuses in the Great Lakes Region of Africa.

The Object of Basic Human Rights

> *Principle 2: Security, subsistence, and liberties of active social participation and physical movement are basic human rights.*

Shue maintains that a right is not a right to enjoy a right; rather, it is a right to enjoy something else. This view is relevant to redressing the failures of governments and the international community vis-à-vis human rights abuses of refugees and IDPs in the Great Lakes Region of Africa.[110] International refugee law as stipulated in the 1951 UN Geneva Convention does not recognize refugees who are victims of social, economic, civil and political, and internal armed conflicts as the subject of rights, so their social, economic, civil and political rights remain legally unprotected. Therefore, due to unstable situations in the region, these groups are vulnerable to human rights' abuses in the region. Unlike the 1951 UN Refugee Convention, the 1969 OAU Refugee Convention, however, recognizes social, economic, civil, and political rights, as the objects of rights in Africa. Furthermore, these rights are explicitly recognized under Article 6 and 22 (1) in the 1981 OAU (Banjul) Charter on Human and Peoples' Rights. If the African regime of rights is implemented, it becomes an effective instrument, which better safeguards social and economic rights in the region.

Shue's understanding that basic human rights are necessary for enjoying the substance of rights is the basis for determining that the priority of basic rights of security, subsistence, and liberties of active social participation and physical movement is critical to redressing human rights' abuses. Implementing this principle contributes to freeing refugees and IDPs from fundamental harm (acts of torture, assaults, physical and sexual abuse, rape, arbitrary arrest and harassment, homelessness, diseases, malnutrition, and ignorance) and able to enjoy basic physical integrity, bodily health, and mental and psychological wellness. Therefore, recognition of these rights should be given legal protection over non-basic rights in international refugee law and policy.

Basic rights of security, subsistence, and liberties of active social participation and physical movement should be exercised interdependently if

---

[110] For further information, see the revised understanding of human rights from the perspective of Shue's theory of basic human rights in section B of chapter 3.

the substance of these rights is to be enjoyed. As shown in chapter 2, the UNHCR in Tanzanian refugee camps has been successful in providing some security and subsistence rights as a result of active social participation.[111] Refugees taking up community leadership roles and introducing self-help projects in agriculture, water, health, sanitation and others, strengthen security and subsistence rights. This strategy of involving refugees, particularly women, in conjunction with governments, the UNHCR and its sister agencies, NGOs, private individuals, and the international community illustrates the positive effect interdependence of basic rights of security, subsistence, and liberty of active social participation has on improving the living standards of refugees in camps. To redress the failures of governments and the international community in dealing with human rights' violations, equal basic rights of security, subsistence, and liberty should take legal priority over non-basic rights in international law and policy. Therefore, priority of equal legal recognition of security, subsistence, and liberties becomes the objective international moral standard in redressing human rights' abuses in the Great Lakes Region of Africa.

The Nature of Basic Human Rights

Principle 3: The moral duty to respect basic rights is the legal priority in international law and policy.

Recognition of basic rights of security, subsistence, and liberty ought to take legal priority over non-basic rights in international refugee law and public policy because basic rights are necessary for enjoying the substance of rights. Shue rejects the dichotomy between positive and negative rights. This is significant because satisfaction of these rights requires positive and negative duties. It is misleading to consider that security rights take priority over subsistence rights because the former are negative, and thus less demanding. Bearing in mind the interdependence of basic rights and that effective social arrangements are critical to enjoying basic human rights, security and subsistence have equal priority.

Humanitarian crises of refugees and IDPs in the Great Lakes Region of Africa have occurred due to the failure of duties by governments, and social institutions to avoid depriving and protect against deprivation.[112] To effectively redress the essential and systematic human rights deprivations

---

[111] The success story of UNHCR demonstrates that active social participation in security and subsistence rights improves standards of living in refugee camps. For further information, see chapter 2, "The Human Rights Situation in Refugee Camps in Tanzania," 48–56.

[112] See the description of nature and scope of humanitarian crises in chapter 1.

in countries like Rwanda and Sudan, the duty to provide refugees and IDPs with basic rights of security, subsistence, and liberties of active social participation and physical movement is a serious moral responsibility from the standpoint of philosophical ethics of basic human rights. Because of the gravity of the situation, implementing the duty to provide refugees and IDPs, particularly women and children, with these basic rights should take a legal priority over other competing moral rights' claims, such as geo-strategic interests, property rights, or states' relative sovereignty. When the lives of these people are at stake, and when less coercive means have failed, the priority of the duty to provide these groups with basic rights of security, subsistence, and liberties of active social participation and physical movement provides legal legitimacy for international humanitarian intervention.[113] This strategic moral principle also should be applied to the humanitarian situation in Uganda in order to redress human rights' abuses of IDPs that are occurring in the northern parts of the country as a result of the Ugandan government's inability to provide IDPs with basic rights.

Moreover, the strategic principle of the duty to provide refugees and IDPs with basic rights of security, subsistence, and liberties is critical for international relations. Any regional or international humanitarian intervention that interferes with domestic affairs of other states, through direct or indirect use of force, is morally and legally illegitimate when the primary aim is to protect geo-strategic interests rather than promote the basic rights of refugees and IDPs. Therefore, legal recognition of the principle of duty to provide basic rights of security, subsistence, and liberties of active social participation and physical movement for these groups becomes the objective international moral standard in dealing with humanitarian crises in the Great Lakes Region of Sub-Saharan Africa.

The Bearer of Correlative Basic Duties

Principle 4: The international community is a bearer of duty to provide assistance to the deprived in international law and policy.

The duty falling upon the international community to provide refugees and IDPs with basic rights of security, subsistence, and liberties of active social participation and physical movement results from the

---

[113] International humanitarian intervention should be conducted under *jus ad bellum* and *jus in bello* criteria. See European Ethics Network, *Ethical Perspectives*, 169–70. The journal stresses that military intervention can be morally justified after less coercive approach has already been exhausted. The justifying factor for the military action is the gross violation of fundamental rights, which affect a national, ethnic, racial or religious group.

failure by governments and social institutions to avoid depriving and to protect against deprivation of these rights. Shue's understanding of basic rights and correlative duties underscores the moral responsibility assigned to governments, social institutions, and the international community. The distinction among duties rather than between positive and negative rights is critical to redressing the failures of governments, social institutions, and the international community. For example, the scenario of the 1994 Rwandan conflict demonstrates neglect of three types of duties: the Rwandan government's failure in resolving inter-ethnic conflicts between the Tutsi minority and Hutu majority (positive duty), and systemic and systematic deprivation of their basic rights through its direct involvement in ethnic cleansing of Tutsis and moderate Hutus during the genocide (negative duty), and the failure of the international community to provide these victims with basic rights of security, subsistence, and liberties of active social participation and physical movement (positive duty).

Moreover, the violator of basic rights cannot be the protector of these rights at the same time. The scenario of conflict in the Western Darfur region of Sudan demonstrates neglect of two types of duties: the Sudanese government's failure to disarm the Arab-militias, the *Janjaweed*, from depriving the civilian populations of security, subsistence, and liberties of active social participation and physical movement (negative duty), and the government's failure to protect the civilians from being deprived of these basic rights (positive duty).

Contrary to the view that negative rights and negative duties (rights to forbearance) should take moral and legal priority over positive rights and positive duties, enjoyment of basic rights not only demands negative actions, but also positive actions through effective social arrangements. As we have seen, the concept of collective moral responsibility for providing refugees and IDPs with basic rights of security, subsistence, and liberties of active social participation and physical movement is quite significant when considering humanitarian tragedy in the Great Lakes Region of Africa. Moral responsibility does not fall upon isolated individual persons but rather on "human communities,"[114] especially when the source of harm is systemic and systematic as the scenarios of Rwanda and Sudan have shown.

---

[114] See the re-interpretation of human rights from the perspective of Shue's analysis under the sub-section "The Bearers of Correlative Duties" in section B of chapter 3, 88–91. For further description of social institutions as the bearers of correlative duties, see Langan, "Defining Human Rights," 77.

Designing effective social institutions is critical in order to redress systemic and systematic deprivations of human rights of refugees and IDPs. International refugee law as stipulated in the 1951 UN Geneva Refugee Convention requires fundamental reform because, unlike the 1969 OAU Refugee Convention, the UN Convention does not fully recognize refugees as the moral subject of equal basic rights to security, subsistence, and active social participation (the object of rights).[115] If these basic rights remain unrecognized as the principal objects of rights in international refugee law and domestic policy, then the moral responsibility of governments, social institutions, and the international community (the bearers of correlative duties) is not adequately assigned. Another reform that both Conventions should undergo is to fully recognize IDPs as the moral subjects of equal basic rights to security, subsistence and active social participation. When these rights are fully recognized, there would be equitable access to resources, and financial crises faced by UNHCR in the region can be resolved. This will contribute significantly to allowing refugees and IDPs to exercise participatory rights in attaining security and subsistence through acquiring skillful training for self-help projects and seeking employment, and thus improves standards of living for families in camps.[116]

To eliminate extreme inequalities, active responses are needed. In order to satisfy basic rights of refugees and IDPs, the priority principle requires that non-basic rights or mere preferences be relinquished. However, it is morally prohibited to relinquish basic rights to satisfy someone's mere preferences (see Table 7).

[115] See chapter 1, where the comparative analysis of both the 1951 UN Refugee Convention and the 1969 OAU Refugee Convention has been made. Also, see section A of chapter 3, under the sub-section "The Subject of Rights" considered under both Conventions.

[116] See in chapter 1, the evaluative description of the responses to humanitarian crises in the Great Lakes Region. There is an acute financial crisis of UNHCR operations in the region because of lower contributions of funds, as illustrated by the 2004 UNHCR's financial report. This shortage of funds is likely to cause a negative impact on the ability to participate in providing security and subsistence rights to millions of refugees and IDPs in the region. For more information, see section A of chapter 3, under the title, "The Respondent of Rights' Moral Claims."

Table 7

	Preference Satisfaction	Cultural Enrichment	Non-Basic Rights	Basic Rights
Basic Rights	Required 1 (Primary)	Required 2 (Secondary)	Required 3 (Tertuary)	Permissible 4
Non-Basic Rights	Permissible 5	Permissible 6	Permissible 7	Permissible 8
Cultural Enrichment	Permissible 9	Permissible 10	Permissible 11	Prohibited 12
Preference Satisfaction	Permissible 13	Permissible 14	Permissible 15	Prohibited 16

Source: Shue, *Basic Rights*, 115.

Governments, NGOs, private individuals, international aid organizations, among others are responsible for carrying out this objective.[117] Involving these groups is essential for providing refugees and IDPs with equal security and subsistence rights through the generous contribution of material and financial resources. Ensuring equal and active participation among the parties concerned, requires a fair distribution of duties, and should reflect the international character of the crises. Although acts of charity by various organizations and private individuals play a significant role in providing the basic rights of refugees and IDPs, these acts alone are incapable of providing basic rights for the ever-growing population of refugees and IDPs that are a consequence of persistent armed conflicts in the Great Lakes Region of Africa. Although it is contrary to the Nozickian view of taxation as forced labor because it interferes with the freedom of property rights, an effective taxation system is a sustainable source of monetary resources that goes hand in hand with the effort of private charities. The combined effort provides a durable solution to the ever-growing financial crisis, and distributes duties more equitably.[118] This approach

---

[117] According to Shue, an affluent person is defined as one who spends considerable large amounts of resources to satisfy non-basic rights such as mere preferences, wants, and desires. The morality of basic rights and correlative duties demands that such persons have a moral responsibility to transfer his or her non-basic rights in order to satisfy the basic rights of those who cannot provide for themselves on the basis of justifiable moral and legal grounds. See Shue, *Basic Rights*, 119. For an in depth discussion of this issue, see section B of chapter 3, under the title, "The Justification of Human Rights."

[118] For the argument provided in favor of effective taxation system as a fare distribution of duties correlative to basic rights, see, Langan, "Defining Human Rights," 77.

enables the parties concerned to contribute resources according to their ability and ensures that duties to provide refugees and IDPs with basic rights of security, subsistence, and liberties of active social participation and physical movement are transnational.

Given the severity of the humanitarian crises in Sudan and Uganda for example, the moral priority of duty to aid refugees and/or IDPs with basic rights provides a legal basis for an international humanitarian assistance. In this context therefore, the moral and legal priority of duty to provide refugees and/or IDPs with basic rights becomes the objective international moral standard, and ought to be the basis of assigning collective moral responsibility for the Great Lakes Region of Sub-Saharan Africa to the international community.

The Justification of Human Rights

Principle 5: Human persons are "dignified objects" of equal respect and consideration

Justifying human rights is critical to re-interpreting human rights of refugees and IDPs from the perspective of the philosophical ethics of rights. The concept of protecting human dignity by fulfilling basic duties correlative to basic rights, especially for those who have been incapacitated to effectively exercise them, is based on Shue's claim that humans are the "dignified objects" of equal respect and consideration.[119] This thesis provides a rationale for transferring non-basic rights from the affluent to satisfying the basic rights of refugees and IDPs, particularly the women and children who are faced with massive human rights' abuses in the Great Lakes Region of Africa. To prevent human degradation, there is need for a collective moral responsibility to provide assistance to the deprived, and this duty falls upon the international community. Extreme inequalities are morally degrading and humiliating to human dignity. This situation is addressed when the concept of basic rights and correlative duties, "the morality of the depths," is applied.

Conclusion

Re-interpreting basic human rights of refugees and IDPs in international refugee law and public policy from the standpoint of philosophical ethics

---

[119] See the re-interpretation of rights of refugees and IDPs in international law and policy according to Shue's theory of basic human rights in section B of chapter 3, under the title, "The Subject of Rights."

of rights is of paramount importance. The revised understanding of basic human rights presented in this section is quite significant, especially at this time when the Great Lakes Region of Africa is experiencing one of the worst humanitarian tragedies in decades. Shue's theory of basic human rights succeeds in offering objective moral and legal criteria for dealing with the failure of governments, social institutions, and the international community. The principle of moral and legal equality in exercising basic human rights provides the basis for implementing the correlative duties of avoiding depriving, protecting from deprivation, and providing assistance to the deprived.

Fundamental reforms are necessary for governments and social institutions to be effective in eliminating essential and systemic deprivation of basic human rights. Moral and legal recognition of refugees and IDPs as equal subjects of basic rights of security, subsistence, and liberties of active social participation and physical movement in international refugee law and public policy becomes an important step towards redressing the human rights' abuse of these groups in the Great Lakes Region of Africa.

The re-interpretation of basic human rights of refugees and IDPs in light of Shue's theory of rights is critical for governments, social institutions, and the international community to deal with humanitarian crises. The theory of basic human rights invokes short, medium, and long-term political responses to the problems of humanitarian crises when resolving conflicts of human rights of refugees and IDPs vis-à-vis other competing moral and legal rights. The theory offers a two-fold solution to the humanitarian crises. It provides the moral and legal basis for international humanitarian action that brings about conflict resolution by making the duty to provide refugees and IDPs with basic rights a priority in international law and public policy. It also prevents humanitarian crises by avoiding actions that can cause human rights' violations, and protects against these violations whenever there is a failure of duty by governments and social institutions to avoid depriving, a situation that is occurring in the Great Lakes Region of Sub-Saharan Africa.

In order to deal with the lacunae of Shue's argument for the justification of rights, theological justification of rights, inculturated into an African social milieu, will be offered in the next chapter.

4

Theological Justification of
Basic Human Rights

Introduction

IN the preceding chapter, the subject, the object, the nature, the respondent of correlative duties, and the justification of rights were examined in light of Shue's theory of basic human rights. In this assessment, it was established that Shue's theory of rights does not offer an adequate account of the justification of human rights.

In this chapter, Roman Catholic social teaching, drawing upon the scriptures, and inculturated in the modern African context, offers an adequate justification for the preceding assessment of human rights, and thus addresses the lacunae of Shue's argument. In the discussion, two fundamental anthropological principles are explored vis-à-vis basic human rights of refugees and IDPs, namely, sacredness or dignity and social nature of the human person. Theologically, recognition of moral and legal priority of duty to aid refugees and IDPs in international refugee law and policy becomes the preferential option for the poor, and thus is an expression of love. Since human dignity can only be fully protected in communal solidarity, then personal rights are essentially social rights, and thus become a question of social justice.

The principle of subsidiarity enables individuals, social institutions, governments, and the international community to foster mutual cooperation to ensure that basic human rights of refugees and IDPs are fully protected in international law and public policy. This principle strengthens communal solidarity of governments, NGOs, individuals, social institutions, and the international community to fully participate in protecting and providing refugees and IDPs with basic human rights. Most importantly, the principle of subsidiarity strengthens communal solidarity of refugees and IDPs by empowering them to fully exercise their basic human rights of security and subsistence. Therefore, the principles of communal solidarity and subsidiarity are intimately related and are critical for promoting human dignity of refugees and IDPs in Africa. The concepts of communal solidarity and subsidiarity depicted by the African model of *cosmotheandrism* are highlighted in order to give an African expression of the theological justification of basic human rights in the Great Lakes Region of Africa.[1]

Theological Justification of Basic Human Rights: From a Perspective of Roman Catholic Church's Social Teaching

In the preceding chapter, it was argued that refugees and IDPs ought to be recognized as human moral subjects and that they are entitled to equal basic human rights of security, subsistence, and liberty of active social participation in international law and public policy. The priority of duty to provide refugees and IDPs with basic human rights remains the moral and legal responsibility of the international community because of the failure of governments and social institutions in their duties to avoid depriving and protect from deprivation. It was also noted that equal recognition of basic human rights in international law and public policy is necessary to address extreme inequalities, which degrade the human person. As a "dignified" object of respect and consideration, refugees and IDPs ought to enjoy the basic rights. In this section, the theological justification that refugees and IDPs are the equal subjects of basic rights in international law and public policy is demonstrated.

The theological justification of basic human rights is grounded on two fundamental anthropological principles: human dignity or sacredness, and the social nature of the human person.[2] The biblical backing provides a rationale for the claim of the human person as *imago Dei*, "God created man in his image; in the divine image he created him; male and female he created them" (Gen 1:27).[3] In *Gaudium et Spes*, the Second Vatican

---

[1] A detailed account of the term, *cosmotheandrism*, will be provided later in the chapter.

[2] Curran, *Catholic Social Teaching*, 131.

[3] The biblical quotation regarding the *imago Dei* is an extract from *The New American Bible, The New Catholic Translation*. All the passages that are cited in this work are drawn from this Bible version. In contrast, Immanuel Kant holds that human dignity is inherent in every human person based on the notion of the autonomy of the will. According to Kant, pure reason is the source of objective and universal moral law; the reason for moral actions. Subjective morality, on the other hand, based on the empirical world, phenomena, passions, emotions, and inclinations, is not the basis for moral law. Universal law based

Council articulates the centrality of the human person based on the language of *imago Dei*. The Council maintains that the human person, as the summit of creation, occupies a central place in the universe and he or she has a unique role to play in it, a view that meets with consensus of most believers and non-believers.[4] Unlike Kantian ethical theory that disregards the material part of the human person, as insignificant in human morality, in Catholic social tradition, the whole human person is at the center of Christian anthropology. "*Gaudium et Spes,*" states:

> For the human person deserves to be preserved; human society deserves to be renewed. Hence the pivotal point of our total presentation will be man himself, the whole and entire, body and soul, heart and conscience, mind and will.[5]

In *"Gaudium et Spes,"* the concept of the centrality of the human person draws its inspiration from the Psalms. In the book of Psalms 8:5–10, the human person is depicted as being higher than the rest of the other creatures on earth.[6] When considering the human person in totality, Christian anthropology takes into account the fullness of *imago Dei* in the person of Jesus Christ in the mystery of Incarnation; Christ is the image of the invisible God and he has restored the *imago Dei* in us, which was disfigured through the sin of Adam (Col 1:15).[7] As the image of the invisible God, Christ is the revelation of God *par excellence*. Therefore, Christ's

---

on pure reason gives rise to the categorical imperative. As a result, every human person has worthiness in oneself and ought to be treated as ends in themselves and not simply as means. All other objects in the world have conditional worth only. Kant sums up the notion of ethical theory in the categorical imperative: "So act as to treat humanity whether in thine own person or in that of nay other, in every case as an end withal, never as means only." However, Kant's ethical theory falls short with regard to the anthropological foundation of the human person. By assigning the absolute and source of moral law to the human person, it overlooks the transcendence and relativity of human dignity and rights. In light of Roman Catholic natural law theory, the Kantian moral theory is flawed because it emphasizes the human person as the ultimate foundation of moral law. Catholic social teaching, however, affirms both the principle of transcendent and immanence in the understanding of the human person, dignity, and rights. See Kant, *Principles of the Metaphysics of Morals*, 46. Also, according to John Rawls, human dignity is grounded in the ability to make free and rational choices. Through the hypothetical method of original position, abstract citizens choose the principles of justice behind the veil of ignorance and must be "treated equally as persons." For further description of the concept of equality of persons and dignity, see Rawls, *Theory of Justice*, 118–22.

4 Vatican II, *"Gaudium et Spes,"* 172, no. 12.

5 Ibid., 167 no. 3.

6 Ibid., 173 no. 12.

7 Ibid., 178 no. 22.

incarnation is the fullest expression of sacredness or human dignity, *par excellence.*

The human person is not a solitary being, and thus human dignity is fully realized only in relationship of love in communal solidarity and mutuality. Drawing upon the Aristotelian–Thomistic philosophical heritage, Catholic social teaching affirms that, "the human being is social and political by nature."[8] "*Gaudium et Spes*" anchors the social and communitarian nature of the human person summed up in Christ's great commandment of love in the model of the Holy Trinity, "that all may be one . . . as we are one." (John 17:21–22).[9] Alluding to the Holy Trinity, this scriptural passage, "Let us make man in our image, after our likeness" (Gen 1:26), affirms the social and communitarian nature of the human person. This affirmation illustrates that creation is an external expression of love of "We-God," the three persons of the Trinity. Therefore, the *imago Dei,* realized in communal solidarity and mutuality, becomes a reflection of the Holy Trinity model of relationship, the exemplary cause.[10] The communitarian nature of the human person, as opposed to individualistic liberalism, demands that the *imago Dei* must be realized in a political community whereby the state and its intermediate institutions are the guardian of human dignity. Catholic social teaching maintains that the human person is prior to the state and its forms (capitalism, socialism, and communism).[11] Therefore, the state and its institutions ought to serve the dignity of the human person and not conversely.

The concept of basic human rights is a highly contested issue not only philosophically but also theologically. In the context of eighteenth-century European Enlightenment and liberal philosophy, for example, interpretation of human rights became more and more subjective and individualistic.[12] Consequently, within the Catholic Church there was suspicion and discomfort with the use of the language of human rights. Faced with the social impact of individualistic liberalism in the twentieth century, human rights language in the Roman Catholic Church took the center stage officially with Pope John XXIII's encyclical, *Pacem in Terris,* in 1963. In this encyclical, Pope John XXIII emphasized human nature as the foundation

---

[8] Curran, *Catholic Social Teaching*, 133.

[9] Ibid., 24.

[10] Vatican II, "*Gaudium et Spes*," 180 no. 24.

[11] See Curran, *Catholic Social Teaching*, 141. Curran makes references to Leo XIII's "*Rerum Novarum*," no. 6, whereby the dignity of the human person must be considered central in society.

[12] See Curran, *Catholic Social Teaching*, 216–17.

of the objective order of human rights and obligations and affirmed that human rights are inviolable and universal.[13] John XXIII acknowledges that rights to life, bodily integrity, food, clothing, and medical care are critical to human dignity.[14] He further emphasized that when the right to life is at stake or threatened, civilians have the rights to immigration and emigration. The Pope argued, "the fact that one is a citizen of a particular state does not detract in any way from his membership in the human family as a whole, nor from his citizenship in the world community."[15] As discussed in chapter 3, the most vulnerable persons are threatened when governments fail in their duties to avoid depriving and protect from deprivation

---

[13] John XXIII, "*Pacem in Terris*," 132 no. 9. For an in-depth historical background analysis of Catholicism and human rights, see Pawlikowski, "Human Rights in the Roman Catholic Tradition," 145–64. Pawlikowski presents an in-depth description of how the social milieu affected the way the Roman Catholic Church perceives human rights. He then describes the socio-political changes that made the Roman Catholic Church shift its emphasis from feudalist society to pluralistic society. The Catholic Church's language of human rights, primarily in terms of duties and obligations, is the legacy of the feudalistic medieval civilization in which rights conceived in terms of duties and obligations are distributed in accordance with the individual's social class. In the seventeenth century, the interpretation of rights took a new turn in the wake of the age of Reason or Enlightenment. In the twentieth century, the movement for religious freedom was championed primarily by the American delegation during the Ecumenical Vatican II Council and "*Dignitatis Humane*" ("Declaration on Religious Freedom") was authorized and published. Similarly, the publication of "*Gaudium et Spes*" marked a major shift from a narrow understanding of Catholicism on human rights to a more comprehensive approach of the contemporary issues, global in nature, particularly affecting the developing world: poverty, political oppression, hunger, housing and the like. Also see Curran, *Catholic Social Teaching*, 215–19. Curran presents an excellent historical evolution of human rights within the Catholic tradition, as a tool to understand the major paradigm shift in the contemporary notion of human rights. For a comparative study of Catholicism and liberalism, see Hollenbach, "Communitarian Reconstruction of Human Rights," 127–50. Also see Hollenbach, *Claims in Conflict*, 127–46.

John XXIII, "*Pacem in Terris*," 134, no. 25. Pope Leo XIII's encyclical, "*Rerum Novarum*," sets a milestone for human rights in the world. The major concern of Leo XIII was not centered on the rights of forbearance, the major tenet of liberal individualism; but rather, the encyclical focuses on the empowerment of employees to participate in exercising social and economic rights by demanding a just wage. A full range of social, economic, civil, and political rights is more developed in John XIII's "*Pacem in Terris*" than in his predecessor, Leo XIII's *Rerum Novarum*.

[14] John XXIII, "*Pacem in Terris*," 132 no. 11.

[15] Ibid., 134 no. 25. It is worth noting that, while John XIII in "*Pacem in Terris*" is emphatic on the rights of refugees and asylum seekers he fails short on the same issues as the 1951 UN Refugee Convention. First, the Pope does not address the complexities and conflicts of human rights and duties involved in fulfilling these rights; and thus lacks the explicit criteria of ranking human rights. Second, he does not consider the importance of addressing the human rights of IDPs, which are critical for the Great Lakes Region of Africa.

of basic human rights. Based on the concepts of *imago Dei* and social nature, refugees and IDPs are entitled to a legal protection of basic rights according their dignity. Since human dignity can only be realized in communal solidarity, the international community becomes a bearer of duty to provide refugees and IDPs with basic rights in international refugee law and public policy.[16]

Often, ideological concerns or personal interests are involved in interpreting and implementing human rights in international refugee law. The *Pontifical Council for the Pastoral Care of Immigrants and Itinerant People* highlights factors that reflect this understanding:

> Despite an increased awareness of interdependence among peoples and nations, some States, guided by their ideologies and particular interests, arbitrarily determine the criteria for the application of international obligation.[17]

When this happens, individuals' biases, geo-strategic interests, state sovereignty, national security concerns, or territorial integrity override the priority of basic human rights, which leads to a great vulnerability of refugees or IDPs, particularly women, children, and the elderly.

As discussed in the preceding chapter, it was argued that governments' and the international community's failure in their duties to protect and provide the deprived has been due a lack of equal recognition of refugees and IDPs as the moral and legal subject of basic human rights in international refugee law and policy. The Catholic Church recognizes the fact that such failure undermines the dignity of refugees and IDPs. Based on the concepts of *imago Dei* and social nature of the human person, recognition of the priority of basic rights and correlative duties in international refugee law becomes extremely important and urgent. Unfortunately during the Cold War, the international community became divided on the question of the priority of fundamental human rights. The Western bloc emphasized the value of civil and political rights and overlooked social, economic, and cultural rights; similarly while the Eastern bloc emphasized

---

[16] Ibid., 135 no. 27. See the detailed discussion on the re-interpretation of human rights in international refugee law and public policy in chapter 3, section B and subsequent section C. This discussion establishes that the international community becomes the bearer of basic human rights of refugees and IDPs in international law when governments and social institutions fail in their duties to avoid depriving and protect from deprivation.

[17] Pontifical Council for the Pastoral Care of Immigrants and Itinerant People, *Refugees: A Challenge to Solidarity*, 7 no. 6.

social, economic, and cultural rights and overlooked political rights and civil liberty.[18]

The conflict of interpretations over the years made the Roman Catholic Church confront the two traditions regarding human rights: individualistic liberalism and collectivistic communism. In *"Pacem in Terris,"* John XXIII strikes a balance between the two major extreme philosophical theories of rights, namely, individualistic liberalism, and collectivist communism.[19] In this document, both kinds of rights: social, economic, and cultural rights, as well as civil and political rights are seen as critical to protecting and promoting the dignity of the human person as an indivisible whole. When ranking human rights, John XXIII gives a top priority to basic rights of security and subsistence.[20] When he addresses the issue of liberty of social participation, he proclaims that, based on human dignity, every person has the right to actively participate in public affairs, and contribute to the promotion of the common good.[21] The rights of security, subsistence, and liberty of active social participation are of paramount importance and crucial to those who are systemically deprived, "through no fault of their own."[22] John XIII maintains that since rights and obligations flow directly from human nature, rights and obligations are inseparable.[23] Promoting human dignity requires satisfying basic rights of security, subsistence, and social participation. John XXIII explains:

> Since men [and women] are social by nature they are meant to live with others and to work for one another's welfare. A well-ordered human society requires that men recognize and observe their mutual rights and duties. It also demands that each contributes generously to the establishment of a civil order in which rights and duties are more sincerely and effectively acknowledged and fulfilled.[24]

---

[18] Hollenbach, *Claims in Conflict*, 33. For a historical analysis of the West-East conflict and its impact on human rights in the international community, see Glendon, *World Made New*, chapter 11, "The Deep Freeze: The Declaration in the Cold War Years," 193–220.

[19] For an in-depth analysis of the concept of human rights both in the secular society and the Catholic Church, see Komonchak, Collins, et al., eds. *New Dictionary of Theology*, 899–904.

[20] John XXIII, *"Pacem in Terris,"* in *Catholic Social Thought*, 133 no. 11.

[21] Ibid., 135 no. 26.

[22] Ibid.

[23] Ibid., 135 no. 30.

[24] Ibid., 135 no. 31.

Because humans are by nature social beings, their rights and duties must be socially guaranteed.[25] In a well-ordered society, fulfilling basic rights of security, subsistence, and social participation, requires "abundant resources."[26] Critical of liberalism, a distinction between positive and negative rights becomes of secondary importance because negative rights require positive duties of providing refugees and IDPs with the rights of security, subsistence, and liberty of active social participation. Social and economic capacity is likewise needed to fully exercise civil and political liberties.[27] This understanding of basic rights and correlative duties includes financial and material contributions needed for the basic needs of refugees and IDPs. Hence, effective social arrangements in international law and policy are critical for promoting basic human rights and dignity.

In *"Pacem in Terris,"* John XXIII expresses opposition to absolute freedom and autonomy of the human person and argues that there must be a proper balance between freedom, truth, and justice.[28] The Pope believes that human dignity must be understood in relation to God, other human persons, and the world itself.[29] He maintains that human rights have a transcendent value. *"Pacem in Terris,"* which depends heavily on the natural law tradition of Thomistic scholasticism as the basis for the objective moral order, affirms that human rights are grounded in God as the giver and the ultimate source of rights.[30] An important element that balances freedom and autonomy is human solidarity through which human dignity is realized, transcending individualistic morality in the pursuit of the common good, namely: the sum total of those conditions of social living whereby people are enabled to achieve their own perfection more fully and more easily. In *Pacem in Terris,* John XXIII calls not only for liberties of forbearance but also for effective social guarantees for the pursuit of the common good:

> For the protection of personal rights is a necessary condition for the active participation of citizens, whether as individuals or collectively, in the life and government of the state.[31]

---

[25] Ibid.

[26] Ibid., 136 no. 33.

[27] See Gewirth, *Community of Rights,* 323.

[28] John XXIII, *"Pacem in Terris,"* 136 no. 35.

[29] Curran, *Catholic Social Teaching,* 220.

[30] John XXIII, *"Pacem in Terris,"* no. 38, in *Catholic Social Thought,* 137.

[31] Vatican II, *"Gaudium et Spes,"* 215 no. 30; ibid., 183 no. 73. See also *"Pacem in Terris,"* 313 no. 29; and U.S. Catholic Bishops, "Economic Justice for All," 595–96 no. 68–76,

Due to the social character of human nature, human dignity can only be realized in communal solidarity.[32] Hollenbach notes, "When the claims of diverse groups in society conflict, the tradition increasingly grants priority to the needs of the weak over the desires and unimpeded liberty of the powerful."[33] As discussed in chapter 3, Shue gives basic rights of security, subsistence, and liberty moral and legal priority over the non-basic rights because they are necessary to enjoy other rights. Since refugees and IDPs, particularly women and children, are most vulnerable to basic human rights deprivation they have the strongest moral claims against other moral and legal rights, for example, state sovereignty.

in *Catholic Social Thought*, 595–96. The Pastoral insists on the community's moral responsibility in defending the dignity of the human person in love and justice. For more reflections and debate on the question of the feasibility of economic rights see Trimiew, "Economic Rights Debate," 85–103. Trimiew presents an interesting debate between two Catholic theologians, David Hollenbach and Michael Novak on John XXIII's "*Pacem in Terris*" and economic rights. Hollebanch is in favor of economic rights as essential for the defense of human dignity as stated in "*Pacem in Terris*," while his rival Novak is skeptical of it. In this debate, Hollenbach's rival, Novak, is skeptical of economic rights because of flaws in Roman Catholic human rights discourse: that these are rights without duties assigned to them and that social arrangements do not exist to support these rights. In addition, Novak argues that some people have to blame themselves for their poverty because of laziness. These people he calls, "depraved" poor. Finally, Novak reluctantly accepts economic rights on condition that they are directed to the "deserving" poor. Hollenbach argues that human dignity is prior to entitlement and achievements, and it is not lost due to laziness because every person is created in the *imago Dei*. In the end, these rivals, Hollebach and Novak, endorse at least subsistence rights, a form of economic rights, as minimum standards of living for all. In my view, this debate refines the concept of human rights, for nothing should be taken for granted in the face of the pluralistic contemporary world of globalization. Novak's criticisms must be seen as a positive sign of growth for Catholics and non-Catholics alike. In fact, refugees and IDPs do not deserve to live in degrading conditions because their right is to not be refugees and IDPs in the first place. They are not what they are due to any fault of their own.

[32] For deeper insights into the concept of *imago Dei*, see Rahner, *Man in the Church*, 238. Karl Rahner distinguishes between "pre-established dignity" and "fulfilled dignity." Fulfilled dignity constitutes "gaining and preservation of the pre-established dignity-the final goal of the human person, which he says, can be lost. However, "the pre-established dignity cannot simply cease or become non-existent, but can exist as something denied, as foundation for damnation and judgment." It is this kind of pre-established dignity that becomes the standard principle for the justification of satisfying economic rights, particularly of refugees and IDPs, whose basic rights of subsistence are imperiled. For further discussion on the theological justification of human rights, see Cahill, "Toward A Christian Theory of Human Rights," 277–80.

[33] Hollenbach, *Claims in Conflict*, 133.

Social, economic, political, and religious factors are to blame for the moral tragedy of humanitarian crises in which refugees and IDPs suffer essential and systematic deprivations of basic rights of security, subsistence, and liberty of active social participation and physical movement. In light of the notions of *imago Dei* and the social nature of the human person, the concept of African spirit of communal solidarity that is expressed by the 1969 OAU Refugee Convention emerges as a critical social institution for protecting security, subsistence, and liberty rights of refugees and IDPs in the Great Lakes Region of Africa. To realize communal solidarity requires active social participation of those involved in the conflict and through the process of liberating both the oppressors and the oppressed[34] who are all children of God, created in the image and likeness of God, and redeemed in Jesus Christ. Hollenbach explains:

> The rights of all human persons are the concern of Christians because they are rooted in universal human dignity. The human rights of all persons are a special concern of Christians precisely because of their ontological foundation in the reality of Christ.[35]

In this context, refugees and IDPs are no longer treated as strangers or aliens, but rather as near and distant neighbors as illustrated in the parable of the Good Samaritan (Luke 10:30–37). Since refugees and IDPs have the strongest moral claims, satisfying their basic rights of security, subsistence, and social participation is an expression of love.

The concept of love for God and neighbor is seen as the Christian virtue of *agape* and thus is characteristic of Christian discipleship. Christian love considers protecting the weakest members of society as the preferential treatment for the poor. As a moral virtue, providing refugees and IDPs with basic rights is an expression of Christian communal solidarity. How critical Christian charity, *agape*, is closely related to justice in resolving conflicts of rights' moral claims in favor of those of the most vulnerable members of society, as preferential option for the poor, is morally significant from the perspective of the justification of human rights.

---

[34] Ellacuria, "Human Rights in a Divided Society," 63–64. The term, "oppressors" is meant those who deprive refugees and IDPs of their basic human rights of security, subsistence, and liberty of social participation and physical movement. The term, "oppressed" is meant refugees and IDPs who are deprived of their basic human rights mentioned above.

[35] Hollenbach, *Claims in Conflict*, 131.

The Catholic Social Justice: Biblical Perspectives

An ethic of Christian discipleship expressed in biblical stories, narratives, and metaphors enables the cultural metaphors of citizens and aliens, and members and strangers to be interpreted as the Christian metaphors of near and distant neighbors.[36] In resolving conflicts of moral rights' claims, the biblical concept of justice is seen as a contribution to this endeavor. In this section, biblically inspired Catholic notions of justice and peace are examined and applied to the basic rights of refugees and IDPs. The concept that personal rights are essentially social rights, and human dignity can only be realized through relationships in community is regarded an expression of covenant fidelity, *sedaqah*.

Both the Old and the New Testaments provide the profound link between rights, justice, peace, and love. From the perspectives of *imago Dei* and the social human nature, every person in community should be treated justly in accordance with one's dignity, particularly refugees and IDPs, who have been deprived of basic rights of security, subsistence, and liberty of active social participation and physical movement.

In biblical language, the terms, "justice," "covenant," "peace," and "love," are closely connected. The biblical notion of justice, *sedaqah*, is best understood as fidelity or faithfulness to the covenant-relationship. *Sedaqah* is also translated as right judgment, fair measure, righteousness, and integrity.[37] The concept of *sedaqah* is equivalent to *mišpat*, justice embodied in a concrete act or deed. The term, *berith* or *diatheke* means covenant.[38] Within the biblical understanding, God is described as the God of justice (Isa 30:18), who loves justice. Justice as a demand of the covenant fidelity is measured by the treatment of four groups in society: the widow, the orphan, the poor, and the stranger in the land (Exod 22:21–27; Ps 146:6–9;

---

[36] The metaphor of "strangers and members" is comparative language used by communitarian philosophers, for example, Michael Walzer, who believes that since membership is a fundamental social good, then membership in community is prerequisite for enjoying basic rights. In this case, refugees, as strangers, are subject to domination by members if membership is not distributed to them. For a further detailed account of the concept of membership, see Walzer, *Spheres of Justice*, 31–35. The metaphor of "citizens and aliens" is a comparative usage drawn upon Rawls's idea of social contract involving abstract citizens in the original position in which principles of justice are chosen behind the veil of ignorance. In the process, refugees are aliens in society and they do not have equal rights as citizens because they are not part of the social contract. For a further detailed account of the concept, see Rawls, *Theory of Justice*, 10–19.

[37] Donahue, *What Does the Lord Require?*, 23.

[38] Baitu, *Covenant as the Foundation of the Old Testament Morality*, 1. For an extensive description of covenant, see Leon-Defour, *Dictionary of Biblical Theology*, 75–79.

Deut 24:6–7; Lev 19:33–34).[39] Justice is also associated with loving kindness and peace, *shalom*. When things go the right way, namely as well-ordered relationships with God and with others, peace results as the fruit of justice.[40] Hence, *sedaqah* and *shalom* are closely interrelated concepts.

The two following biblical passages illustrate the point that justice and peace are closely linked: "Justice will bring peace and right will produce calm and security" (Isa 32:17); "I will appoint peace your governor and justice your ruler" (Isa 60:17). Justice, *sedaqah*, and love, *hesed*, as stipulated in the Torah, are interrelated because fidelity to the demands of the covenant is an expression of faith and love for God and for others. The chosen people of Israel enjoyed a special bond with God, Yahweh, through the covenant at Mt. Sinai. Faithfulness to the covenant implies obedience to the Decalogue when applied to socio-political and economic life as reflected in various Codes of the Old Testament. In the Cultic Code, holiness and social justice are intertwined.[41] Israel's ethos is summed up in the Torah, the legal expression of faith, love, and practice of the covenant morality that distinguishes Israel as a nation different from other neighboring nations. This difference makes Israel a "contrast society."[42]

The prophets did not preach a different ethos apart from the covenant morality. They continued to refer to the covenant made with Yahweh at Mt. Sinai by reminding Israel, a contrast society, to be righteous and remain faithful to the demands of the covenant-relationship, *sedaqah*, being especially mindful of the poor, the widow, the orphan, and the stranger in the land.

Over time, Israel drifted away from the covenant fidelity, *sedaqah*. During the monarchic period, moral decadence set in and there was a misuse of power and the growth of material prosperity during which the ownership of the land was in the hands of a few people and the upper class suffocated the lower class. Consequently, there was a paradigm shift:

> [From land as a] primary social good, from the function of support
> to that of the capital; the orientation of social goals from personal

---

[39] The term *stranger* is translated as *ger*. In Hebrew language, *ger* literary means "sojourner or resident alien." For an analysis of *gerim*, see Schaeffer, *Sanctuary and Asylum*, 14–15. Also see Crüsemann, "You Know the Heart of a Stranger," 101–4.

[40] Donahue, *What Does the Lord Require?* 23.

[41] Ibid., 27.

[42] Ibid., 25.

values to personal profit; to subordination of judicial process to the interest of the entrepreneur.[43]

Of course it is an illegitimate claim to maintain that wealth in itself is wrong. But to acquire wealth at the expense of oppressing the afflicted is contrary to justice, *sedaqah*. The prophetic literature summed up the four groups as the "poor or the powerless." In the Bible, there are a number of terms that describe or stand for the "poor." But the most common term is *anawim*, which is derived from, *aniyyim*, "bent down" or "afflicted."[44] A further clarification of the term, *anawim,* is warranted here when it is linked with the term, *Yahweh.* The term *anawim* acquires a fuller more profound meaning when it is linked with the term *Yahweh* and becomes the *poor of Yahweh.* It must be noted however, that "not every poor person merits the title of poor of Yahweh; the poor with the disposition of humility, fear of God, with faith and fidelity merit the name of POOR OF YAHWEH,"[45] the *anawim of Yahweh*. Israel, the afflicted in Egypt, could be called the poor of Yahweh if it remained faithful to the demands of the covenant. Subsequently, *sedaqah* and *anawim* embrace and become the expression of the covenant morality.

The New Testament gives a special concern for the "*anawim*."[46] The New Testament concept of justice, *sadaqah*, is embodied in Christ's mission for the Kingdom of God in which he identifies himself with the needy, the poor, and the sinner. In his inaugural speech in the synagogue, Jesus proclaims the good news to the poor and the afflicted and promised liberation (Luke 4:18–19).[47] The parable of the rich man and Lazarus (Luke 16:19–31) highlights the loving and compassion of God for the poor. The Christians in the early Church lived in community of love, *agape*, in communal solidarity, *koinonia*, for the service, *diakonia*, of windows, orphans, the poor, and strangers. It may be surmised that in such a community, the four groups were protected by the moral principles of *koinonia* and *diakonia* (Acts 2:41–47; 4:32–37). The practice of *koinonia* and *diakonia* is an expression of *agape*.

---

[43] Ibid., 34.

[44] Ibid., 31. See Isa 1:17–18, in which the powerless must be protected, "search for justice, help the oppressed, be just to the orphan and plead for widow.

[45] For further analysis of *anawim,* see Amewowo, "Poor of Yahweh," 59.

[46] Donahue, *What Does the Lord Require?* 50.

[47] See Dulles, "Christianity and Humanitarian Action," 9. Dulles refers the inaugural speech by Jesus as the humanitarian dimension of Jesus' ministry.

The twin commandments of love for God and neighbor, as depicted in the parable of the Good Samaritan, convey the demands for an ethic of discipleship. When love for God is expressed concretely in the love for neighbor, the former becomes intertwined with the latter. Hence "the knot they tie is where spirituality is situated."[48] Carroll Stuhlmueller reminds us of the reason for being compassionate by recalling the loving acts of God when Israel was liberated from slavery in Egypt and was in exile in Babylon. Stuhlmueller maintains that because Israel was enslaved and oppressed that it became the object of God's compassion and intervention. "Called to be compassionate persons like God in the Hebrew Scriptures and like Jesus the Messiah, we have no other option than to respond to the outcry and affliction of the poor."[49]

The Moral Significance of Biblically Inspired Catholic Social Justice: The Preferential Option for the Poor

Applying the biblical notion of justice, modern Catholic social teaching maintains that *sedaqah* can be expressed concretely in three major ways that govern human relationships: commutative justice, distributive justice, and social justice. Because personal rights are essentially social rights in this tripartite typology of justice, the forms of justice are intimately connected. Commutative justice governs the domain of private agreements and contracts made between individuals, groups or associations. Equal basic rights and dignity are the criteria for these relationships.[50] Because personal rights are social rights, the principle of distributive justice is needed to regulate and resolve conflicts of moral rights in the domain of commutative justice. This kind of justice governs the public domain, which demands that all persons be accorded equal opportunity and access to basic human rights.[51] Necessary social arrangements are critical to protecting and promoting these rights. Social justice governs institutional arrangements that are necessary to enable all people to have equal participation in realizing distributive justice.[52]

Human rights have personal, social, and institutional aspects. However, these rights need to be regulated in the face of competing de-

---

[48] Gutierrez, *We Drink From Our Own Wells*, xxi.

[49] Stuhlmueller, "Option for the Poor," 21.

[50] Hollenbach, *Justice, Peace and Human Rights*, 26–27.

[51] Ibid.

[52] Ibid.

mands and conflicts of rights-claims. Social justice regulates and resolves claims-rights in society through government's institutional arrangements and legal guarantees.[53] Resolving these conflicts is possible through the principles of justice because of the intrinsic correlation between rights and justice.[54] Rights are regarded as claims of one's due according to equal dignity. Fulfilling these claims requires effective social arrangements and legal guarantees, and thus becomes a matter of social justice.

The tripartite typology of justice is morally significant to resolving conflicts of rights for the defense of human dignity of refugees and IDPs in the Great Lakes Region of Africa. In chapter 3, section B it was argued that the primary duty of governments is to avoid depriving people of their basic rights, and the secondary duty is to protect the people it governs from deprivation of basic rights. However, the government's failure to protect from depriving results in humanitarian crises. In order to effectively deal with humanitarian crises, distributive justice demands that refugees and IDPs ought to have equal access to basic human rights in international law and policy. To make it happen, social justice demands that effective social institutions must be in place to not only provide refugees and IDPs with basic human rights to security and subsistence but also to provide them with access to liberty of active social participation in exercising security and subsistence rights.

There is an ever-growing awareness of the fact that international treaties remain inadequate in addressing the basic rights of refugees particularly "the victims of armed conflicts, erroneous economic policy or natural disasters."[55] Moreover, it is regrettable that IDPs, who do not fall under international refugee law, are the most vulnerable. The Catholic Church reaffirms the commitment that the need for legal recognition of IDPs remains necessary for the protection of their dignity:

> For humanitarian reasons these displaced people should be considered as refugees in the same way as those formally recognized by the 1951 Convention because they are victims of the same type of violence.[56]

---

[53] Ibid.

[54] Ibid., 144–45.

[55] Pontifical Council for the Pastoral Care of Migrants and Itinerant People, *Refugees: A Challenge for Solidarity*, 6 no. 4.

[56] Ibid., 7 no. 5.

In order to effectively protect the basic rights of refugees and IDPs, Catholic social justice calls for a review of international law.[57] This legal process would ensure that priority is placed on the rights of refugees and IDPs over the rights of state sovereignty or national interests.[58] Effective protection of these groups remains the collective responsibility of the international community. Fostering an international solidarity requires economically developed states to assist the affected countries deal with the situation of "extreme marginalization."[59] For an effective international solidarity, there is need for "joint initiatives of humanitarian assistance and cooperation for development."[60] Furthermore, searching for 'durable solutions' to the problems of forced migrations and humanitarian crises is considered to be a comprehensive measure and a long-term strategy.[61]

In *"Rerum Novarum,"* Leo XIII notes affirming the moral responsibility of social institutions. ". . . When there is question of protecting the rights of individuals, the poor and the helpless have a claim to special consideration."[62] Christian *agape* is a tangible way of allowing the demands of justice and rights to become a reality. In the same vein, in *"Quadragesimo Anno,"* Pius XI observes that love is paramount for binding all people together in solidarity within political institutions in the realization of justice and rights.[63] Based on the parable of the Good Samaritan, Christian *agape* is discriminatory and partial to those who are most in need. David Hollenbach writes, "When the claims of diverse groups in society conflict, the tradition increasingly grants priority to the needs of the weak over the desires and impeded liberty of the powerful."[64]

In Africa, the concept of basic human rights is a top priority. The African Banjul Charter on Human and Peoples' Rights, in which duty rests upon member states, places strong emphasis on the rights to economic, social and cultural development.[65] Similarly, in *Justice in the World,*

---

[57] Ibid., 8 no. 8.

[58] Ibid., 8 no. 9.

[59] Ibid., 13 no. 20.

[60] Ibid. On similar international initiative for protecting refugees and IDPs, see the introductory remarks, Pontifical Council for the Pastoral Care of Migrants and Itinerant People, *Extracts from Speeches by the Holy Father,* accessed 3/20/2005.

[61] Pontifical Council for the Pastoral Care of Migrants and Itinerant People, *Refugees: A Challenge for Solidarity,* 12 no. 18. See John Paul II, *"Redemptor Hominis"* no. 17.

[62] Leo XIII, *"Rerum Novarum,"* 28 no. 29.

[63] Pius XI, *"Quadragesimo Anno,"* 47 no. 137.

[64] Hollenbach, *Claims in Conflict,* 133.

[65] "African [Banjul] Charter," accessed 12/20/2003.

the 1971 Synod of Bishops affirmed that love and justice are intimately related, "For love implies an absolute demand for justice, namely a recognition of the dignity and rights of one's neighbor."[66] The Synod maintains that the right to development is a justice issue not only for the states, but also for the Church, making obligations of justice constitutive to Christian evangelization. The Synod explains:

> Action on behalf of justice and participation in the transformation of the world fully appears to us as constitutive dimension of the preaching of the Gospel, or, in other words, of the Church's mission for the redemption of the human race and its liberation from every oppressive situation.[67]

Perhaps, conscious of the global refugee crisis back then, the Synod acknowledged the fact that the refugees, asylum seekers, and IDPs are victims of persecution, injustice, and oppression. The Synod noted that ethnocentrism and tribalism lead to civil strife, conflict, and "genocide,"[68] a scenario that came to pass twenty-three years later in Rwanda. In their document, the Synod identified refugee basic rights of security, subsistence, and liberty of social participation as a moral priority and that protection of these rights is regarded the preferential option for the poor. What can be drawn from *Justice in the World* is that liberation from human rights' abuses and protecting human dignity is constitutive to Christian evangelization.

Earlier, it was established that humanitarian crises are a social disorder and a moral tragedy. In the face of the catastrophe, the weakest groups: women, children, and the elderly suffer the most from human rights' violations such as violence and abuse.[69] In *"Sollicitudo Rei Socialis,"* John Paul II observes that refugees are victims of persecution, discrimination, conflict and war. He argues that the preferential option for the poor is "the special form of primacy in the exercise of Christian charity, to which the whole tradition of the Church bears witness."[70] The preferential option for the poor is a moral choice to accord equal respect, dignity, and rights to the powerless. Donal Dorr expounds on this point by arguing, "It is clear

---

[66] Synod of Bishops, "Justice in the World," 293.

[67] Ibid., 289. Also see Dorr, *Option for the Poor,* 289.

[68] Ibid., 292.

[69] See the analysis of the nature and scope of humanitarian crises in the Great Lakes Region of Africa in chapter 1.

[70] John Paul II, *"Sollicitudo Rei Socialis,"* 409 no. 24; ibid. 425, no. 42. For an in-depth analysis of preferential option for the poor, see Dwyer, *New Dictionary of Catholic Social Thought,* 755–59. See O'Neill, "No Amnesty for Sorrow," 650–55.

that lack of power of one kind or another is both an essential part of being poor and is also the key cause of poverty."[71] The term 'poor' as powerless can be described in several ways. In the context of humanitarian crises, refugees and IDPs are considered poor because they are powerless: they are deprived of basic human rights of security, subsistence, and liberty of social participation and physical movement.

Before proceeding, a few thoughts should be considered in connection with the expression, preferential option for the poor. This expression is a "discriminatory principle," which is expressed in a non-derogatory sense. To clarify this concept, a distinction between the right to "identical treatment," and the right to "equal treatment" must be made. The right to equal treatment or "treatment as an equal" is a matter of a complex egalitarian ethic that calls for equal basic rights as a moral minimal standard for all. The right to "identical treatment" however, is a matter of a simple egalitarian ethic, which calls for the same kind and number of duties, particularly with regard to distribution of resources, benefits, burdens, or opportunity.[72] With respect to the former, treating others as equals does not necessarily imply the right to receive "identical treatment." Consequently, refugees and IDPs, orphans of the state system, have the right to treatment as equals, respect and dignity, as a "preferential treatment" because their basic human rights of security, subsistence and liberty of social participation and physical movement are most imperiled. It follows, therefore, that they have the right to moral and legal privilege. The moral and legal privilege means that basic human rights of security, subsistence, and liberty of social participation and physical movement have top moral and legal priority over other rights, such as state sovereignty, geopolitical interests, property rights, preferences, or wants.

At times priority must be given to rights that demand utmost attention for implementation. For example in cases of humanitarian catastrophe: famine, floods, earthquakes, armed conflicts, and such, the rights of liberty may be compromised by the need for bread. "This means that the states are morally bound to respect and promote the basic human rights of both citizens and resident alien, especially the most vulnerable."[73] When states fulfill this moral and legal duty, they form a community of rights because enjoying the substance of basic human rights requires fulfilling positive and/or negative duties. Consequently, refugees and IDPs are re-

---

[71] Dorr, *Mission in Today's World*, 150.

[72] Dworkin, *Taking Rights Seriously*, 227.

[73] O'Neill and Spohn, "Rights of Passage," 99.

garded as bearers of basic human rights and states become bearers of correlative duties.[74] As they become a community of rights, states may overcome xenophobia: racism, ethnocentrism, tribalism, clanism, sexism, and nationalism. The political communal solidarity of governments and social institutions (both local and international) that results is, from a Christian perspective, an expression of *agape*.[75]

Christian *agape*, apart from considering the material welfare of refugees and IDPs, forges the formation of moral bonds, unites all human persons and strengthens interdependence between people and nations.[76] This universal love, which expresses the demands of the new covenant community of disciples in Jesus Christ, in communal solidarity with all the parties concerned, promotes the common good. Christian *agape* inspires participation; creating international justice that forges a commitment in global solidarity between the rich and the poor, the weak and the strong through which mutual respect and human dignity is realized. This universal love and communal solidarity allows human persons to take their proper place in human community and become authentic and productive moral agents. In this manner, the values of freedom and autonomy are regulated in justice and in truth.

The implementation of policy for refugees and IDPs by governments, the right to protection, asylum and voluntary repatriation in times of persecution, is an expression of the moral bonds of persons, with those whose basic rights of security, subsistence and liberty of active social participation are essentially and systematically denied or threatened. The universal love and communal solidarity requires Christian faith and grace to surrender individual self-centered preferences, desires, and wants for the benefit of those whose basic rights are denied or threatened. Shue notes that although no one is required to surrender basic rights to aid those in need, it is permissible however, as an act of heroism, to do so:

> The reason for judging the sacrifice of one's own basic rights for the basic rights of someone else to be permissible, not prohibited, is to leave open the possibility of heroism. Although people cannot be expected to surrender their basic rights, surely they are at liberty to

---

[74] Gewirth, *Community of Rights*, 86.

[75] The virtue of solidarity connotes not only promoting and sharing material goods with the needy, but also spiritual goods of faith and love, as the engine for the former. See *Catechism of the Catholic Church*, 471 no. 1942.

[76] Hollenbach, *Claims in Conflict*, 76.

do so, if they choose, and we might consider a knowing and will-
ing sacrifice of this magnitude admirable and heroic.[77]

Shue places the choice of surrendering basic rights to satisfy the basic
rights of someone else at liberty, however, Christian liberty, *agape*, and
justice require no less. This does not mean giving away only what is not
needed or surplus, but rather surrendering the most basic as an expression
of authentic Christian sacrificial love, justice, and faith. Mere "impartiality fails to accommodate the characteristic Christian stress on self-denial
and cross bearing, on a love that goes the second mile and turns the other
cheek."[78]

Such self-sacrifice shares some similarity with St. Paul's notion of self-
emptying, *kenosis*, in the model of Christ. In Paul's words, ". . . rather,
humbly regard others as more important than yourselves, each looking
out not for his own interests, but [also] everyone for those of others" (Phil
2:4). Hence, Paul's notion of *kenosis* indeed is self-love inverted, the preferential option for the poor, par excellence. In light of *kenosis*, heroic and
sublime love, the communal solidarity, transforms members and citizens,
into near and distant neighbors in the model of the Good Samaritan.
Through the international communal solidarity, basic rights are guaranteed and protected as a moral and legal priority in international law and
policy. Likewise, in *kenosis*, when refugees and IDPs are treated with equal
dignity, they are transformed into members and citizens in the political
community of rights. This wonderful transformation leads to a paradigm
shift of burden sharing to responsibility sharing where refugees and IDPs
are no longer seen simply as a resource drain and burden, but as active
participants in social development in their political communities.

The words of John Paul II, marking the 89th World Day of Migrants
and Refugees, reflect *kenosis* as sharing in the Paschal Mystery of Christ's
death and resurrection, using the parable of the last judgment, where Jesus
identifies himself with the needy (Matt 25:31–46). Providing refugees and
IDPs with their basic needs within a political community and social arrangement is a demand of Christian discipleship of solidarity, sacrificial
love, compassion, faith, and justice. John Paul II remarks, "In some cases

---

[77] Shue, *Basic Rights*, 116. See John Stuart Mill's notion of Classical utilitarianism in *Utilitarianism*, 193. Although Mill reduces every thing to the principle of Utility, his moral
theory recognizes the role of sacrifices not as an end but as a means to increase the greater
happiness for the greatest number.

[78] Outka, "Universal Love and Impartiality," 17.

[living an ethic of Christian discipleship] is a real Way of the Cross."[79] In the next section, biblically inspired African Catholic social teaching and its significance in responding to the plight of refugees and IDPs is discussed.

Catholic Social Teaching and the African Christian Justification of Human Rights

In the preceding sections, it was argued that human dignity is fully real-ized in communal solidarity. Protecting refugees and IDPs in commu-nal solidarity is seen from the perspective of Catholic social teaching as a preferential option for the poor, and thus is constitutive to the Church's mission. Biblically inspired Catholic social teaching understood from the perspective of an African Christian theology known as *cosmotheandrism* expressed in communal solidarity and subsidiarity is discussed in this sec-tion. The relationship between *cosmotheandrism* and Christian anthropol-ogy is established, and how this relationship provides a framework for African Catholic social teaching for responding to humanitarian crises is demonstrated. Therefore, it can be argued that the implementation of *cos-motheandrism* is seen as a means for building the Church as the *Family of God* and a community of rights, and thus becomes an expression of the African Christian theology of the justification of human rights.

The African Concept of Cosmotheandrism

The term, *cosmotheandrism*, is not African in origin. Rather, the meaning it conveys suits the African social milieu.[80] A product of academic creativity, *cosmotheandrism* consists of three Greek words: *cosmos* (earth), *theos* (God), and *anthropos* (human). In Africa, it is believed that the earth, God, and the human person are related to form a triad in a *cosmotheandric* manner (horizontal and vertical) so that fulfilling one's duties towards human so-ciety and the earth is considered to be a fulfillment of one's duties towards God, the creator. Based on the African concept of creation, every human person is a member of the human community regardless of social status or political affiliation.[81] In black Africa, ethics and religion, as well as politics

---

[79] John Paul II. "Message for the 89th World Day of Migrants and Refugees 2003," ac-cessed 2/25/2004.

[80] It must be noted that it is not the scope of this study to focus on *cosmotheandrism* in relation to a particular African community. The concept of *cosmotheandrism* is general in nature, representing the common feature of most black African cultures.

[81] Bujo, *Foundations of an African Ethic*, 65. The concept of human community is all-embracing and counteracts extreme or closed communitarianism: exclusivism, clanism,

and philosophy are so closely interrelated that the dichotomy between the sacred and profane, as well as the spiritual and material is virtually non-existent.[82] Laurenti Magesa explains:

> The realization of sociability or relationships in daily living by the individual and the community is the central moral and ethical imperatives of African Religion. Relationships receive the most attention in the adjudication of what is good and bad, what is desirable and undesirable in life . . . .[83]

From this perspective, the human person is regarded as an indivisible whole, a concept, which does not admit dualism. Consequently, social, economic, and cultural rights cannot be separated from civil and political rights.[84]

Moreover, in Africa, there is a strong sense of affinity with the earth, the sole source of livelihood. Threats to this relationship such as conflicts, violence, civil wars, natural disasters and forced migrations often destroy life and disrupt social harmony. The concept of *cosmotheandrism* is so central to African society that the entire community in solidarity must meet internal and external enemies of life.[85] In Magesa's words, "What falls on one, falls on all."[86] Sharing resources is a moral imperative and an expression of *cosmotheandrism* made possible through hard work and care for one's family including members of the extended family. Sharing one's resources is the prima facie duty of every member of that community; not simply a matter of individual choice, but rather as an expression of being African as stated in the 1981 OAU Charter on Human and Peoples' Rights, Article 21(4):

---

tribalism, ethnocentrism, or nationalism.

[82] It should be noted that *cosmotheandrism* should not be mistaken for the Greek-Stoic pantheon in which the *cosmos* and *theos* are one and the same, a concept grounded in the philosophy of emanation. The African view of *cosmotheandrism* is that, while the three components namely, *cosmos*, *theos*, and *anthropos* are interrelated, they are, however, distinct. Hence, both the transcendence and immanence of *cosmotheandrism* are clearly distinguished.

[83] Magesa, *African Religion*, 65.

[84] See Ilesanmi, "Civil-Political Rights," 191–212. For further analysis of these rights, see Hollenbach, "Solidarity, Development, and Human Rights," 315.

[85] For an in-depth understanding of internal and external enemies of life, see the section of the root causes of humanitarian crises in the Great Lakes Region of Africa in chapter 1. Chapter 2 is a demonstration of how the enemies of life can be prevented both locally and internationally.

[86] Magesa, *African Religion*, 66.

States party to the present Charter shall individually and collec-
tively exercise the right to free disposal of their wealth and natural
resources with a view to strengthen African unity and solidarity.[87]

Moreover, because Africans believe that God is the ultimate author
of the earth's resources, readiness to share as an expression of hospitality,
is at the heart of moral living and this is why "refusal to share is wrong."[88]
The sense of community brings about the sense of duty in sharing with
those in need:

> Since in African Religion the individual can exist as a person in
> community, his or her well-being can be assured only in the con-
> text of the well-being of the community . . . the ethical dimension
> of community, which forms part of the life-style of all members,
> assures that sharing takes place when necessary.[89]

However, in the face of modernity, the sense of community and social
integration is weakening and industrialization, urbanization, population
growth, as well as globalization are having an adverse impact on Africa's
cosmotheandrism. In spite of the wave of changes upon modern Africa, the
sense of community in the many countries that have been affected by violence, war, conflicts and civil war is still cherished in rural areas where the
majority of Africans live. A rediscovery of *cosmotheandrism* may reclaim
the African social ethos of communal solidarity.

The concept of God as the creator and giver of life is the basis of
cosmotheandrism. Because the dignity of the human person is rooted in the
transcendent origin of life, human dignity is the basis and end of rights.[90]
What seems inexplicit in black Africa, however, is the concept of God as
savior revealed in Jesus Christ, the fullest expression of human dignity, *par
excellence*. How can the concept of God as creator and savior be integrated
and transform *cosmotheandrism*, and thus become an authentic expression

---

[87] "African Charter," in John, 141.

[88] Magesa, *African Religion*, 66.

[89] Ibid., 243–44. Critics of African communitarian philosophy argue that community
tends to absorb individual's identity, freedom, and rights. Simeon Ilesanmi argues, "Rights
were not entitlements that a person had by virtue of her [his] intrinsic worth as an individual but only because she [he] was a part of the whole." For an in-depth analysis of
this concept, see Ilesanmi, "Human Rights Discourse," 306. It must be noted, however,
that a proper balance between individual rights and community or groups rights must be
maintained. Moreover, since rights and duties are intimately related, individual rights are
essentially social rights because enjoying basic rights require effective social arrangements
and legal guarantees.

[90] Ilesanmi, "Human Rights Discourse," 300.

of an African Catholic social justice? When it is claimed that, in light of Catholic social justice, *cosmotheandrism* is transformed, it means that, in the words of Benezet Bujo:

> . . . There is only one vocation of the human person, a vocation with God as its goal. This means that African anthropology, which envisages the earthly (secular) and the religious (sacred) together, does not require a distinction between world ethos and ethos of salvation leading to the mutual autonomy of the two. Christian faith does not mean a quantitative addition to African anthropology, but it is qualitatively different although it points in the same direction.[91]

Bujo continues by arguing that because the concept of ancestor is central to African social ethos, to use St. Paul's language, Christ is considered the proto-ancestor through whom all other human ancestors receive the vital force (Col 1:15). Whenever this vital force is abused or threatened through violence, conflicts and wars in Africa, the perpetrators, who are considered to be the enemies of life, are challenged by the concept of Christ, the proto-ancestor and the giver of life, *par excellence*:

> In Black African tradition, a chief or king is assessed according to his success in transmitting to the people entrusted to him the life that comes from the ancestors. This means, in keeping with African tradition, that the modern state must be so organized that an unworthy politician will be de-posed by the people as a whole, both in the name of the ancestors and with an appeal to the proto-ancestor, Jesus Christ.[92]

African Catholic social justice demands that, through *cosmotheandrism*, abuses of human rights and dignity can be effectively addressed in order to protect and promote the lives of refugees and IDPs in the Great Lakes Region of Sub-Saharan Africa.[93] Because the concepts of *imago Dei* and redemption in Christ makes the African social ethos qualitatively different, the biblically inspired Catholic social teaching can be inculturated by employing *cosmotheandrism*, and thus becomes an expression of

---

[91] Bujo, *Foundations of an African Ethic*, 102–3.

[92] Ibid., 105.

[93] The decadence of *cosmotheandrism* in the Great Lakes Region of Africa may have contributed to the lack of respect for human life and dignity. Hence, the re-discovery of *cosmotheandrism* can effectively assume a mediating role of holistically defending human dignity, and thus establish a personalist-centered human rights discourse in Africa.

an African justification of human rights and a preferential option for the poor in the region.[94]

The African Catholic Social Teaching and the Response to Humanitarian Crises in Africa

In this chapter, it was shown that the 1971 Synod of Bishops' document, *Justice in the World*, declared the right to development to be considered a measure for fighting poverty and powerlessness. With respect to this understanding, the right to development is a justice issue not only for states, but also for the Church; hence obligations of justice are constitutive to Christian evangelization. It follows, since the Catholic Church upholds the defense of human dignity, protecting basic rights of refugees and IDPs is constitutive of Christian evangelization. In this section, this understanding is further discussed in the context of the African Catholic Church.

The 1994 Synod for Africa affirmed that the problems of famine, war, racial and tribal tensions, political instability, and human rights violations are threats to contemporary African society.[95] It was cited that the plight of refugees and IDPs, caused by the factors above, are challenges that the Synod faces. In his *Post-Synodal Exhortation*, John Paul II's theme, "The Church in Africa and Her Evangelizing Mission Towards 2000," is a clear message for the Church in Africa. The message of hope is central to John Paul's theme for the Synod. This message, which is rooted in the Pascal Mystery for liberation from oppression and slavery, emphasizes that integral human development, spiritually and materially, is at the very heart of Christian evangelization, especially for the weak, the poor, and the voiceless. In other words, conversion of heart, *metanoia,* and reconciliation are the *conditio sine qua non* of an authentic liberation. John Paul writes, "Integral development, the development of every person and of the whole person, especially of the poorest and most neglected in the community, is at the heart of evangelization."[96]

---

[94] It is beyond the scope of this study to explore all the aspects of *cosmotheandrism*: the earth, God, and humans. It must be noted throughout this section that the concept of *cosmotheandrism* will be employed analogically vis-à-vis basic rights of refugees and IDPs. The sense of communal solidarity is the main feature as demonstrated by a triad of relationships: humans, God, and the earth. It is significantly important that, because from Catholic social teaching, human dignity can be fully fulfilled in relationships with others, the concept of *cosmotheandrism* can best express the sense of community and interdependence of rights from an African perspective, and thus becomes an African theology of social justice.

[95] John Paul II, *Church in Africa*, 51 no. 51.

[96] Ibid., no. 68. Also see John Paul II, *Church in America*, 97–98. The message, "prefer-

According to Julius Nyerere, the notion of integral human development is critical to protecting human dignity. When Nyerere addressed a Congress of Maryknoll Sisters on October 16, 1970 in New York, he succinctly stated:

> We say that [the human person] was created in the image and likeness of God. I refuse to imagine a God who is poor, ignorant, superstitious, fearful, oppressed, wretched—which is the lot of the majority of those He created in his own image. Humans are creators of themselves and their conditions, but under the present conditions we are creatures, not of God, but of our fellow humans.[97]

Nyerere believes that degrading conditions of poverty, ignorance, and others in which the majority of people live today in the developing world contradict human dignity. He underscores the importance of liberation from oppressive conditions for a good standard of living in keeping with human dignity. Human development is considered the way forward to eradicate these degrading living conditions, and thus improve standards of living. Contributing to this subject, Pope John Paul II stresses that a thick description of liberation is warranted. He maintains that although there is a close link between evangelization and human advancement, as well as development and liberation, the latter must be understood in totality and cannot be restricted to the domain of economics, politics, social or cultural life. From a *cosmotheandric* perspective, authentic liberation, however, must entail the development of the whole human person in all his or her dimensions, physical and spiritual.[98] Since refugees and IDPs are subject to essential and systematic deprivations of basic human rights, authentic liberation of these groups is constitutive of the mission of the Catholic Church.

With regard to the mission of the Church, Dorr, writes, "Authentic development is an integral part of true liberation."[99] Liberation can be described as a two-fold process: first, liberation from personal wickedness or sinfulness, and second, liberation from "sinfulness, which has become embodied in most of traditions and institutions of our nations and our

---

ential option for the poor" features in the 1999 American Synod of Bishops, as well as the 1994 African Synod of Bishops. Similar views have been expressed by Hessel in "Solidarity Ethics," 96.

[97] Nyerere, *Freedom and Development*, 216.

[98] John Paul II, *Church in Africa*, 71–72 no. 68.

[99] Dorr, *Mission*, 120.

world."[100] Dorr claims that personal and social sins are closely connected. This is based on the view that corporate sin is the cause of personal sin because the latter tends to contaminate the former.[101] Dorr argues, "The social sin is not only an effect, but also a cause of the personal sinfulness."[102] Of course, it is indisputable that personal and social sins are intimately connected.[103] At this juncture, it can be argued that the preferential option for the poor involves an integral commitment: total liberation from personal and social sin. Because humanitarian crises are a result of essential and systematic deprivation of basic human rights of security, subsistence, and social participation, social institutions that embody these deprivations must be liberated from both the personal and social sin in order to effectively protect the basic human rights of refugees and IDPs, and thus promote their dignity in the Great Lakes Region of Africa.

The notion of total liberation from essential and systematic deprivations of basic human rights is fulfilled in Christ Jesus, as illustrated in his inaugural speech in the synagogue: releasing captives, liberating the oppressed, and proclaiming the acceptable year of the Lord (Luke 4:18–19; cf. Isa 61:1–2). Concretely, Christ Jesus fulfilled this proclamation in his public ministry by healing people from every kind of sickness (Matt 8:17).[104] By carrying out the ministry of Christ Jesus, the Church, as the *Family of God*, proclaims the Kingdom of God to be the kingdom of peace and justice.[105] In this way, the Church becomes a living witness of Christ's message and community of rights in solidarity for defense of human dignity; for every person is created in the image and likeness of God and redeemed in Christ Jesus.[106] The prophetic role of the Church is to become

[100] Ibid.

[101] Ibid., 113

[102] Ibid.

[103] The manner in which Dorr makes a distinction between social and personal sin based on a cause-effect argument is morally disputable. If freedom and knowledge are the necessary requirements for a moral action, then the human person is the cause of personal sin and social sin is not the cause of personal sin. Nevertheless, whatever is personal can be social. Corporate sinfulness simply provides a favorable environment and condition for social sin to thrive. However, it is beyond the scope of this study to give a detailed account of the origin of personal and social sin.

[104] John Paul II, *Church in Africa*, 71 no. 68.

[105] The Church as the "Family of God" is the ecclesiological model adopted by the 1994 Synod for Africa. The adoption of this model was based on the fact that a sense of traditional family value of communal solidarity, *cosmotheandrism*, is central to ethical and religious way of life in Africa.

[106] John Paul II, *Church in Africa*, 73 no. 69.

the voice of the voiceless as the preferential option for the poor, particularly women, children, and the elderly who are refugees and IDPs in camps and in armed conflict areas. John Paul II urges the Church to protect human dignity by providing refugees and IDPs with material and pastoral support.[107] The Synod additionally made a special reference to all customs and practices that deprive women of their rights and duties to actively participate in full development of the Church and society.[108] This holistic approach to evangelization tends to bid farewell to the "salvation of souls" model. Implementing the African Synod's holistic model of *Family of God* realized in communal solidarity, *cosmotheandrism*, the Church becomes the source of hope for the liberation of the afflicted, *anawim*, and faithful witness to the covenant fidelity, *sedaqah*.

To make the task effective, the African Synod for Bishops urges "national, regional and international organizations to find long-lasting solutions to the problems affecting refugees and [internally] displaced persons."[109] Addressing the problems of refugees and IDPs is a mutual solidaristic symbiosis and dialogical process, which calls for the cooperation of governments and NGOs, private individuals, international organizations, and the international community to defend human dignity. Nevertheless, in order to fully protect human dignity of refugees and IDPs, it is imperative that mutual solidaristic symbiosis be fostered between the Church and those groups. Based on the words of the 1971 Synod of Bishops, and the 1994 Special Assembly of the Synod of Bishops for Africa, the authenticity of the Church is realized when it calls for justice among its own members as the witness, inspiration, and shining example for governments, NGOs, international organizations, and the international community.

Gustavo Gutierrez, drawing upon the Latin American experience, stresses the importance of the spiritual experience with Christ in the ecclesial community and its actions in the world as the source of authentic liberation. The spiritual experience resulting from an encounter with Christ is the spirituality of liberation theology. This spiritual experience is the driving force that makes the followers of Christ "walk with and committed to the poor; when they do so, they experience and encounter with the Lord who is simultaneously revealed and hidden in the faces of the

---

[107]   See similar concerns expressed by the Pontifical Council for Pastoral Care of Migrants and Itinerant People, *Refugees: A Challenge to Solidarity*, 16 nos. 28–29.

[108]   John Paul II, *The Church in Africa*, 124 no. 121.

[109]   Ibid., 122 no. 119.

poor (Matt 25:31–46)."[110] Gutierrez believes that the strength for liberation comes from this encounter, which allows people and the Church to
experience mutual solidaristic symbiosis "in defense of human rights and,
in particular, the rights of the poor."[111] The experience leads to "an irrup-
tion of the poor," as Gutierrez calls it, and enables them to take control of
their history and destiny as a people. The Church, the *Family of God* and
the messianic community, must accompany the dispossessed and marginalized in their journey for total liberation from all forms of essential and
systematic deprivations of basic human rights. It must be noted, however,
that solidarity is a gift not only from individuals and community, but also
the dispossessed, which cannot be taken for granted; it is indeed not paternalism, *noblesse oblige*. Dorr writes:

> It is a gift, which cannot be presumed or demanded from [refugees
> and IDPs]. They give it in their own time and in their own degree,
> and only to one who comes to them with no air of superiority
> paternalism.[112]

Mutual solidaristic symbiosis is key to a successful commitment to preferential option for the poor.

The Church's solidarity with the dispossessed, in cooperation with
governments and NGO's, as well as the international community, should
not only take the victims' side as in the parable of the Good Samaritan, but
should also make "their experience their own." According to Gutierrez,
"any other response will be a halfway response."[113] A similar commitment
to solidarity with the dispossessed was made during the Conference of
the Latin American Church held in Medellin, Colombia in 1968. In this
conference, "the bishops say that solidarity with the poor means that we
make ours their problems and their struggles."[114]

Liberation from essential and systematic deprivation of basic human
rights is regarded the spirituality of liberation theology. Often misunder-

---

[110] Gutierrez, *We Drink from Our Own Wells*, 38.

[111] Ibid., 21. The phrase, "solidaristic symbiosis" is derived from two terms, "solidarity,"
and "symbiosis." The phrase connotes the intimate relationship that should be fostered
between the poor and the church.

[112] Dorr, *Mission in Today's World*, 155.

[113] Gutierrez, *We Drink from Our Own Wells*, 31. When the experience of refugees and
IDPs become our own, their way of seeing, feeling, and thinking becomes our seeing, feeling, thinking, and acting. This "social intercourse" makes liberation from the essential and
systematic deprivation of basic rights of refugees and IDPs become a reality.

[114] Dorr, *Option for the Poor*, 207.

stood by critics who perceive this theology as a politico-economic ideology and sectarian revolutionary movement[115]devoid of sound spirituality, liberation theology is, in fact, an authentic, all-embracing Christian spirituality. This Christ-centered spirituality of liberation theology, a reflection of Christian experience, is not a class struggle as perceived in Marxist ideological circles, because Christ loves both the oppressed and the oppressor.[116] Liberation theology becomes the model for the Church's struggle and commitment for liberation of the dispossessed. Understanding the concept of liberation in the Latin America Church can be an inspiration to the rest of the church and those who are committed to the cause of basic human rights, justice, and peace in the Great Lakes Region.

The 1994 African Synod conceived a model of the African Church as the *God's Family* and called for solidarity as well as care and sharing resources with others, regardless of ethnicity or tribe.[117] This model is designed to bring about reconciliation, communion, and peace among various social and political groups in the war-torn countries of the Great Lakes Region of Sub-Saharan Africa. Like its counterpart in the Latin American Church, the Church in Africa is faced with the problems of marginalization. If the African Church is to be true to its mission and model, the *Family of God*, it must forge a *cosmotheandric* model of solidarity with refugees and IDPs, and accompany them in their journey for the African total liberation from human rights' deprivation. To do so, the African Church, as the *Family of God*, must make deprived people's experiences, journeys, and struggles its own, thus realizing the theme of the 1994 African Synod, *You will be my witnesses to the ends of the earth.*

Catholic Episcopal Conferences and relief organizations in the Great Lakes Region of Africa have demonstrated the spirit of *cosmotheandrism* with refugees in different ways. Demonstrating *cosmotheandrism* with the dispossessed is Caritas Tanzania, one of the departments of the Tanzania Episcopal Conference (TEC) dealing with refugees and other emergencies.[118] Since 1994, Caritas Tanzania has assisted 100,000 Rwandan refugees in the area of camp management, health, and community services. The Caritas Network, in conjunction with the Government of Tanzania and the UNHCR, supports this initiative. In 1995, a total of Tshs.

---

[115] *Liberation Theology and The Vatican Document*, 137.

[116] Gutierrez, *We Drink from Our Own Wells*, xi.

[117] John Paul II, *The Church in Africa*, 64–65 no. 63. See "African Charter," in John, 141.

[118] *Caritas* is a Latin word equivalent to " love" or "charity." It is also equivalent to a Greek word, *agape*, or "love," and not to *eros*.

695,832,688 (US $695,832.688) was granted to the refugee operations located in Kigoma and Kagera Regions of Tanzania. In 1996, a total of Tshs. 1,497,252,859 (US $1,497,252.859) was spent to provide humanitarian services in these regions.[119] Also Caritas Tanzania works in conjunction with several private relief organizations such as the Jesuit Refugee Service (JRS). JRS offers human and pastoral services to thousands of refugees including programs of pastoral care, education for children and adults, social services and counseling and health care. In Ngara District of Kagera Region, Tanzania, JRS has established Radio Kwizera. It broadcasts both to refugees and local population on educational programs, reconciliation, and peaceful co-existence.[120]

In 2002 the 14th Plenary Assembly of Regional African Catholic Bishops, *Association of Member Episcopal Conferences of Eastern Africa (AMECEA)*, which met in Dar-es-salaam, Tanzania, reiterated the message from the 1994 Synod for Africa on the rights of refugees and IDPs. The main theme, *Deeper Evangelization in the New Millennium*, puts the question of refugees and IDPs at the top of the agenda. According to the assembly, deeper evangelization connotes total evangelization, involving personal interior and communal transformation, as well as that of the world's social, cultural, political, and economic structures. These transformations must be inspired by the values of the kingdom of God, namely, love, mercy, compassion, justice, and peace. Led by the example of Christ's ministry for the dispossessed and marginalized, deeper evangelization means profound commitment to a preferential option for the poor not only through material assistance but also denunciation of the structures of evil in society. The Church, as the *Family of God*, is called to forge communal solidarity with the poor; not only to be in favor of the poor and against their poverty, but also to take up their cause and uncover the root causes of the essential and systematic deprivations of basic human rights. Consequently, protection of refugees and IDPs within the AMECEA countries is constitutive of the African Catholic social teaching. The Assembly called for a durable solution of conflicts to end displacement, and humanitarian crises in the AMECEA countries.[121] Moreover, in December 2001, prior to the plenary assembly, the AMECEA delegation visited IDPs located in various camps

---

[119] The Tanzania Episcopal Conference, *Report on Caritas* (1995–1999), accessed 3/25/2003.

[120] Jesuit Refugee Service, *2000 Report*, accessed 5/9/2003.

[121] "Main Decisions," accessed 8/20/2004.

in Sudan, as a demonstration of their *cosmotheandric* communal solidarity with the oppressed.[122]

Earlier in 2002, the 12th Plenary Assembly of Continental African Catholic Bishops, *Symposium of Episcopal Conferences of Africa and Madagascar (SECAM)* held in Rome, Italy, expressed similar concern about political injustices and internal armed conflicts leading to refugees in Africa. Unfortunately, the question of IDPs did not feature in this assembly. Under the theme, *Christ our Peace: Church as Family of God, Place and Sacrament of Reconciliation, Forgiveness and Peace in Africa*, the assembly highlighted the root causes of political instability and internal armed conflicts as deprivation of fundamental rights of civil and political liberties: freedom of speech and association, and freedom to choose a government. These human rights deprivations contribute to tensions and dissatisfactions between government leaders and civilian populations.[123] The assembly pledged for peace, justice, and reconciliation within the Church as well as within the political and economic sectors. More importantly, the Church was called to give witness to justice within itself by avoiding ethnocentrism, favoritism, and excessive particularism in order to foster communal solidarity, unity, and credibility inside and outside the Church.[124]

The communal solidarity with the marginalized and dispossessed is the preferential option for the poor, and portrays the Church, the *Family of God*, as a protector of the basic human rights of refugees and IDPs in Africa. Communal solidarity with refugees and IDPs is liberation from extreme inequalities to recognition of equal dignity and basic rights. The evangelical witness of the Church's solidarity with refugees and IDPs becomes exemplary to social institutions; it is a significant signal to governments, NGOs, international organizations, and the international community to continue their mutual support of providing these groups with basic human rights of security, subsistence, and liberty of active social participation in the Great Lakes Region of Sub-Saharan Africa.[125]

---

[122] For detailed information on this issue, see AMECEA Delegates, "In Solidarity," 125–52.

[123] "Message from the 12th Plenary Assembly of SECAM," accessed 8/20/2004.

[124] Ibid., no. 43–44.

[125] The call for communal solidarity between the Church and refugees and/ or IDPs is critical at a time when some Church members were implicated in the massacre of thousands of Tutsis and moderate Hutus in the 1994 Rwandan genocide. In this scenario, those who sought shelter and asylum in church buildings fell into a trap. Finally, they were mercilessly tortured and killed by their captors. This incident is contrary to the covenant fidelity, *sedaqah*, and the ethics of Christian discipleship. The ecclesiastical model of the Af-

Basic Rights of Refugees and IDPs and Relationship between Communal Solidarity and Subsidiarity

As stated earlier, the principle of communal solidarity (*cosmotheandrism*) demands that all the parties in the international community be morally responsible for the provision of equal basic human rights of refugees and IDPs in Great Lakes Region of Africa. This recognition of equality of basic rights demonstrates equal dignity and respect of refugees and IDPs, and thus becomes an expression of the commitment to a preferential option for the poor. In order to effectively fulfill the commitment, all the key players in the international community are required to work together for and with refugees and IDPs. The function of the principle of subsidiarity strengthens the principle of communal solidarity by clearly defining moral and legal responsibility for member states in the international community regarding the basic rights of refugees and IDPs. When the principle of subsidiarity is respected and observed through the communal solidarity of every member state in the international community, resolving conflicts of basic rights between refugees and IDPs and state sovereignty, and preventing humanitarian crises are made possible in the region. Most importantly, redressing the conditions that cause large numbers of citizens to flee their homes is a long-term strategy and an investment to achieving a just and peaceful society. To achieve this objective, exercising the principles of communal solidarity and subsidiarity both locally and internationally is key to this project. In this section, under the principles of communal solidarity and subsidiarity, the roles of governments, NGOs, individuals, groups, international agencies, and the international community in resolving conflicts of basic human rights and preventing humanitarian crises in international law and public policy are examined in light of the Catholic Church's social thought.

According to Catholic social teaching, effective institutional arrangements and legal guarantees are required to protect basic human rights and dignity. The human person is prior to the state, therefore political institutions must be structured and developed to protect the common good. When one considers the social nature of the human person, it follows

---

rican Church, the *Family of God*, is called to foster communal solidarity, *cosmotheandrism*, with refugees and IDPs. Moreover, fostering communal solidarity with refugees and IDPs sends a powerful signal to local and international organizations, especially the peacekeeping forces, which have been implicated in the physical and sexual abuses of refugees and/or IDPs in Africa and elsewhere. Such actions contradict their code of ethics for protecting these groups against essential and systematic deprivation of basic human rights of security, subsistence, social participation and physical movement.

that the state is natural, necessary, and good. The Catholic Church seeks to avoid extreme liberalistic individualism and totalitarian socialism by perceiving the state as a limited political order.[126]

The Catholic Church has persistently taught that the political and moral order are interrelated and that effective social institutions are prerequisite for the enjoyment of basic human rights; a stand that is based on a positive image of state. Bearing in mind the fundamental anthropological principles stated above, the Catholic Church takes a middle stand between liberal capitalism and state socialism. The church's stand, which will be highlighted in the discussion, uses Catholic documents related to political order.

The Catholic Church acknowledges the limitations of the state when it comes to understanding the moral vision of the dignity of the human person. Individualistic liberalism, which considers the priority of negative freedom is opposed to the Catholic Church's social tradition, which affirms the centrality of the human person: the human person is essentially social, and human dignity can only be realized in communal solidarity.

In *Pacem in Terris*, John XXIII maintains that civil government should exercise its authority according to right reason; keeping the best interest of its citizens in mind and promoting the common good. The common good is promoted when each individual fulfills his or her rights and duties in the community. Because God created social nature, "authority must derive its obligatory force from the moral order, which in turn has God for its first source and final end."[127] Hence, one of the fundamental duties of civil authority is to coordinate social relations to safeguard free exercise of rights and duties and restore them when threatened.[128]

---

[126] Curran, *Catholic Social Teaching*, 138. It is worth noting that the Catholic view of the state is not accepted universally by other Christian religions. The Lutheran view, for example, is that the state is of divine origin. Based on the concept of the original sin and its impact in the world, Lutheran doctrine considers the state to be a God-given institution set up to contain the power of sin; keeping humans away from sin and from destruction. By contrast, according to Catholic doctrine, the state is a political institution that advances social justice and promotes personal and social good rather than simply preventing people from sinful actions. Because it is based on the positive notion of creation, the Catholic view of state is more optimistic than the Lutheran view, which regards the state as coercive in nature. Nevertheless, the danger with the Catholic anthropology lies in the optimistic notion of creation, which may easily overlook the reality of sin in society. For further information about the comparative notion of state, see Curran, *Catholic Social Teaching*, 139–40.

[127] John XXIII, "*Pacem in Terris*," 138 no. 47.

[128] Ibid., 94 no. 62. This claim made by the Synod of Bishops is consonant with the findings in chapter 1 regarding the root causes of forced migration and humanitarian crises under the title, "Political Leadership and Governance in Africa."

In *Ecclesia in Africa*, The Synod of Bishops for Africa expressed a similar concern about the need for good governance in political and economic spheres. Although some of the continent's problems can be attributed to external factors, the Synod noted that other problems are a result of corruption and bad governance by African leaders.[129] The Synod maintained that sound institutional arrangements are necessary to "protect the rights and define obligations of the citizens."[130] The Synod acknowledged that in Africa, armed conflicts, civil wars, political strife, violence, and the tragedy of refugees and IDPs, and humanitarian catastrophes have been caused by ethnic conflicts, political repression, injustices, and human rights abuses. To avoid deprivation of basic human rights, "authentic democracy, which respects pluralism" is a pre-requisite for the restoration of political stability and economic prosperity in Africa.[131] When sound social arrangements are in place, equal dignity is protected and promoted in community. Nevertheless, the Synod's view of authentic democracy, which respects pluralism, is susceptible to ambiguity; it is unclear what pluralism means in the context of Africa. Furthermore, if political pluralism in Africa simply means political parties and structures, which primarily reflect liberties of forbearance, then the political process is bound to fail if it ignores the concept of *cosmotheandrism*, which considers the holistic nature of the human person critical to the understanding of human rights in contemporary Africa. Most importantly, in light of *cosmotheandrism*, which rejects the dichotomy between ethics and religion, social and economic rights as well as civil and political rights are intimately related, and thus are critical to a life of dignity.

In *Gaudium et Spes*, the Second Vatican Council maintains the centrality of the human person in society. The Council affirms that the justification of state as a political community exists for the service of the common good, which embraces all those conditions that enable individuals and communities to achieve fulfillment.[132] In order to promote social justice, the civil authority has the duty to create the necessary conditions and structures every citizen needs to actively participate in social, political,

---

[129] John Paul II, *Church in Africa*, 113 no. 110.

[130] Ibid., no. 112. The Lutheran tradition shares similar views with the Catholics on the foundation of human rights: dignity and social nature of the human person. The Lutheran tradition maintains that "human rights cannot be realized unless social conditions and political structures are justly ordered at the same time." Lutheran World Federation, *Theological Perspectives on Human Rights*, 11.

[131] Ibid.

[132] Vatican II, "*Gaudium et Spes*," 216 no. 74.

and economic life. Bearing in mind the signs of the times and rapid changes in the contemporary world, institutional arrangements should take into
account the social milieu: the historical developments and the particular character of a people, society, and culture.[133] In this regard, successful
political reforms in Africa must take into account the *cosmotheandric* view
of society.

Protecting human rights cannot be fully achieved if left to the state
alone. Although the state, family, cultural groups, associations, and religious organizations are independent entities, they all serve the common
good in political community by the justification of the principle of subsidiarity. This principle, as stipulated in Pius XI's *Quadragesimo Anno,*
maintains that the state and its mega institutions have the primary duty of
protecting the common good without subsuming or absorbing the functions and roles of lesser groups or intermediate associations. Moreover,
transferring social functions to the state and its mega institutions, which
can be carried out by lesser or intermediate social institutions, is inappropriate. Pius XI states:

> . . . It is fundamental principle of social philosophy, fixed and un-
> changeable, that one should not withdraw from individuals and
> commit to the community what they can accomplish by their own
> enterprise and industry. So, too, it is an injustice and at the same
> time a grave evil and a disturbance of right order to transfer to the
> larger and higher collectivity functions which can be performed
> and provided for by lesser and subordinate bodies. Inasmuch as ev-
> ery social activity should, by its very nature, prove a help to mem-
> bers of social body, it should never destroy or absorb them.[134]

The social arrangements that the principle of subsidiarity defends allow
individuals, the state, NGOs, African Union (AU), UNHCR, and other
agencies to freely and interdependently perform the primary duties proper
to each one's status and role. Most importantly, the closer the principle
of subsidiarity is faithfully followed, the more effective, efficient, and efficacious the society becomes, thereby maintaining hierarchical order that
allows for the flourishing of the common good.

Developing relationships of interdependence within the state's mega
institutions and the lesser or intermediate social institutions brings about
a moral bond of communal solidarity and mutuality in the community of
rights. Bearing in mind that the African community of rights is a broad,

---

[133] Ibid.

[134] Pius XI, "*Quadragesimo Anno,*" 60 no. 79.

embracing, and encompassing concept of regulated social relationships, *cosmotheandrism*, is the best expression of the principle of subsidiarity in Africa. It regulates and orders personal and social relationships, distributes rights, and defines duties and institutional arrangements. These communal relationships operate in the African traditional intermediate social institutions of families (both nuclear and extended), kinships, clans, tribes, and ethnicity. The bonded relationships of material and spiritual, political and moral, bring about cosmic order and ecosystem equilibrium. Hence, *cosmotheandrism* is the basis of African ethos. Generally, one can say that because the principle of subsidiarity promotes mutual cooperation and communal solidarity in the state and in the world, the principles of subsidiarity and solidarity are critical to protecting and promoting basic rights of security, subsistence, and liberties of social participation.

Often, ethno-centricity is seen as a contributing factor to violence, armed conflicts, civil wars, forced migration, and humanitarian catastrophe in Africa, particularly in the Great Lakes Region.[135] Although ethnocentricity plays a role in the conflicts in the region, ethnicity as such is not necessarily negative. In the message of the SECAM Bishops to the Churches of the Great Lakes Region and the rest of Africa and Madagascar, Gabriel Gansum Ganaka, president of SECAM, explains the theological significance of ethnicity:

> . . . Ethnicity indicates a gift of God, which makes us different one from the other for our mutual enrichment. It is God who makes each one what one is. Ethnicity gives us our social and cultural identity as well as our personal identity. The individual finds his [her] roots and values in his ethnic group.[136]

Through subsidiarity, ethnicity can be a useful institution when it is used to promote social participation, and advance the values of self-identity, inclusion, spirit of tolerance, mutual understanding and the common good. In support of the principle of subsidiarity, Hollenbach writes:

> The principle of subsidiarity embodies a pluralistic model of social interaction. It envisions society as composed of many groups with many different purposes, needs, and legitimate claims.[137]

---

[135] See chapter 1 with regard to the analysis of the root causes of the forced migrations and humanitarian crises in the region.

[136] Ganaka, "Message of the SECAM Bishops," 67. A similar view has been expressed by Ngabirano, "National Justice," 234.

[137] Hollenbach, *Claims in Conflict*, 159. On the issue of subsidiarity in Africa, see also Achermann, *Cry Beloved Africa*, 189–90.

Under the principle of subsidiarity, African intermediate institutions such as families, clans, tribes and ethnic groups, can be good sources of positive values and effective vehicles to promote communal solidarity and the common good. Communal solidarity and the common good can be promoted as long as the intermediate social institutions reflect *cosmotheandrism*, as the example of the Burundian social institution, *Ubushingantahe* demonstrates.[138] Hence, the principle of subsidiarity strengthens the communal solidarity.[139]

In the same vein, John Paul II, in *Centesimus Annus*, reiterates that state's intervention in the intermediate institutions is justifiable when their actions become a threat to the common good. Moreover, in exceptional cases, the state can exercise a substitute function when the intermediate institutions are too weak to function.[140] The Church expresses great concern about an excessive intervention by the state, which "can threaten personal freedom and initiative."[141] The principal function of subsidiarity is that it is "opposed to all forms of state collectivism," and thus limits state intervention.[142] Since these intermediate bodies are instrumental to the promotion of the common good, public authority should empower them to become more effective and productive. The Second Vatican Council warns that the state should not be tolerated when its actions stifle the duties and rights of intermediate social institutions.[143]

Although the Church, as an intermediate institution, is committed to the promotion of the common good, it should not be confused with the political community, nor be bound to any political system.[144] Based on the fundamental anthropological principles of dignity and social nature, the Church is the defender of the transcendence of the human person; it

---

[138] The rediscovery of the concept of *Ubushingantahe*, a term in Burundian language, stands for local council, intermediate social institution, in Burundian society. The institution aims at promoting communal solidarity in addressing social, political, economic, and cultural issues. Encouraging all people to take active social participation at all levels of society, illustrates the importance of *Ubushingantahe* in the *cosmotheandric* model of communal solidarity. For further information about the concept of *Ubushingantahe*, see Bujo, *Communal Dimension of Community*, 167–68.

[139] From the African perspective of the principles of communal solidarity and subsidiarity, see Baitu, "Christian Ethical Principles," 4–5.

[140] John Paul II, "*Centesimus Annus*," no. 48 in *Catholic Social Thought*, 475–76.

[141] *Catechism of the Catholic Church*, 460 no. 1883.

[142] Ibid., 460 no. 1885.

[143] Vatican II, "*Gaudium et Spes*," 217 no. 75. See John Paul II, "*Centesimus Annus*," 475–76 no. 48.

[144] Vatican II, "*Gaudium et Spes*," 218 no. 76.

is not a political-economic ideology, which may threaten human dignity and human rights.

The Moral and Legal Significance of the Principles of Communal Solidarity and Subsidiarity in International Law and Policy

In the preceding section the Catholic Church's social teaching regarding the principles of communal solidarity and subsidiarity were examined. In this section, the moral significance of these principles in protecting the basic human rights of refugees and IDPs in international law and policy for the Great Lakes Region of Africa is undertaken.

Under the principle of subsidiarity, any intervention by government, the mega institution, is regarded morally and legally legitimate when such actions protect the most vulnerable groups from essential and systematic deprivation of basic human rights of security, subsistence, and liberties of active social participation and physical movement. Implementing this principle ensures that equal dignity and rights of every person are respected by all in the state through the principle of communal solidarity. However, government's intervention is regarded illegitimate when it deprives individuals, groups, or intermediate institutions' ability to exercise the basic human rights.

To confront humanitarian crises, the principle of subsidiarity is deployed to resolve conflict of rights by overriding the rights of state sovereignty in favor of basic human rights of refugees or IDPs when no less coercive policy is possible. In such cases, the duty to provide basic human rights becomes the moral and legal basis for international humanitarian intervention.[145] For humanitarian operations to be successful, the principle of subsidiarity calls for communal solidarity of the international community to provide these groups with basic human rights. For an effective protection of refugees and IDPs, all the key players in the international community should take their active role in providing basic human rights by contributing financial and logistic support to the successful mission of UNHCR in the Great Lakes Region of Africa. To avoid paternalism, the principle of communal solidarity demands that all the parties concerned

---

[145] The use of force for protecting the most fundamental human rights of refugees and IDPs ought to be carried out under the just-war criteria; *jus ad bellum* and *jus in bello*. For a detailed account of the morality of the just-war criteria considered from a perspective of Catholic social teaching, see "Challenge of Peace," 510–17 nos. 80–110. For further analysis of humanitarian intervention, see Himes, "Morality of Humanitarian Intervention," 82–105.

(governments, NGOs, UNHCR, UNICEF, WHO, WFP, and other aid organizations) make the necessary social arrangements and legal guarantees to empower refugees and IDPs to exercise security and subsistence rights. These social arrangements are key to improving living standards of these groups in camps.[146]

It is worth noting that the principle of subsidiarity is not confined to conflict resolution of basic human rights. Rather, this principle plays a significant role in preventing humanitarian crises. Under the principle of subsidiarity, international intervention is morally unjustifiable and legally illegitimate when it threatens the common good of refugees and/or IDPs. Such threats may take place when international humanitarian intervention is closely associated with *Realpolitik* or geopolitical interests.[147] To prevent this situation, such interventions should be conducted under the rule of international law through the communal solidarity of the international community. By implementing the principles of communal solidarity and subsidiarity, *cosmotheandrism*, equal dignity and rights are respected and protected, and thus express a profound commitment for the preferential option for refugees and IDPs in the Great Lakes Region of Sub-Saharan Africa.

Conclusion

The Catholic Church's view of human rights completes the philosophical argument for basic human rights and correlative duties by providing it with a solid theological ground. In general, the Church considers that social and economic rights (security and subsistence), as well as civil and political rights (social participation) are critical to the integral development of the human person. Although these rights are distinct, however, they are inseparable. By invoking the fundamental anthropological principles of *imago Dei*, and social nature the theological justification of basic human rights is established.

Given the fact of conflict of rights, the biblically inspired notion of justice, becomes a regulatory moral principle in key human relationships: commutative justice, distributive justice, and social justice. As such, these principles function interdependently. When the basic rights of the most vulnerable persons are imperiled, the principles of justice demand that the duty to protect these persons becomes a top moral priority. Since refugees

[146] For further information regarding the cooperative venture of UNHCR, governments and NGOs, see chapter 2, "The Human Rights Situation in Refugee Camps in Tanzania."
[147] Taylor, "Role of the United Nations," 147.

and IDPs in general, and women and children in particular, suffer from essential and systematic deprivations of basic human rights they have the strongest moral claims in the Great Lakes Region of Africa.

Effectively satisfying basic human rights requires commitment to have in place effective social arrangements and legal guarantees. Hence, the principles of communal solidarity and subsidiarity, *cosmotheandrism*, are key to such an endeavor. Inasmuch as implementing these principles provides effective protection for the deprived, recognition of the priority of basic human rights in international law and social policy is a commitment to preferential option for the poor.

The philosophical and theological analyses of the concept of human rights demonstrate that the priority principle of basic human rights and correlative duties of providing refugees and IDPs, orphans of state system, is the ultimate moral criterion for responding to humanitarian crises in the region. The study of basic human rights invokes short, medium, and long-term political responses to forced migrations and humanitarian crises in the region. The priority principle of the duty to protect refugees and IDPs is critical for resolving conflicts of rights vis-à-vis state sovereignty. With respect to these points, in the next chapter, concrete proposals and recommendations are made.

PART IV

Concrete Proposals and
Recommendations

5

Toward a Liberation Ethic of Public Policy for Refugees and IDPs

Introduction

IT was established that humanitarian crises are a manifestation of social disorder in the Great Lakes Region of Sub-Saharan Africa.[1] Finding the long lasting resolution to the unprecedented humanitarian crises in the region evokes the need for concrete actions.[2] Philosophical and theological analyses of basic human rights remain an empty rhetoric unless they illumine the appropriate short, medium, and long-term moral and legal responses to the humanitarian crises in the region.[3]

In light of these analyses, in this chapter, a set of moral priorities is proposed as a framework in formulating public policy for refugees and IDPs in the area. Effective implementation of these moral priorities redresses governments' and the international community's failure to adequately protect and aid refugees and IDPs. This task, under the auspices of UNHCR, becomes a crucial challenge not only to governments and the international community, but also to the Sub-Saharan Regional Church of the AMECEA.

---

[1] See the nature and scope of the humanitarian crises in the Great Lakes Region of Sub-Saharan Africa in chapter 1.

[2] The concern is related to the shortcomings of governments, social institutions, and the international community in responding to the humanitarian crises in the region described in chapter 2.

[3] See the moral and legal significance of basic rights from philosophical and theological perspectives discussed in chapters 3 and 4 respectively.

Ethics, International Law, and Public Policy

Based on the philosophical analysis of basic human rights, the principal legal and moral limitations that contribute to governments' and the international community's failure to effectively respond to the humanitarian crises in the Great Lakes Region of Africa are brought to light in chapter 3. Using Shue's theory of basic human rights, in this chapter, I argued that in order to protect and aid refugees and IDPs, objective moral standards are needed in international law and policy.[4] It was established in chapter 4 that a biblically inspired Roman Catholic social teaching, inculturated into an African social milieu, *cosmotheandrism*, provides an adequate account for the justification of human rights, and thus addresses the lacunae of Shue's argument regarding justification. Because human rights are grounded in the transcendent origin of life, satisfying such rights requires not only social arrangements and legal guarantees but also effective implementation in communal solidarity and subsidiarity rooted in *cosmotheandrism*.

The prophetic mission of the Church in Africa becomes irrelevant unless a high moral and legal priority is placed on protecting and aiding refugees and IDPs, whose basic rights are most imperiled. In so doing, the Church "contributes with her ethical and religious vision to restore and uphold the dignity of every human person."[5] Moreover, in the course of history the church has acquired a mass of human experience and can contribute significantly to "formulating adequate laws."[6] To this end, objective moral standards, drawn upon both philosophical and theological analyses of rights, paves the way for action by proposing a set of moral priorities, the moral minima, which become the basis of formulating effective laws and public policy for refugees and IDPs in the Great Lakes Region of Sub-Saharan Africa.

Public Policy and Moral Priorities

Bear in mind that the immediate objective of this chapter is not to propose a public policy for refugees and IDPs in the Great Lakes Region of Africa. Rather, the objective is to identify key moral priorities that can be demanded of governments, social institutions, and the international com-

---

[4] See the objective moral standards, which were discussed in chapter 3, section C.

[5] The Pontifical Council for the Pastoral Care of Migrants and Itinerant People, *Refugees: A Challenge to Solidarity*, 18 no. 36.

[6] Ibid.

munity.[7] In this section, four moral priorities are proposed as the basis of public policy for refugees and IDPs in the region.

1. *Official recognition that refugees and IDPs are moral subjects of rights and ought to enjoy equal legal entitlements*

It was argued in chapter 3 that the failure of the international community in preventing the 1994 Rwandan genocide demonstrates a fundamental lack of recognizing the moral principle that Rwandans, particularly Tutsis are the moral subjects of rights, and ought to enjoy equal legal entitlements in international law and policy regardless of race. The Sudanese government's failure to protect IDPs in the Western Darfur region as well as in southern Sudan demonstrates a fundamental lack of recognizing the moral principle that IDPs are moral subjects of rights, and ought to enjoy equal legal entitlements in domestic law and policy regardless of race and religion.

As noted in the preceding section, the philosophical and theological analyses of human rights offers the objective moral and legal criteria in effectively dealing with humanitarian crises. The proposition that refugees and IDPs are moral subjects of rights is based not only on the principles of equality and freedom, as stipulated in the Universal Declaration of Human Rights and expressed in the International Bill of Rights, but also on the belief that God is the ultimate foundation and justification of human rights. Biblically inspired Roman Catholic social teaching, inculturated into an African milieu, *cosmotheandrism*, espouses that the human person is at the center of the cosmos because he/she is created in the image and likeness of God, and redeemed in Christ, the proto-ancestor.[8] Bearing in mind that human dignity can be realized in communal solidarity and subsidiarity, formulating effective policies fulfills the demands of *cosmotheandrism*, which is critical to protecting refugees and IDPs, the subjects of rights.

It must be taken into account that the 1951 UN refugee law was adopted to deal with the aftermath of the post–World War II conflict half a century ago. For this reason, there is a need to re-examine and re-evaluate this law to reflect the aftermath of the conflict in post–Cold War Africa. The moral failure to prevent human rights abuses in Rwanda, for example, calls for the necessary reforms in international law and policy as a matter of high priority. Institutional reforms must broaden the legal definition of refugee to include both refugees and IDPs, the subjects of rights, who

---

[7] See Hollenbach, *Claims in Conflict*, 188–89.

[8] See the description of the concept, "Christ, the proto-ancestor," in chapter 4.

are victims of social and economic deprivations as well as internal armed conflicts and political instability in Africa. For the institutional reforms to become a reality, this process should be conducted in a spirit of solidarity and subsidiarity. This means that the international community, in conjunction with UNHCR, should set aside their political differences and geo-strategic interests and adopt a measure to reform international law and policy and officially recognize refugees and IDPs as the moral subjects of rights in the region.

On the regional level, the AU extends legal protection to refugees resulting from social and economic deprivations as well as internal armed conflict and political instability in Africa. IDPs, however, whose number keeps growing due to ongoing-armed conflicts, do not enjoy the same legal protection. Given the scope of humanitarian crises in the Western Darfur region, southern Sudan, and in northern Uganda, heads of state and government, in conjunction with the AU, should *cosmotheandrically* adopt a legislation that considers IDPs as equal subjects of rights in domestic law, and made into an effective policy in the Great Lakes Region of Sub-Saharan Africa.[9]

2. Official recognition that security, subsistence, and liberties of social participation and physical movement are basic rights and ought to enjoy a lexical priority over non-basic rights

It was established that security, subsistence, and liberties of social participation and physical movement are the principal objects of rights because they are necessary to enjoy the substance of rights.[10] The failure of the international community to prevent the 1994 Rwandan genocide demonstrates that security, subsistence, and liberties were not regarded as the principal objects of rights, and thus were not accorded a top moral priority in international law and policy.[11] The scenarios in the Western Darfur region and in southern Sudan demonstrate that these rights were not re-

[9] Take note that the 1969 OAU Refugee Convention is the source of the international regional law and policy for Africa. It may be thought that the phrase, "international law" applies only to a global community. However, in this case, it applies to the African nation-states as well. The word, *cosmotheandrically*, is used to signify a collective action of solidarity. For a detailed account of *cosmotheandrism*, see chapter 4.

[10] See the re-interpretation of basic human rights in international law and policy in section B of chapter 3.

[11] On the question of governments' and the international community's achievements and failure in the Great Lakes Region of Africa, see chapter 2.

garded as the principal objects of rights, and thus were not accorded a top moral priority in domestic legal policy.[12]

Biblically inspired Roman Catholic social teaching, inculturated into African social milieu, *cosmotheandrism*, maintains that basic security, subsistence, and liberties of social participation and physical movement are critical to safeguard human dignity.[13] Acts of torture, arbitrary arrests and intimidation as well sexual abuse and rape fundamentally violate the personal integrity of refugees and IDPs. Basic security rights are essential for the physical and psychological well-being of refugees and IDPs, and basic subsistence rights are essential for ensuring adequate nutrition and safe water, shelter, sanitation, clothing, and education. Hence, freely exercising these basic rights should be accorded a top moral priority in international legal policy, thus overrides state sovereignty.

Since basic security, subsistence, and liberties of social participation and physical movements are a moral priority there is a need to safeguard these rights by establishing internationally recognized standards. Drawing upon the 1969 OAU Refugee Convention, which extends security, subsistence, and liberty of social participation as part of the broader social, economic, and cultural rights, as well as civil and political rights to refugees, efforts must be made to officially recognize these rights in international law and public policy. While the IDPs Guidelines developed by UNHCR are an important step, they are not legally binding for states. This situation calls for internationally binding principles to guarantee the basic rights of IDPs. Hence, making the necessary reforms to recognize these rights both in the 1951 UN Refugee Convention as well as in the 1969 OAU Refugee Convention becomes a high priority in the Great Lakes Region of Africa.

3. *Official recognition of positive and negative duties correlative to basic rights of security, subsistence, and liberties of social participation and physical movement*

In the preceding section, it was established that the official recognition of basic rights is a top moral priority in international law and domestic policy. Forced migrations and humanitarian crises are seen as "a constant attack on essential human rights;"[14] thus fulfilling the duties correlative to

---

[12] For domestic response to humanitarian crises, see chapter 2.

[13] See chapter 4, "Theological Justification of Basic Human Rights," 110–18.

[14] Pontifical Council for the Pastoral Care of Migrants and Itinerant People, *Refugees: A Challenge to Solidarity*, 18 n. 35.

basic rights is a significant step toward restoring human dignity for millions of refugees and IDPs in Africa.[15]

It is worth noting that the priority of basic duties stems from the priority of basic rights. The need to fulfill the moral duties to provide and aid refugees and IDPs is a consequence of governments and social institutions failing in their duties to avoid depriving and to protect from deprivation. For this reason, the moral duties to provide these groups with basic rights ought to be a top moral priority in international law and policy. Because the life of dignity requires not only liberties of forbearance, but also social arrangements and legal guarantees, implementing effectively the duties to aid the displaced becomes the preferential option for the poor. Preventing a catastrophe like the 1994 Rwandan genocide from occurring in the future requires the international community to officially recognize and adopt the objective moral standard of the priority of duties to protect and to provide assistance to the displaced as an integral part of the international law and public policy.

The priority of duties to protect the deprived is relevant on the domestic level as well. The failure of duty to resolve the conflict of rights between state sovereignty and IDPs in Western Darfur region of Sudan is a consequence of the refusal to recognize IDPs priority of rights by the Sudanese government. Therefore, the priority of duty to protect IDPs from attacks by the *Janjaweed* ought to be an integral part of the Sudanese legal policy.

The priority of duties should be recognized in public policy in a lexical order. When they are thus ranked, the most basic needs of refugees and IDPs are taken into account. As shown in chapter 3, the dichotomy between positive and negative rights is no longer considered of primary ethical importance because both positive and negative duties are essential to satisfy positive and negative rights.

Although basic duties correlative to security and subsistence rights have equal legal priority they command differing degrees of urgency when being implemented. The tragic scenarios in chapter 2, illustrate the fact that due to inadequate security in areas of the armed conflict and in refugee camps in northern Uganda and in Sudan Darfur region, IDPs, particularly women and children are victims of torture, exploitation, sexual abuse, and rape. Consequently, insecurity adversely affects their subsistence rights because they are unable to engage in occupations that

---

[15] See the section in chapter 2 titled, "The Nature and Scope of UNHCR and the Global Picture of Refugees and IDPs," 31–35.

sustain their livelihood. Moreover, insecurity debilitates IDPs from exercising freedom of physical movement, which is needed to search for food, firewood, water, or work outside the camps. Therefore, officially recognizing basic duties to security rights should be accorded first priority both in international and domestic policy for refugees and IDPs in the Great Lakes Region of Africa.

It was argued that security and subsistence rights are closely interrelated.[16] Adequate security allows refugees and IDPs to engage in self-help projects such as farming, health, water, and education programs. Adequate security allows humanitarian agencies and human rights groups to bring relief supplies to the affected populations and monitor the living conditions of refugees and IDPs in these areas. These measures alleviate malnutrition and prevent disease and deaths among refugees and IDPs, particularly children, women, and the elderly. Therefore, basic duties to subsistence rights should be accorded second priority in international and domestic policy, and be officially recognized as such.

Fulfilling the duty of liberties of social participation and physical movement creates an environment that enables refugees and IDPs to exercise security and subsistence rights by becoming actively involved in leadership roles in camps. This strategy breaks the traditional African barrier of gender inequality, and empowers women to become active participants in the social, economic, cultural, and political life in camps.[17] Therefore, basic duties to participatory rights should be officially recognized as an integral part of effectively enjoying basic security and subsistence rights in the region.

The analyses of human rights illumines short, medium, and long-term solutions to humanitarian crises in the region. It was established in chapter 3 that the duty to provide and aid the deprived is a result of double failure of the duty to avoid depriving, and the duty to protect from deprivation. On the one hand, international humanitarian assistance is seen as a short-term strategy to resolve the conflict of rights by overriding state sovereignty. On the other hand, recognizing the duty to avoid depriving basic rights prevents future humanitarian crises like those caused by the Hutu government sponsored *Interahamwe* in the 1994 Rwandan genocide as well as the Sudanese government sponsored *Janjaweed* in the Western Darfur region of Sudan. Therefore, officially recognizing the duty to avoid

---

[16] See chapter 3, section B, 77–97.

[17] For a detailed account of the success story of satisfying subsistence rights in the Tanzanian refugee camps, see chapter 2.

depriving basic rights by governments and social institutions should be an integral component of the domestic policy for the Great Lakes Region of Africa.

The duties to avoid depriving are considered universal,[18] so recognizing these duties is not confined only to national governments and their social institutions. Rather, as the world becomes increasingly global and interdependent it is critical to recognize these duties by implementing the principles of solidarity and subsidiarity rooted in *cosmotheandrism*. When foreign governments and international institutions interfere with the internal affairs of states it leads to political instability and threatens basic security, subsistence, and social participation of citizens.[19] Trading in diamonds, gold, uranium, and oil for arms with oppressive regimes or rebel groups demonstrates the failure of duty of non-interference by nations, which contribute significantly to violence, armed conflicts, and civil wars, and leads to political instability in the Great Lakes Region of Africa. The bill passed by the U.S. House of Representatives in April 2003 to ban the import and export of diamonds, which may sponsor conflicts and terrorism, is a crucial step in the right direction. Implementing this bill is seen as a demonstration of non-interference, and thus promotes justice and peace in Africa in general, and in the Great Lakes Region in particular.[20] Officially recognizing the duty of non-interference with internal affairs of states should be an integral part of international and domestic policy for Africa. At the same time, international assistance aimed at strengthening the capacity of states to effectively promote social, economic, and political rights should be encouraged.[21] In the long-term, ratifying the UN Covenants on Social, Economic, and Cultural Rights as well as Civil and Political Rights remains an effective way of recognizing basic rights of security, subsistence, and social participation.[22]

---

[18] See the section of chapter 3 titled "The Bearers of Correlative Duties," 88–91.

[19] See Shue, *Basic Rights*, 161.

[20] Associated Press, "Bill Bans Blood Diamond," A5.

[21] Shue, *Basic Rights*, 163.

[22] See a detailed discussion by Shue, *Basic Rights*, 155–61. The U.S. Government, for example, ratified the UN Covenant on Civil and Political Rights in 1992. However, the UN Covenant on Social, Economic, and Cultural Rights is yet to be ratified. For a detailed account of this question, see, "U.S. Finally Ratifies," accessed 10/22/2004. China signed the UN Covenant on Civil and Political Rights. In 2001, China ratified the UN Covenant on Social, Economic, and Cultural Rights. For further information, see "EU-China Network," accessed 10/22/2004.

To eliminate or minimize the essential and systematic deprivations of basic rights, national governments must design effective and sustainable institutions that can prevent humanitarian crises. Bearing in mind that marginalization polarizes societies from enjoying civil liberties, implementing the duty of equal social participation in political life is key to exercising basic security and subsistence rights. When all citizens are allowed to participate in society humanitarian crises such as those occurring in the Western Darfur region, Rwanda, Uganda, and others, can be prevented. Shue remarks, "It is not possible to enjoy full rights to security or subsistence without also having rights to participate effectively in the control of security and subsistence."[23] To Shue, the emphasis of civil liberties on "effective participation" affects individual choices and bears on the operations of fundamental social institutions and policies and the control of these on security and subsistence.[24] In exercising effective social participation, civil liberties should be viewed as generating both positive and negative duties. Democratic institutions where social participation is practiced bear three kinds of duties: the duties to refrain from interference, the duties to protect from interference and the "duties to assist persons to make use of their civil liberties in certain ways that can achieve certain ends."[25]

Since it was argued that basic liberties and political democracy are intimately connected, political democracy is justified on the basis of enjoying equal social participation.[26] It was argued in chapter 1 that colonial legacy and bad governance contribute to political instability and economic stagnation. The introduction of multi-party democracy in Africa in 1980's is believed to have failed partly due to an inadequate consideration of the African social milieu. A pragmatic approach to democracy in the African continent, particularly the Great Lakes Region, must consider important principles of solidarity and subsidiarity rooted in *cosmotheandrism*, with its great emphasis on active involvement of the local intermediate institutions. The Burundian local council of elders known as *Ubushingantahe*, and the Rwandan reconciliatory courts known as *gacaca* demonstrate this approach.[27] Blending modern democracy with African indigenous politi-

---

[23] Shue, *Basic Rights*, 71.

[24] Ibid.

[25] Also see Gewirth, *Community of Rights*, 337.

[26] Ibid.

[27] The term, *elders*, in Africa connotes a group of people who are regarded as being wise and endowed with the ability to lead others in community. For a person to be called an *elder*, he or she has to undergo a particular rite of initiation in leadership responsibility. The meaning of the Rwandan reconciliatory courts, *gacaca,* will be explained later in the up-

cal institutions remains, in the long-term, a durable solution to violence and conflicts, and can prevent future humanitarian crises in the region.[28] Therefore, recognizing *cosmotheandric* models of political institutions should be an integral part of the international and domestic policy for the Great Lakes Region of Africa.

4. Moral responsibility assigned to the international community as a bearer of the duties to aid and to provide refugees and IDPs with basic rights ought to be officially recognized and enforced

To understand the position of refugees and IDPs, the subject of rights, in international law and policy the assigned moral responsibilities correlative to basic rights must be taken into account. As seen in the preceding section, duties correlative to basic rights ought to be officially recognized in both international and domestic policy. Implementing these duties requires the communal solidarity of the international community. This section focuses on the moral responsibility assigned to the international community including religious institutions.

SOLIDARITY OF SECULAR COMMUNITY: INTERNATIONAL COMMUNITY AND INSTITUTIONS

As argued in the preceding section the failure of the duty to avoid depriving and the failure of the duty to protect the most vulnerable from deprivation generate the duty to aid and provide the deprived. In principle, this moral responsibility does not fall upon isolated individuals, but rather, it rests with the international community, particularly when there are essential and systematic deprivations of human rights.[29] Because personal rights are essentially social rights, basic rights of refugees and IDPs are satisfied in communal solidarity and subsidiarity, *cosmotheandrism*.

Protecting refugees and IDPs according to equal dignity is an ethical criterion for evaluating the international and domestic legal policy.[30] Preventing moral failure similar to the 1994 Rwandan genocide requires establishing a new sustainable international order. When other appropriate means are exhausted, the moral principle of the duty to provide and

coming section on "Solidarity of Religious Community: Church and Others," 164–67.

[28] The lack of social participation in political life contributes to humanitarian crises as demonstrated in chapter 1. A rediscovery of the intermediate institutions will help bring about social participation at the grass-root levels.

[29] See chapter 3, "The Bearer of Correlative Basic Duties," 102–6.

[30] See the unequal treatment of women in the Tanzanian judicial court system in chapter 2.

aid IDPs and refugees becomes the basis for international humanitarian assistance.[31] Implementing the moral principle by the international community becomes the sole strategy for avoiding inconsistency and double standards in international law and policy. Therefore, the moral responsibility assigned to the international community should be officially recognized in international law and policy, and enforced through the UN. International solidarity is needed to aid and provide refugees and IDPs, and the material and financial contributions by governments, NGOs, international aid agencies as well as religious institutions are vital for this to happen. The shortfall of US $407,952,974 reflected in the 2004 UNHCR budget report of US $1,177,488,731 showed that the number of contributors (countries and private organizations) dropped from 94 in 2003 (US $957,093,313) to 66 in 2004 (US $769,535,757). These financial crises demonstrate the need for an improvement in international cooperation.[32] Moreover, the persistent conflicts and protracted wars contribute to the financial crises facing the UNHCR, and affect the quality of life in camps.

It was argued that it is unfair to provide security to property rights while subsistence rights are unprotected.[33] When this occurs, extreme inequalities are not addressed and the dignity of refugees and IDPs becomes degraded. Private donations and charities are inadequate to provide the Great Lakes of Africa with the necessary financial assistance. Effective social arrangements and legal guarantees through taxation are appropriate to maintain a fair share of moral responsibility for providing refugees and IDPs with subsistence rights in the region. The least that can be demanded from affluent nations, institutions, and private individuals fulfill their moral duty is to surrender or relinquish their non-basic rights to satisfy the basic rights of refugees and IDPs. However, going an extra mile by giving

---

[31] Take note of the shift in the order, which provides priority to IDPs over refugees by considering IDPs the immediate beneficiary of the international humanitarian assistance. IDPs do not have legal status in international refugee law, and thus are most vulnerable to human rights violations by governments or rebel groups. Refugees, being the direct beneficiaries of the international legal system, have an advantage over IDPs because they can seek asylum in a third country when the host country experiences conflicts or violence. For this reason, IDPs ought to be the first beneficiary of the international humanitarian assistance.

[32] See the 2004 UNHCR financial requirements for Africa in chapter 2. Inadequate resources are partly to blame for poorly trained security forces and court personnel in the Tanzanian refugee camps described in chapter 2, "Security Rights" and "Subsistence Rights."

[33] See the section of chapter 3 titled "The Bearers of Correlative Duties," 88–91, as well as section C of the same chapter, "The Justification of Human Rights," 106.

away basic rights to satisfy those of refugees and IDPs is regarded as *kenotic heroism*. Moreover, duties to aid refugees and IDPs are considered transnational; hence restitutive justice demands that governments and social institutions that are complicit in regional conflicts become more cooperative by generously providing humanitarian assistance to the people that are being displaced.[34]

Although the moral responsibility to protect and aid refugees and IDPs may seem too ambitious, burdensome, and unrealistic to implement, one must bear in mind that the recognition of human rights is a major breakthrough, resolving a fundamental hermeneutical question of great moral significance in international law and public policy. The tragedy in Rwanda can be directly attributed to the narrow interpretation of rights (the subject, the object, the nature, the bearers of correlative duties, as well as the justification of rights) in international law and policy. The moral responsibility assigned to governments, social institutions, and the international community regarding the crises in the Great Lakes Region of Africa is clarified when the priority of duties correlative to basic rights are officially recognized.

A transition from theory to ortho-praxis is often cumbersome, and thus requires the active participation of all stakeholders in the international community. Implementing the principles of communal solidarity and subsidiarity by which governments, NGO's, as well as private agencies and religions organizations should *cosmotheandrically* participate in providing and aiding refugees and IDPs in the Great Lakes Region of Africa is the most critical aspect of this transition.[35]

SOLIDARITY OF RELIGIOUS COMMUNITY: CHURCH AND OTHERS

Considering that the concept of human dignity is the leitmotif of the Roman Catholic social teaching, aiding refugees and IDPs becomes a pastoral challenge for the Church in Africa.[36] Moreover, the 1994 Synod of Bishops for Africa affirmed that liberation of the whole person is constitutive of the Church mission as *family of God*. Therefore, as part of the international community, the Church, the community of rights, should

---

[34] It is argued in chapter 1 that external forces such as colonialism and neo-colonialism, as well as the Cold War politics contribute to forced migrations and humanitarian crises in the Great Lakes Region of Sub-Saharan Africa.

[35] In this case, the term, "*cosmotheandrically*," is used to signify interdependence of duties and collective responsibility.

[36] See Pontifical Council for Pastoral Care of Migrants and Itinerant People. *Refugees: A Challenge for Solidarity*, 15 no. 25.

be active in the duty of aiding refugees and IDPs. The reality of the *family of God,* through which the Church becomes a living witness to Christian discipleship and exemplary to government and social institutions, is demonstrated through the solidarity of love, compassion, and care for refugees and IDPs. However, when the Church becomes part of the social and political establishment in which it operates its credibility is compromised, putting the prophetic mission of defending the basic rights of refugees and IDPs in jeopardy.[37]

In 2000, the 14th AMECEA Plenary adopted a theme, *Deeper Evangelization in the Third Millennium,* which advocates for a profound commitment of the preferential option for the poor, particularly refugees and IDPs. This is a theme that should be translated into concrete deeds. In light of Christian solidarity of love, commitment to protecting and aiding refugees and IDPs falls upon the local Church. First, personal contact with refugees and IDPs, demonstrated by the AMECEA Bishops' delegation to IDPs camps in Sudan, should be encouraged. Second, action for defending the rights of refugees and IDPs should be encouraged, as should denouncing violence, revenge, and conflicts that perpetuate humanitarian crises. One of the effective ways of doing this is issuing pastoral letters to the general public and using the media to disseminate information about refugees and IDPs. Forming and empowering the *Justice and Peace Commission* at all Church levels encourages active participation for the defense and promotion of basic rights.[38] Third, the Church ought to lobby for the necessary legal reforms and encourage national governments to adopt effective public policy; that with support from the AU and UN would be effective in guaranteeing their protection. Fourth, bearing in mind that tribalism, ethnocentrism, sexism, religious sectarianism, as well as racism are at the root of humanitarian crises, the Church should continue in its effort to advocate for education against xenophobia. Fifth, the Church should work with local and international aid organizations to create groups of volunteers and establish emergency funds and gather material resources, which will support and supplement the efforts of UNHCR. Sixth, efforts should be made to provide pastoral counseling for the victims of violence and

---

[37] Dorr, *Mission in Today's World*, 157. In 1994, some Catholic leaders in Rwanda were accused of directly becoming involved or being complicit in the genocide. This allegation paints a gloomy picture of the Church, and affects its credibility in the country.

[38] See Resolutions 69 and 70 of the 2002 AMECEA 14th Plenary in *AFER* 44 (2002) 283–84.

persecution, particularly women and children suffering from trauma and loss of self-esteem.[39]

Based on the global nature and scope of the humanitarian crises, commitment for aiding refugees and IDPs should be carried out ecumenically.[40] This effort will be an invitation to people of all faiths to participate in protecting victims of human rights abuses. Implementing the principles of solidarity and subsidiarity requires Catholics and non-Catholics, Christian and non-Christian to share their experiences, knowledge, resources, wisdom and expertise to aid the good cause of promoting basic rights. Implementing this ecumenical spirit helps protect and promote basic rights of security, subsistence, and social participation, and thereby providing refugees and IDPs in the Great Lakes Region of Africa with comfort, hope, and optimism.[41]

It was seen in chapter 4 that fostering solidarity and subsidiarity among governments, international organizations, and religious institutions brings about liberation of refugees and IDPs from essential and systematic deprivations of basic rights. As a necessary pre-condition for achieving holistic liberation from these deprivations, and as an essential part of the biblically inspired notion of justice not only is restitution needed; but also forgiveness, reconciliation, and peace.[42] Conflict resolution of basic rights of refugees and IDPs, through the principle of justice, is an important step toward achieving peace and political stability in the region. This strategy, however, does not go far enough to eradicate hatred, revenge, and resentments that lead to humanitarian crises.[43] Forgiveness (of both personal and social sin) and reconciliation will, in the long-term, put to rest the humanitarian crises in the Great Lakes Region of Africa. This process implies that "both the victim and oppressor must acknowledge the evil that has occurred. Only then can they reach out to each other in complete honesty and openness to be reconciled."[44]

Nevertheless, one must bear in mind that genuine reconciliation is a gift and grace from God by which a change of heart by both op-

---

[39] See Pontifical Council for Migrants and Itinerant People, *Refugees: A Challenge to Solidarity*, 15 no. 26.

[40] Ibid., 17–18 no. 34.

[41] Ibid., 18 no. 37.

[42] See Gutierrez, *We Drink from Our Own Wells*, 92. Also see the spirituality of liberation theology in chapter 4.

[43] Dorr, *Mission in Today's World*, 129.

[44] Ibid., 132. For a discussion regarding various aspects of reconciliation, namely the religious, the psychological and the political, see Dorr, *Mission in Today's World*, 131–43.

pressor and victim becomes a reality as reminded by the 2002 SECAM Plenary Session in its theme, *Christ Our Peace: The Church as Family of God, Place and Sacrament of Reconciliation.*[45] To put in place an effective mechanism through which the grace of God can be experienced leads to a successful process of reconciliation and healing. The South African Truth and Reconciliation Commission under the leadership of the Archbishop Desmond Tutu demonstrated this approach. As a way of implementing the African solidarity and subsidiarity, *cosmotheandrism,* the Rwandan Government has adopted a traditional model of settling disputes through *gacaca.*[46] This model plays a significant role in resolving conflicts among Rwandans, leading to reconciliation between Tutsis and Hutus.[47] Models similar to *gacaca* and *Ubushingantahe* should be established and promoted by the Church in the AMECEA region and beyond to bring about holistic liberation, and thus prevent future humanitarian crises. Therefore, promoting these *cosmotheandric* models becomes a strategy to implement the AMECEA plenary theme, *"Deeper Evangelization in the Third Millennium," for the Great Lakes Region of Sub-Saharan Africa.*[48]

Conclusion

An inadequate interpretation of human rights in international law and domestic policy as well as insufficient or the lack of political good will

[45] See a detailed account of the 2000 SECAM Plenary in chapter 4. With regard to the emphasis made on the relationship between reconciliation and grace, see Uwe, "Together We Have a Future," 28. Christine Uwe states, "There was a time when a South Africa open to all in a spirit of dignity and equality was nothing more than a utopia. Today that utopia has become flesh and blood. In our opinion we cannot evade the effort, but, at the same time, we need an attitude of waiting, of availability-dare we say-of grace."

[46] Through *gacaca* the Rwandan Government tries to encourage those who committed atrocities during the genocide to come forward and speak up in the presence of the victims or their families. It must be noted, however, that *gacaca* can only handle small-scale crimes and it does not in any way replace "The International Tribunal for Rwanda" in Arusha, Tanzania, which is responsible for prosecuting the ringleaders and their accomplices in the genocide.

[47] For a detailed description of the reconciliation method, *gacaca,* see Kamanzi, "Reconciliation?" 20–21.

[48] See AMECEA Delegates, "Deeper Evangelization," 264. The countries of Rwanda, Burundi, and D.R. Congo in the Great Lakes Region do not belong to the *Association of Member Episcopal Conferences in Eastern Africa (AMECEA).* Its members include Sudan, Ethiopia, Eritrea, Kenya, Uganda, Tanzania, Malawi, and Zambia. Since the humanitarian crises of refugees and IDPs affect all countries in the region either because they generate refugees or host them, the Church in AMECEA region can contribute to resolving conflicts by fostering solidarity with the Church in Rwanda, Burundi, and D.R. Congo, and others.

contribute significantly to the failure of governments, social institutions, and the international community to effectively respond to humanitarian crises in the Great Lakes Region of Africa. The critique deriving from Shue's theory of basic rights provides governments, social institutions, and the international community with objective moral criteria for effectively responding to the crises. Biblically inspired Catholic social teaching, inculturated into an African social milieu, *cosmotheandrism*, provides adequate grounding for the justification of human rights. This approach eventually leads to establish a set of moral priorities as the basis of public policy of refugees and IDPs for the region.

By implementing moral priorities, the moral failure is redressed, and thus the basic rights of refugees and IDPs are effectively protected and promoted. These moral priorities are:

First, refugees and IDPs are the moral subjects of rights and they ought to enjoy equal legal entitlements. Second, basic rights of security, subsistence, and liberties of social participation and physical movement are the principal objects of rights, and they ought to enjoy moral and legal priority over non-basic rights. Third, considering that the human person is an indivisible whole, positive and negative duties are essential to exercising basic rights. Fourth, the international community, in conjunction with UNHCR, governments, NGO's, the Church, and international aid agencies, is the final bearer of the duty to protect and provide assistance to refugees and IDPs.

Implementing these moral priorities illumines short, medium, and long-term solutions to the humanitarian crises. Employing international humanitarian assistance resolves, in the short-term, conflict of rights between refugees and IDPs, and state sovereignty, or geo-strategic interests, *Realpolitik*. Designing effective and sustainable government institutions provides, in the long-term, social participation of all citizens in political life, and thus prevents violence, conflicts, and civil wars. While social participation is an integral part of preventing the crises, non-interference with internal affairs of states is regarded as a medium-term strategy to prevent them.

Finally, successful implementation of these priorities requires a holistic liberation from both the personal and social sin for achieving forgiveness, reconciliation, and promoting justice, and peace in the Great Lakes Region of Sub-Saharan Africa.

General Conclusion

POLITICAL persecution, armed conflicts, and civil wars that have rocked countries of the Great Lakes Region of Sub-Saharan Africa are a manifestation of social disorder. The devastating effect of the violence is illustrated by the unprecedented humanitarian catastrophe of the 1994 Rwandan genocide that caused deaths, homelessness, despair, poverty, political instability, and economic stagnation in this country. In the aftermath of this catastrophe, governments and the international community realized that timely intervention is essential for saving lives. The response to the humanitarian crises in both the south and the Western Darfur region of Sudan, although falling short of what is needed, is a result of governments' and the international community's awareness created by the genocide in Rwanda. Ultimately, however, the only way to resolve current conflicts and prevent humanitarian crises in the future is to find the root causes of conflict; an approach that previously has not been adequately used. This study underscores the importance of the concept of basic human rights in international law and public policy and its contribution in addressing the plight of refugees and IDPs, and restoring justice and peace in the region. The study was undertaken to provide short, medium, and long-term solutions to the humanitarian crises in the region.

The root causes of humanitarian crises in the Great Lakes Region of Sub-Saharan Africa were the focus of chapter 1. Contrary to the oversimplified view that internal factors are solely to blame for the crises, the study reveals that conflicts, violence, and civil wars triggering humanitarian crises are a product of multi-faceted phenomena and are closely interrelated. For example, both tribalism and colonialism contributed to the 1994 Rwandan genocide. The crises in Sudan illustrate interrelations between politics, race, and religion. It was demonstrated that finding the solution to multi-dimensional problems requires a multi-dimensional approach. In other words, finding the root causes, rather than treating the symptoms, is the right course towards a durable solution to the problems of the humanitarian crises of refugees and IDPs in Africa.

The focus of chapter 2 was governments' and the international community's humanitarian response to the crises in the Great Lakes Region of Africa. It was established that, because refugees and IDPs are orphans of the state system, they are vulnerable to human rights abuses, and thus have the strongest moral claims for adequate protection by governments and international community. Under the umbrella of UNHCR, refugees and IDPs are provided with some security, subsistence, and liberties of active social participation and physical movement. Ensuring active participation of refugees and IDPs in exercising security and subsistence rights is the key to improving the standards of living in camps. Despite the achievements, however, the failure of governments and the international community to adequately provide security, subsistence, and liberty generated human rights' abuses of refugees and IDPs in the region, particularly women and children.

Chapter 3 addressed the failure of governments and the international community and offered a critical assessment of the interpretation of human rights of refugees and IDPs in international law and public policy. It was demonstrated in this chapter that a major factor in the poor or the lack of response to the humanitarian crises in the Great Lakes Region of Africa is an inadequate understanding of human rights of refugees and IDPs in international law. The manner in which governments and the international community responded to the humanitarian crises demonstrates major legal and moral limitations in interpreting the subject, the object, the nature, the respondent of rights, and the justification of human rights in international refugee law and public policy. Refugee law as stated in the 1951 UN Geneva Convention and its 1967 Protocol illustrates this shortcoming. Under this law, refugees and IDPs in Africa are not fully recognized as moral subjects and therefore, are not guaranteed equal social and economic rights and civil and political rights. They are not considered to be a top priority in international law and domestic policy because of this oversight, so assigning bearer of correlative duties to protect and provide assistance to these groups is fundamentally lacking. This inadequate interpretation of human rights of refugees and IDPs partly explains the cause of the failure by governments and the international community in effectively responding to the humanitarian tragedy as the scenario of the 1994 Rwandan genocide demonstrates. From the standpoint of philosophical ethics of human rights, such situations raise serious moral and legal concerns, and thus provide a rationale for developing a reinterpretation of human rights in international law and public policy for refugees and IDPs in the Great Lakes Region of Sub-Saharan Africa.

Re-interpreting human rights in international law and public policy from the standpoint of Shue's theory of basic human rights is considered under the formal elements of the subject, the object, the nature, the respondents of correlative duties, as well as the justification of rights. This analysis provides the international law and public policy with objective ethical standards to redress the failure of governments and the international community, and thus promotes the basic human rights of refugees and IDPs in the region. Shue's concept of the priority of basic human rights and their correlative duties of avoiding depriving (negative), protecting from deprivation (positive), and providing for the deprived (positive) is morally significant in dealing with the moral concerns raised by the failure of governments and the international community in the region. The governments' failure in the duty to avoid depriving and the duty to protect from deprivation generates a corresponding moral and legal responsibility for the international community to protect and to provide refugees and IDPs with basic rights of security, subsistence and social participation. The priority of the duty to protect and the duty to provide these groups with basic human rights overrides state's sovereignty and territorial integrity. When displaced people are considered as moral subjects of rights, their equal legal protection is guaranteed through international law and public policy; thus the moral failure of governments and the international community is redressed. Fulfilling this moral and legal priority demands governments and the international community design effective social arrangements and legal guarantees to eliminate essential and systematic deprivations of social, economic, and civil-political rights. Unlike the 1951 UN Refugee Geneva Convention, the 1969 OAU Refugee Convention is a regional institutional model that extends the social and economic rights, as well as civil-political rights to refugees in Africa. However, both conventions share a common shortcoming; they do not extend these rights to IDPs on a legal basis. IDPs ought to be recognized as human moral subjects and enjoy equal basic rights of security, subsistence, and liberties of active social participation and physical movement under both conventions.

In general, the question of whether or not humans have basic human rights is not a highly contested issue. What is highly contested, however, is the moral criterion for the justification of human rights in international law and policy. It must be noted that Shue does not offer an independent criterion for the justification of rights. Shue, however, tackles the question of the justification of rights in the context of the priority of basic rights and correlative duties. Shue believes that humans are dignified objects of honor and respect. Shue, therefore, argues that extreme inequalities are morally unacceptable because they are degrading to human dignity. Shue's principle of degrading prohibition, aimed at redressing extreme inequalities, is regarded as the justification of basic human rights. Although Shue believes that, from philosophical ethics of rights, the "degradation prohibition principle" promotes equality and dignity of the human person, Shue does not offer grounding for human dignity. In order to address the lacunae of Shue's argument, the theological justification of human rights was offered in the next chapter.

In chapter 4, support for the theological justification of basic human rights of refugees and IDPs from the perspective of modern Roman Catholic social teaching, inculturated into an African social milieu, *cosmotheandrism,* was offered. The *imago Dei* that was tainted by original sin has been redeemed through the person of Christ, the proto-ancestor, and the image of the invisible God, par excellence. As a reflection of the Holy Trinity, human dignity or sacredness can only be effectively realized in community through the principles of communal solidarity and subsidiarity. Based on the biblically inspired notion of justice, *sedaqah,* the quality of human relationship is measured by how faithfully we are committed to the cause of refuges and IDPs. Hence, it is a moral imperative that refugees and IDPs are accorded the respect and consideration that corresponds to human dignity. Because the human person is an indivisible whole, understanding the interrelation, unity, and interdependence of basic human rights is required, as expressed by the African model of communal solidarity and subsidiarity, *cosmotheandrism.* Thus, the dichotomy between positive and negative rights is no longer of primary importance because social and economic rights, as well as civil and political rights demand positive and negative duties.

In light of the concepts of creation and redemption, refuges and IDPs are considered moral subjects entitled with equal basic rights. As victims of essential and systematic deprivation of basic human rights, refugees and IDPs, particularly women and children, are most vulnerable to human rights' abuses. Hence, the priority of duty to protect and the duty to provide refugees and IDPs with basic human rights of security, subsistence, and liberties of active social participation and physical movement through international refugee law is the preferential option for the poor.

Rooted in the biblically inspired notion of justice, the principles of communal solidarity and subsidiarity, *cosmotheandrism,* demands compassion and love by having in place effective social arrangements and legal guarantees. Governments, social institutions, and the international community cooperating to protect and provide refugees and IDPs with basic human rights becomes an expression of love for neighbor. Most importantly, social justice demands that refugees and IDPs be given equal opportunity to actively participate in community, and thus contribute to the common good. To do so, the principle of subsidiarity demands that these groups actively participate in public life by freely exercising social, economic, and civil-political rights without unnecessary intervention or interference from governments, social institutions, individuals, and the international community.

Chapter 5 offers four fundamental moral priorities that can be demanded of governments, social institutions, and the international community, and thus become the basis of evaluating public policy for refugees and IDPs in the Great Lakes Region of Africa. First, the official recognition of refugees and IDPs, the moral subject of rights, aims at guaranteeing their equal legal entitlement. Second, the official recognition of basic security, subsistence, and liberties of social participation and physical movement, the principal objects of rights, places legal priority of these rights over non-basic rights. Third, the official recognition of priority of positive and negative duties demands that social arrangements and legal guarantees are essential for exercising basic rights to security, subsistence, and liberties of social participation and physical movement. Fourth, in the spirit of solidarity and subsidiarity, *cosmotheandrism*, the official recognition that the international community, in conjunction with UNHCR, governments, NGOs, private organizations, as well as the Church, is the final bearer of correlative duties to protect and aid refugees and IDPs, provides the moral and legal legitimacy for international humanitarian intervention as a last resort. This priority aims at resolving conflict of rights between refugees and IDPs, and state sovereignty, national security, or geo-political interests.

Moreover, the analyses of basic human rights offer not only effective strategies for resolving conflict of rights, but also offer the prevention of humanitarian crises in the region. Implementing the duties of non-interference with internal affairs of states is seen as essential for preventing the prevailing crises. Furthermore, non-interference with exercising basic rights is not only confined to foreign governments and institutions, but also to national governments and institutions. Designing effective and sustainable social institutions are seen as essential for civilian populations to exercise civil liberties rooted in *cosmotheandric* model of African political organizations. Provision of equal opportunity for the civilian populations to participate in political life minimizes tribalism, ethnocentrism, sexism, racism, religious sectarianism, and totalitarianism, and thus prevents conflicts, forced migrations, and humanitarian crises in the Great Lakes Region of Africa.

Bear in mind that this study is not intended to solve every problem related to refugees and IDPs in the region. On the one hand, the study underscores the importance of recognizing basic human rights of refugees and IDPs in international law and public policy. This recognition remains critical for governments, social institutions, and the international community to effectively deal with humanitarian crises, and thus promotes human dignity in the Great Lakes Region of Sub-Saharan Africa.

On the other hand, a successful implementation of these strategies requires a holistic liberation of both the personal and social sin. Victims of human rights abuses and their perpetrators are called upon to make a change of heart and embrace each other as children of God, who are created in his image and likeness and redeemed in Christ, the proto-ancestor.

Bibliography

Achermann, Eduard. *Cry Beloved Africa: A Continent Needs Help*. Kinshasa: African University Studies, 1994.

"African [Banjul] Charter on Human and Peoples' Rights." In *Africa's Refugee Crisis*, translated by Michael John, 137–41. London: Zed, 1986.

"African Charter on Human and Peoples' Rights." University of Minnesota Human Rights Library. http://wwwl.umn.edu/humanrts/instree/ratz1afrchar.htm. Accessed 12/9/2004 and 12/20/2004.

African Exodus: Refugee Crisis, Human Rights and the 1969 OAU Convention. New York: Lawyers Committee for Human Rights, 1995.

"African Refugees Face Severe Food Shortages." International Refugee Committee. http://www.intrescom.org/index.cfm?section+news&wwwwID=1663. Accessed 5/9/2003.

AMECEA Delegates. "Deeper Evangelization in the New Millennium: A Challenge for AMECEA." AMECEA Fourteenth Plenary. *AFER* 44 (December 2002).

———. "In Solidarity with a Church under Persecution." *AFER* 44 (2002) 125–52.

Amewowo, Wynnand. "The Poor of Yahweh, the Poor of the Messiah." In *Towards African Christian Maturity*, edited by A. Shorter, J. M. Waliggo, and A. Amewowo. Nairobi: St. Paul Publication Africa, 1992.

Arrupe, Pedro. *The Refugee Crisis in Africa: Opportunity and Challenge for the Church*. A Survey Undertaken for the VI SECAM General Assembly in Younde, Cameroon, June 28–July 6, 1968. Rome: Privately Printed, 1981.

Associated Press. "Bill Bans Blood Diamond." *San Francisco Chronicle*. April 9, 2003, A5.

Baitu, Juvenalis. "Christian Ethical Principles and Societal Problems in Sub-Saharan Africa." *ACS* 15 (1999) 1–16.

———. *The Covenant as the Foundation of the Old Testament Morality*. Moral Theology Series 1. Nairobi: The Catholic University of Eastern Africa, 2000.

"Basic Facts." In *Refugees by Numbers, 2004* (2003 edition). http://www.unhcr.ch/cgibin/texis/vtx/basics/+AwwBmeLqZw_ww. Accessed 7/11/2004.

"Basic Facts, Sunday, February 1, 2004." http://www.unhcr.ch?cgibin/texis/vtx/basics/+DwwBm7ewAbdwww. Accessed 1/31/2004.

Blakley, Mike. "Somalia, Case Preview." http://www.unhcr.ch/cgi-bin/texis/vtx/basics/+AwwBmeLqZw_ww. Accessed 7/11/2004.

Bloomer, David R. "Violence in the Congo: A Perspective on United Nations' Peacekeeping." http://http://www.globalsecurity.org/military/library/report/1984/BDR.htm. Accessed 9/20/2004.

Bujo, Benezet. *The Communal Dimension of the Community: The African Model and the Dialogue between North and South*. Nairobi: Paulines Publications Africa, 1997.

———. *Foundations of an African Ethic: Beyond the Universal Claims of Western Morality*. Translated by Brian McNeil. New York: Crossroad, 2000.

Bulcha, Mekuria. "Historical, Political and Social Causes of Mass Flight from Ethiopia." In *Refugees and Development in Africa*, edited by Peter Nobel, 19–36. Uppsala: Scandinavian Institute of African Studies, 1987.

———. "Sociological and Economic Factors in Refugee Integration: The Case of Ethiopian Exiles in the Sudan." In *Refugees and Development in Africa*, edited by Peter Nobel, 73–90. Uppsala: Scandinavian Institute of African Studies, 1987.

"Burundian Women Abused in Tanzanian Refugee Camp." *World Report*. September 28, 1999. Human Rights Watch. http://www.afrol.com/categories/women/wom004_refugee. Accessed 3/16/2003.

Cahill, Lisa S. "Toward A Christian Theory of Human Rights." *JRE* 8 (1990) 277–96.

Carens, Joseph H. "States and Refugees: A Normative Analysis." In *Refugee Policy: Canada and the United States*, edited by Howard Adelman, 18–29. Toronto: Centre for Refugee Studies, York University, 1999.

Casperson, Pia. "Impoverished Tanzania Still Bears Heavy Refugee Burden." January 10, 2003. http://www.reliefweb.int/rwb.nsf/9ca659/ee22658ecl12566300408599/4e0a. Accessed 3/16/2003.

Catechism of the Catholic Church. Washington. D. C.: United States Catholic Conference, 1994.

"Chronology of U.S/U.N Actions: 100 Days of Slaughter." *Frontline*. http://www.pbs.org/wgbh/pages/frontline/shows/evil/etc/slaugher.html. Accessed 2/12/2004.

"Convention against Torture and Other Cruel, Inhuman or Degrading Treatment or Punishment." A/Res/39/46, 10 Dec. 1984. In *The United Nations and Human Rights: 1945–1995*. 151–53. United Nations Blue Book Series iv.vii. New York: United Nations Department of Public Information, 1995.

Crüsemann, Frank. "You Know the Heart of a Stranger (Exodus 23.9). A Reconciliation of the Torah in the Face of New Nationalism and Xenophobia." In *Migrants and Refugees*, edited by Dietmar Mieth and Lisa Cahill, 95–109. Concilium. Maryknoll, NY: Orbis, 1993.

Curran, Charles E. *Catholic Social Teaching 1891–present: A Historical, Theological, and Ethical Analysis*. Washington D.C.: Georgetown University Press, 2002.

Donahue, John R. *What Does the Lord Require?: A Bibliographical Essay on the Bible and Social Justice*. St. Louis: Institute of Jesuit Sources, 1993.

"Donors/Partners, Sunday, March 21, 2004." http://www.unhcr.ch/cgi-bin/texis/vtx/partners/+wwFqzvK+vx856x. Accessed 3/20/2004.

Donors/Partners, "Situation as of June 25, 2004." http://www.unhcr.ch/cgibin/texis/vtx/home/opendoc.htm. Accessed 8/4/2004.

Donnelly, Jack. *Universal Human Rights: In Theory and Practice*. 2d ed. Ithaca: Cornell University Press, 2003.

Donnelly, John. "Government, Rebels Sign Peace Agreement." *San Francisco Chronicle*, May 27, 2004, A23.

Dorr, Donal. *Option for the Poor: A Hundred Years of Catholic Social Teaching*. Maryknoll, NY: Orbis, 1983.

———. *Mission in Today's World*. Maryknoll, NY: Orbis, 2000.

Dulles, Avery C. "Christianity and Humanitarian Action." In *Traditions, Values and Humanitarian Action*, edited by Kevin M. Cahill, 5–20. New York: Fordham University Press and the Center for International Health and Cooperation, 2003.

Dworkin, Ronald. *Taking Rights Seriously*. Cambridge: Harvard University Press, 1977.

Dwyer, Judith, editor. *A New Dictionary of the Catholic Social Thought*. Collegeville, MN: Liturgical, 1994.

Ellacuria, Ignacio. "Human Rights in a Divided Society." In *Human Rights in the Americas: The Struggle for Consensus*, edited by Alfred Henelly and John Langan, 52–65. Washington, D.C.: Georgetown University Press, 1992.

European Ethics Network. *Ethical Perspectives: Journal of the European Ethics Networks*. 11: 2/3 (June–September 2004) 97–212.

"The EU-China Network for the Ratification and Implementation of the UN Covenants." http://www.nuigalway.ie/human_rights/china.html. Irish Center. Accessed 10/22/2004.

Fanon, Frantz. *Toward the Africa Revolution: Political Essays*. Translated by Haakon Chevalier. New York: Grove, 1967.

Ferris, Elizabeth G. *Beyond Borders: Refugees, Migrants, and Human Rights in the Post Cold War Era*. Geneva: WCC Publications, 1993.

Financial Requirements for 2004. Revised July 14, 2004. UNHCR. http://www.unhcr.org. Accessed.

Ganaka, Gabriel G. "Message of the SECAM Bishops to the Churches of the Great Lakes Region and the Rest of Africa and Madagascar." *ACS* 13 (June 1997) 63–75.

Gasarasi, Charles P. "The Tripartite Approach to the Resettlement and Integration of Rural Refugees in Tanzania." In *Refugees: A Third-World Dilemma*, edited by John R. Rogge, 99–114. Totowa, NJ: Rowman and Littlefield, 1987.

George, William P. "International Regimes, Religious Ethics, and Emergent Probability." *ANSCE* (1996) 145–70.

Gewirth, Allan. *Human Rights: Essays on Justification and Application*. Chicago: University of Chicago Press, 1982.

———. *Reason and Morality*. Chicago: University of Chicago Press, 1978.

———. *The Community of Rights*. Chicago: University of Chicago Press, 1996.

Glendon, Mary A. *A World Made New: Eleanor Roosevelt and the Universal Declaration of Human Rights*. New York: Random House, 2001.

Gourevitch, Philip. *We Wish to Inform You That Tomorrow We Will Be Killed with Our Families: Stories from Rwanda*. New York: Farrar, Straus and Giroux, 1998.

Gutierrez, Gustavo. *We Drink from Our Own Wells: The Spiritual Journey of a People*. 20th anniversary edition. Maryknoll, NY: Orbis, 2003.

Hessel, Dieter T. "Solidarity Ethics: A Public Focus for the Church." In *Selected Papers from the Eighteenth Annual Meeting*, edited by Max L. Stackhouse, 90–99. AMSCE, 1977.

Himes, Kenneth R. "The Morality of Humanitarian Intervention." *TS* 55 (1994) 82–105.

Hollenbach, David A. *Claims in Conflict: Retrieving and Renewing the Catholic Human Rights Tradition*. New York: Paulist, 1979.

———. *Justice, Peace, and Human Rights: American Catholic Social Ethics in a Pluralistic World*. New York: Crossroad, 1988.

———. "A Communitarian Reconstruction of Human Rights: Contribution from Catholic Tradition." In *Catholicism and Liberalism*, edited by R. Bruce Douglass and David A. Hollenbach, 127–50. Cambridge Studies in Religion and American Public Life. New York: Cambridge University Press, 1994.

———. "Solidarity, Development, and Human Rights: The African Challenge." *JRE* 26 (1998) 300–315.

"How Does Humanitarian Law Protect Refugees and Internally Displaced Persons?" International Committee for the Red Cross. http://www.icrc.org.web/eng/siteeng0. nsf/htmlaII/ 5KZLXB. Accessed 5/25/2004.

Humanitarian Update Uganda 6 no. 4 (April 2004). OCHA. http://www.reliefweb.int/w/rwb.nsf/480fa8736b88bbc3c12564f6004c. Accessed 6/14/2004.

Ilesanmi, Simeon O. "Civil-Political Rights or Social Economic Rights for Africa? A Comparative Ethical Critique of a False Dichotomy." *ANSCE* 17 (1997) 191–212.

———. "Human Rights Discourse in Modern Africa: A Comparative Religious Ethical Perspective." *JRE* 24 (1995) 293–316.

"Internally Displaced by Far Outnumber Refugees in Africa." *Afrol News.* http://www.afrol.com/News2002/afr004_idp-stats.htm. Accessed 3/14/2003.

"Interview, Refugee Nduta Camp. In the Name of Security, May 31,1998." Human Rights Watch. http://www.hrw.org/reports/1999/Tanzania/. Accessed 3/14/2003.

Jesuit Refugee Service. *2000 Report.* http://www.jesref.org/jrs/ar2000/eaf/tza2000.htm. Accessed 5/9/2003.

John, Michael, translator. *Africa's Refugee Crisis: What's To Be Done?* London: Zed, 1986.

John XXIII. "*Pacem in Terris.*" In *Catholic Social Thought: The Documentary Heritage*, edited by David J. O'Brien and Thomas A. Shannon, 129–62. Maryknoll, NY: Orbis, 2001.

John Paul II. *The Church in Africa: Post-Synodal Apostolic Exhortation.* Washington D.C.: United States Catholic Conference, 1999.

———. *The Church in America: Post-Synodal Apostolic Exhortation.* Washington, D.C.: United States Catholic Conference, 1999.

———."*Sollicitudo Rei Socialis.*" In *Catholic Social Thought: The Documentary Heritage*, edited by David J. Brien and Thomas A. Shannon, 393–436. Maryknoll, NY: Orbis, 2001.

———. "*Centesimus Annus.*" In *Catholic Social Thought: The Documentary Heritage*, edited by David J. O'Brien and Thomas A. Shannon, 437–88. Maryknoll, NY: Orbis, 2001.

———. "Message for 89th World Day of Migrants and Refugees 2003." Vatican, October 24, 2002. http://www.vatican.va/roman_curia/pontifical_councils/migrants/s_in. Accessed 2/25/2004.

Josephat, Sosthenes L. "Crises in the Great Lakes and the Dilemma of Humanitarian Intervention in the Era of Globalization: A Reflection on Principles, Ethics, and Contradiction." Licentiate in Sacred Theology thesis, Jesuit School of Theology at Berkeley, California, 2002.

Kamanzi, Michael S. "Reconciliation?" *PI* 20–21.

Kant, Immanuel. *Fundamental Principles of the Metaphysics of Morals.* Translated by Thomas K. Abbot. Indianapolis: Bobbs-Merrill, 1999.

"Key Events in Congo's Post-Independence History." *Facts on File.* http://www.facts.com/wnd/conevent.htm. Accessed 9/13/2004.

Kibread, Gaim. *African Refugees: Reflection on the Refugee Problem.* Tenton, NJ: African World, 1985.

Knight, Thomas G. *Seminar Course 5601, Fundamentals of Strategic Logic*, Janet Breslin-Smith and Col. Jack McDonald, Advisors. National Defense University National War College.

Komonchak, Joseph, Mary Collins, et al. *The New Dictionary of Theology.* Wilmington, DE: Glazier, 1987.

Lacey, Marc. "Uprooted Sudanese Tell of Atrocities by Arab Militias." *New York Times*, May 8, 2004, A3.

———. "Sudan Frustrated as Militias Hide in Plain Sight." *New York Times*, August 6, 2004, A6.

Langan, John. "Defining Human Rights: A Revision of Liberal Tradition." In *Human Rights in the Americas: The Struggle for Consensus*, edited by Alfred Hennelly and John Langan, 69–101. Washington, D.C.: Georgetown University Press, 1982.

Leave None to Tell the Story: Genocide in Rwanda. Human Rights Watch Report. http://www.hrw.org/reports/1999/rwanda/Gonol5-8-03.htm. Accessed 2/22/2004.

Lebacqz, Karen. *Six Theories of Justice*. Minneapolis: Augsburg, 1986.

"Legal Protection of Internally Displaced Persons." Geneva Conventions Placing Limits on War. International Committee for the Red Cross. http://www.lcrc.org/web/eng/siteeng0.nsf/htmlaII/5DHD82. Accessed 5/25/2004.

Leo XIII. "*Rerum Novarum*." In *Catholic Social Thought: The Documentary Heritage*, edited by David J. O'Brien and Thomas A. Shannon, 12–39. Maryknoll, NY: Orbis, 2001.

Leon-Defour, Xavier, editor. *Dictionary of Biblical Theology*. Translated by P. Joseph Cahill. New York: Descles, 1967.

"Let Barlonyo Camp Attack Be the Last." http://www.allafrica.com/stories/200402270078. Accessed 2/29/2004.

Liberation Theology and the Vatican Document. Volume 3, *Perspectives from the Third World*. No. 67. Quezon City, Philippines: Claretian Publications, 1987.

Lobe, Jim. "Rwanda-US: Papers Imply Hutu Hard-Liners Downed President's Plane." *Inter Press Service News Agency*. http://www.pbs.org/newshour/bb/religion/july-decoo/rwanda_8-31.html. Accessed 2/21/2004.

Lutheran World Federation. *Theological Perspectives on Human Rights: Report on an LWF Consultation on Human Rights, Geneva, June 29–July 3, 1976*. Geneva: Lutheran World Federation, 1976.

Mabuwa, Rumi. *Seeking Protection: Addressing Sexual and Domestic Violence in Tanzania's Refugee Camps*. New York: Human Rights Watch, 2000.

MacIntyre, Alasdair. *After Virtue*. 2d ed. Notre Dame, IN: University of Notre Dame Press, 1984.

Magesa, Laurenti. *African Religion: The Moral Traditions of Abundant Life*. Nairobi: Paulines Publications Africa, 1997.

———, and Zablon Nthamburi, editors. *Democracy and Reconciliation: A Challenge for African Christianity*. Nairobi: Acton, 1999.

"Main Decisions of AMECEA General Assembly 2002." Dar es Salaam, Tanzania. http://www.africamission_mafr.org/ameceal.html. Accessed 8/20/2004.

"Major Refugee Arrivals 2002." UNHCR. http://www.unhcr.ch/cgibin/texis/vtx/basics/+AwwBmeLqZw_ww. Accessed 7/11/2004.

Mbande, Laurent. *Committed to Conflict: The Destruction of the Church in Rwanda*. London: SPCK, 1974.

Menkhaus, Ken. "Somalia at Crossroad of American Foreign Policy, January 28, 2002." http://www.selfdetermine.org/crisiswatch/0201somalia_body.html. Accessed 2/21/2004.

"Message from the 12th Plenary Assembly of SECAM, the Symposium of Episcopal Conferences of Africa and Madagascar." Rome, Italy, September 30–October 9, 2000. http://www.nccbuscc.org/sdwq/international/pasinya.htm. Accessed 8/20/2004.

Mill, John Stewart. *Utilitarianism; and On Liberty*. 2d ed. Edited by Mary Warnock. Malden, MA: Blackwell, 2003.

Nelson, Jack A. *Hunger for Justice: the Politics of Food and Faith*. Maryknoll, NY: Orbis, 1980.

New American Bible, New Catholic Translation. Nashville: Catholic Bible Press, 1987.

Ngabirano, Maximiano. "National Justice: A Challenge to the Great Lakes Region of Africa." *AFER* 43 (August–October 2001) 229–49.

Nozick, Robert. *Anarchy, State, and Utopia.* New York: Basic, 1974.

Nuhu, Alpha. "Refugee Camps Attract Sex Workers and AIDS." Panafrican News Agency, January 5, 2001. http://www.hartford-hwp.com/archives/36/3/74. Accessed 3/16/2003.

Nyerere, Julius K. *Freedom and Development: A Selection from Writings and Speeches, 1968–1973.* London: Oxford University Press, 1973.

"OAU Convention Governing the Specific Aspects of Refugee Problems in Africa." University of Minnesota Human Rights Library 1001. http://www1.umn.edu/humnrts/instree/z2arcom.htm. Accessed 6/13/2003.

O'Brien, David J., and Thomas A. Shannon, editors. *Catholic Social Thought: The Documentary Heritage.* Maryknoll, NY: Orbis, 2001.

Okumu, Stephen O. "Land Clashes in Burnt Forest." Licentiate in Sacred Theology thesis, Jesuit School of Theology at Berkeley, California, 2002.

O'Neill, William R. "No Amnesty for Sorrow: The Privilege of the Poor in Christian Social Ethics." *TS* 55 (1994) 638–56.

———, and William C. Spohn. "Rights of Passage: The Ethics of Immigration and Refugee Policy." *TS* 59 (1998) 84–106.

Outka, Gene. "Universal Love and Impartiality." In *The Love Commandments: Essays in Christian Ethics and Moral Philosophy*, edited by Edmund N. Santurri and William Werpehowski, 1–103. Washington, D.C.: Georgetown University Press, 1992.

Pawlikowski, John T. "Human Rights in the Roman Catholic Tradition." *Selected Papers From the Twentieth Annual Meeting*, edited by Max L. Stackhouse, 145–64. AMSCE, 1979.

Pius XI. "*Quadragesimo Anno.*" In *Catholic Social Thought: The Documentary Heritage*, edited by David J. O'Brien and Thomas A. Shannon, 40–80. Maryknoll, NY: Orbis, 2001.

Pontifical Council for the Pastoral Care of Migrants and Itinerant People. *Refugees: A Challenge to Solidarity.* Vatican City, 1992.

———. *Extracts from Speeches by the Holy Father and Positions taken by the Holy See concerning Refugees and Internally Displaced Persons.* January 1, 2002—January 31, 2003. http://www.vatican.va/roman_curia/pontifical_councils/migrants/s_in. Accessed 3/20/2005.

"Protecting Refugees, 2002." http://www.unhcr.ch/cgibin/texis/vtx/protect/+cwwBm SelBvdwwwi. Accessed 12/19/2003.

Rahner, Karl. *Theological Investigations.* Vol. 2, *Man in the Church.* Translated by Karl-H. Kruger. Baltimore: Helicon, 1963.

Rawls, John. *A Theory of Justice.* Rev. ed. Cambridge, MA: Belknap, 1971.

Refugees by Numbers 2003. UNHCR. http://www.unhcr.ch/chbin/texis/vtx/basics/+AwwBmeLqZw_ww. Accessed 9/11/2004.

Reliefweb. "Uganda: Mass Displacement to Uprooted Camps." Norwegian Refugee Council. http://www.reliefweb.int/w/rwb.nsf/yID/66C64867BA769320C1256. Internet. Accessed. 6/14/2004.

———. "Uganda: Mass Displacement to Unprotected Camps." Norwegian Refugee Council. http://www.reliefweb.int/w/rwb.nsf/yID/66C64867BA769320C1256. Accessed 12/30/2003.

"Religion and Conflicts in Rwanda." *Online News Hour.* August 31, 2000. http://www.pbs.org/newshour/bb/religion/july-dec00/rwanda_8-31.html. Internet. Accessed 2/21/2004.

Rodney, Walter. *How Europe Underdeveloped Africa.* Washington, D.C.: Howard University Press, 1974.

Rorty, Richard. "The Priority of Democracy to Philosophy." In *The Virginia Statute for Religious Freedom: Its Evolution and Consequences in American History,* edited by Merrill D. Peterson and Robert C. Vaughan, 257–88. New York: Cambridge University Press, 1988.

"Rwanda: OAU." *Africa Policy E-Journal.* http://www.africaaction.org/docsoo/rwan0007. htm. Accessed 9/11/2004.

"Rwanda-UNAMIR Mandate." http://www.un.org/Depts/dqko/co.mission/unamirM. htm. Accessed 2/22/2004.

"Rwanda 2002." USCR. http://www.refugee-org/world/countryrpt/Africa/rwanda.htm. Accessed 10/4/2004.

Sadi, Jean-Pierre K. "Rwanda: The Sacred and Political Violence." Licentiate in Sacred Theology thesis, Jesuit School of Theology at Berkeley, California, 2002.

Schaeffer, Jill. *Sanctuary and Asylum: A Handbook for Commitment.* Geneva: World Alliance of Reformed Churches, 1990.

Schreiter, Robert J. *The New Catholicity: Theology Between the Global and the Local.* Maryknoll, NY: Orbis, 2000.

Schmucker, Reinold. "Can War Be a Moral Action? Towards a Normative Theory of Humanitarian Intervention." *Ethical Perspectives* 11: 2/3 (2004) 162–74.

Sen, Amartya. *Development as Freedom.* New York: Knopf, 1999.

Sengupta, Somni. "Sudan's Ethnic Strife Spurs Bush, Annan to Voice Worry." *San Francisco Chronicle,* April 18, 2004, A20.

Shirbon, Estelle. "Sudan Signs Peace Deal with Darfur Faction." http://www.news.yahoo. com/s/nm/20060505/ts_nm. Accessed 6/1/2006.

Shue, Henry. *Basic Rights.* Princeton: Princeton University Press, 1990.

Smith, Bryan. "The Need for Humanitarian Intervention in Central Africa." http://www. wcl.american.edu/hrbrief/v3i3/rwanda33.htm. Accessed 2/15/2004.

Stuhlmueller, Carroll. "Option for the Poor: Old Testament Directives." In *Economic Justice: CTU's Pastoral Commentary on the Bishops' Letter on the Economy,* edited by John Pawlikowsk and Donald Senior, 19–27. Washington, D.C.: Paulist, 1988.

Symser, W. R. *Refugees: Extended Exile.* Washington D.C.: Center for Strategic and International Studies, 1987.

Synod of Bishops. "Justice in the World." 1971. In *Catholic Social Thought: The Documentary Heritage,* edited by David J. O'Brien and Thomas A. Shannon, 287–300. Maryknoll, NY: Orbis, 2001.

Tanzania Episcopal Conference. "A Report on Caritas, 1995–1999." AMECEA Assembly, 25 July–8 August, 1999. http://www.re.net/tanzania/tec/caritas.htm. Accessed 3/25/2003.

"Tanzania in the Name of Security-Forced Round-Ups of Refugees in Tanzania." July 1999. Human Rights Watch. http://www.hrw.org/reports/1999/Tanzania. Accessed 3/14/2003.

Taylor, Paul. "The Role of the United Nations in the Provision of Humanitarian Assistance: New Problems and New Responses." In *Human Rights and International Relations in the Asia Pacific,* edited by James T. H. Tang. London: Pinter, 1995.

Tenui, Prisca T. "Conflict in the Sudan." *AFER* 44 (2000) 96–123.

"Text of the 1967 Protocol Relating to the Status of Refugees," in *Sanctuary and Asylum: A Handbook for Commitment,* ed. Jill Schaeffer. Geneva, Switzerland: World Alliance of Reformed Churches, 1990.

"Text of the United Nations' 1951 Convention Relating to the Status of Refugees." In *Sanctuary and Asylum: A Handbook for Commitment*, edited by Jill Schaefer, 96–138. Geneva: World Alliance of Reformed Churches, 1990.

Trimiew, Darryl M. "The Economic Rights Debate: The End of One Argument, the Beginning of Another." *ANSCE* (1991) 85–108.

"Uganda Complex Situation Report #3. Fiscal Year (FY) July 3, 2003." United States Agency for International Development. http://www.usaid.gov/hum_response/ofda/situation.html. Accessed 6/13/2003.

"Uganda General Election, 2006." *Wikipedia.* http://www.en.wikipedia.org/wiki/Uganda_general_election,_2006. Accessed 6/1/2006.

"Uganda Rebels Feeling the Heat." http://www.iol.co.za/index.php?click_id=68.Accessed 2/29/2004.

"UN Urges Urgent Aid for Refugees in Africa." Reuters, February 14, 2003. http://www.agriculture.com/worldwide/IDS/2003-02-14T170438Z_01_L1469662_. Accessed 3/14/2003.

"UNFPA Sponsors Services for Refugees in Tanzania." June 1999. UNFPA. http://www.unfpa.org/modules/dispatch/issues99/tanzania.html. Accessed 3/14/2003.

UNHCR Global Report 2002. UNHCR. *http://www.unhcr.ch/cgi-bin/texis/vtx/protect/+cwwBmSelBvww.* Accessed 12/19/2004.

United Kingdom Committee for Human Rights. *Human Rights: A Study Guide for the International Year for Human Rights.* London: Heinemann, 1967.

United Nations General Assembly Resolution 217A (III), section 3 article I, United Nations General Assembly Resolution 71, United Nations Document A/810 (1948). In *The United Nations and Human Rights: 1945–1995.* 153–56. United Nations Blue Book Series iv.vii. New York: United Nations Department of Public Information, 1995.

"United Nations' 1948 Universal Declaration of Human Rights." In *Sanctuary and Asylum: A Handbook for Commitment*, edited by Jill Schaeffer, 83–88. Geneva: World Alliance of Reformed Churches, 1990.

United Nations Economic and Social Council. *Situation of Human Rights in Somalia: Advisory Services and Technical Cooperation in the Field of Human Rights.* E/CN.4/200/110 January 2000, original: English.

Update on the Work of the Jesuit Refugee Service Geneva (UN) Office, 2002–2003. JRS.http://www.jesref.org/report.php?lang=en&repld=un03528en. Accesssed 12/19/2003.

U.S. Catholic Bishops. "The Challenge of Peace: God's Promise and Our Response." In *Catholic Social Thought: The Documentary Heritage*, edited by David J. O'Brien and Thomas A. Shannon, 492–571.

———. "Economic Justice for All." In *Catholic Social Thought: The Documentary Heritage*, edited by David J. O'Brien and Thomas A. Shannon, 572–680. Maryknoll, NY: Orbis, 2001.

"U.S. Finally Ratifies Human Rights Covenant." Carter Center. http://www.cartercenter.org/doc1369.htm. Internet. Accessed 10/22/2004.

U.S. Senate. Congressional Research Service. Library of Congress. *World Refugee Crisis: The International Community's Response.* Ninety-Sixth Congress, First Session. Washington, D.C.: U.S. Government Printing Press, 1979.

Uwe, Christine. "Together We Have a Future," *PI* 83–84 (2004:2/3) 28.

Van Selm, Joanne, et al., editors. *The Refugee Covention at Fifty: A View from Forced Migration Studies.* Lanham, MD: Lexington, 2003.

Vatican II. "*Gaudium et Spes*." In *Catholic Social Thought: The Documentary Heritage*, edited by David J. O'Brien and Thomas A. Shannon, 164–237. Maryknoll, NY: Orbis, 2001.

Walzer, Michael. *Spheres of Justice: A Defense of Pluralism and Equality*. New York: Basic, 1983.

"WFP Emergence Report No. 20." May 14, 2004. http://www.jesref.org/report.php?lang= en&repld=un30528en. Accessed 6/24/2004.

www.ingramcontent.com/pod-product-compliance
Lightning Source LLC
Chambersburg PA
CBHW061736270326
41928CB00011B/2253